BUILDING STUDENTS' HISTORICAL LITERACIES

"At the heart of this book, Jeffrey Nokes draws a key distinction between historical knowledge and historical literacy. . . . A historical literate person knows how to evaluate the quality of information, rather than just regurgitate it on a test. This book provides a road map for creating a generation of historically literate students. Its chapters lay out in rich detail the many ways that forward-looking teachers are preparing students for the 21st century. It combines salt-of-the-earth wisdom with concrete examples from real schools and real teachers. It draws on insights from the latest research on historical thinking, but never loses site of the fact that creative teachers much shape these insights to fit their own unique circumstances. Jeffery Nokes has performed a great service in writing this book. It is now our turn to put it into practice."

Sam Wineburg, Margaret Jacks Professor of Education and (by courtesy) History, Stanford University, USA. From the Foreword

". . . Compelling, relevant, and interesting. . . . An essential resource for teacher educators, education students, and practicing teachers concerned with history learning and literacy, this book provides a wealth of insight, resources, and concrete ideas on how to engage students in the critical historical literacy practices so important to civic participation and deep, conceptual learning. Thank you, Dr. Nokes!"

Darin Stockdill, University of Michigan, USA

How can teachers incorporate the richness of historical resources into classrooms in ways that are true to the discipline of history and are pedagogically sound? This book explores the notion of historical literacy, adopts a research-supported stance on literacy processes, and promotes the integration of content-area literacy instruction into history content teaching. It is unique in its focus on the discipline-specific literacies of historical inquiry. Literacy is addressed from a historian's rather than a literacy specialist's point of view. A broad range of texts is surveyed, including those that historians and non-historians both use and produce in understanding history. The book features a wide variety of practical instructional strategies immediately available to teachers.

History teachers who read this book will receive the practical tools they need in order to help their students reach the national standards for history teaching. With the recent inclusion of a historical literacy component of the English Language Arts Common Core Standards Initiative, this book is also highly relevant to English, language arts, and reading teachers, who are expected, under the new guidelines, to engage their students in historical reading and writing.

Visit **www.historicalliteracies.byu.edu** for additional information and resources on teaching historical literacies.

Jeffery D. Nokes is Assistant Professor, Department of History, Brigham Young University, USA.

BUILDING STUDENTS' HISTORICAL LITERACIES

Learning to Read and Reason with Historical Texts and Evidence

Jeffery D. Nokes

Routledge
Taylor & Francis Group

NEW YORK AND LONDON

First published 2013
by Routledge
711 Third Avenue, New York, NY 10017

Simultaneously published in the UK
by Routledge
2 Park Square, Milton Park, Abingdon, Oxon OX14 4RN

Routledge is an imprint of the Taylor & Francis Group, an informa business

© 2013 Taylor & Francis

The right of Jeffery D. Nokes to be identified as author of this work has been asserted
by him in accordance with sections 77 and 78 of the Copyright, Designs and Patents Act
1988.

Library of Congress Cataloging in Publication Data has been applied for

ISBN: 978-0-415-80897-2 (hbk)
ISBN: 978-0-415-80898-9 (pbk)
ISBN: 978-0-203-13732-1 (ebk)

Typeset in Bembo and Stone Sans
by RefineCatch Limited, Bungay, Suffolk, UK

Printed and bound in the United States of America
by Edwards Brothers Malloy

To Gina

CONTENTS

FOREWORD

In 1892, an election year, the incumbent Benjamin Harrison issued the following proclamation four months before his countrymen went to the polls.

> I Benjamin Harrison ... do hereby appoint Friday, Oct. 21, 1892, the four hundredth anniversary of the discovery of America by Columbus, as a general holiday for the people of the United States.... Let there be expressions of gratitude to Divine Providence for the devout faith of the discoverer, and for the Divine care and guidance which has directed our history and so abundantly blessed our people.
>
> *New York Times*, July 22, 1892, p. 8

In a study we did some years ago, we gave this document to several dozen high school students. We asked them to place the document "in historical context," that is, to think about the proclamation as a historical artifact: who produced it and why, what might have been the motivations behind it, and what might have been the broader circumstances that influenced its creation. Our interviewees included a group of bright juniors and seniors, all of whom had recently sat for the most rigorous history examination in the country: the three-hour-and-five-minute Advanced Placement (AP) exam.

One student stands out. Jacob, a 17-year-old senior, had strong opinions about Harrison's proclamation.

"The first thing that jumps out," he noted, "is that Columbus is a pioneer of 'progress and enlightenment.'" But Jacob had his own take on the "discoverer": "From what I've learned, his goals were not entirely noble. Just get rich, whatever; ... he claimed to be a true Christian, but he also captured and tortured Indians, so he wasn't maybe as noble as this is having him be."

Jacob's stance was typical of what we heard from this group of students. These young people, who had just completed months of preparation for a high stakes exam, had myriad facts at their disposal. Jacob, for example, knew about Columbus, knew about the slaughter of the Arawaks, knew that the Genoan not only hacked the hands off of those who failed to meet their gold quota, but penned others to ship to Spain as slaves to pay back investors. For most of these AP students, this document prompted outrage at the whitewashing of a figure today viewed at best with ambivalence, and, at worst, with opprobrium.

We interviewed a second group as well: a half-dozen PhD students representing an array of different historical interests and specialties. Their responses to this document couldn't have been more different. One of the grad students summarized Harrison's proclamation as "an expansion of the heroic pantheon to include former undesirables." Another added: "it's a shameless appeal to super-heroes in order to gain votes in urban centers." Nothing about 1492. Nothing about the Indians. Columbus' name never even mentioned. What in the world were these future historians talking about?

Let's listen in on Matt, a 23-year-old history grad student, whose first words immediately set him on a different course from the high school interviewees:

> "Okay it's 1892; So it's the 400th anniversary. Benjamin Harrison ... the 1890s, the beginning of the Progressive Era, end of the century, closing of the frontier ... biggest wave of immigration in U.S. history. Hmm... *That's it.*"[1]

The first thing Matt does is situate the document in the coordinates of time and place. Although Harrison's proclamation refers to events of 1492 it is a creature of America in the 1890s. Matt puzzles his way through the document. Initially his path is unclear, hesitating. He notes the Progressive Era and the closing of the frontier, and then takes a long pause. He seems to be asking himself why a sitting president would go out of his way in an election year to make a big deal out of Columbus. In other words, what about the context of 1892 might shed light on this proclamation? And then Matt zeros in: "the biggest wave of immigration in U.S. history," a wave that brought in millions of immigrants from Italy, Poland and other countries in Eastern Europe, the majority of whom practiced a religion different from the dominant Protestantism of America in the Gilded Age. These immigrants were Catholics, the same religion as "the discoverer." And they and their relatives in the United States constituted a new voting bloc, especially in urban centers. "That's it" was Matt's way of calling attention to the fact that presidential proclamations are *interested* acts – they don't come out of nowhere.

---

[1] For more on this study, along with classroom lesson plans based on it, see Sam Wineburg, Daisy Martin, and Chauncey Monte-Sano (2011), *Reading like a historian: Teaching literacy in middle and high school history classrooms*. New York: Teachers College Press.

And this proclamation seemed to be a calculated move to appeal to Catholics by crowning their co-religionist as a national hero.

Matt's reading differs from Jacob's in key ways. To be sure, Matt has more factual knowledge at his disposal; he has, after all, made the decision to pursue history as his career. But remember, Jacob is no slouch, either. He earned a very respectable "4" on his AP exam, which qualifies him for college credit at many universities. He brought to this document a great deal of historical knowledge – not only about Columbus, but when we interviewed him later, it turns out, about the 1890s, immigration, the countries from which these immigrants came, and even what religion they practiced. But none of this knowledge was perceived as relevant when Jacob confronted this document. For Jacob and his peers, the proclamation was all about 1492 and Christopher Columbus. For Matt and his fellow graduate students, on the other hand, this document was about 1892 and Benjamin Harrison. These two groups looked at the same document but saw two completely different things. For one, a "Columbus button" immediately went off, and judgments were issued about this controversial historical figure. For the other, the document was an opportunity to think about historical context and raise questions about presidential decision making in an election year. One kind of reading yielded stock answers; the other, fresh questions.

The book you are holding helps us understand what is at stake in these two different approaches to historical texts. Jeffery Nokes writes that in no subject is there a greater gap between the work of professionals and how that subject is taught in schools. "In science," Nokes writes, "Students do labs. In gym class, they play sports. In English class, they write poetry . . . . and in industrial arts they work with the same tools carpenters use." But in history, Nokes continues, the main activities are listening to lectures and memorizing information. When Nokes sat down with a group of 5th graders and asked them how historians spent their time, students imagined historians "surfing Wikipedia, watching the history channel, or listening to lectures, all processes more closely associated with the way students learn history than with actual historical inquiry." Most students simply had no idea about what historians do. Nothing in their experience with learning history in school had prepared them for this question.

At the heart of this book, Jeffery Nokes draws a key distinction between *historical knowledge* and *historical literacy*. "Historical literacy," he explains, "is not the possession of encyclopedic knowledge of historical facts, but the ability to glean appropriate information about the past from resources of many genres. It is the ability to engage in historical processes – to not simply possess knowledge, but to know how to build it."

Historical literacy is, if you will, a way of seeing the world. To be historically literate means that we know how to ask questions about where information comes from, about how it comes into our hands in the first place, and the question of utmost importance, whether we should believe it. In an age where going to the library is equivalent to pointing one's browser to Google, such questions are of paramount importance. The Internet readily provides documents "proving" that President Obama was born in Kenya, that the Holocaust didn't happen, and that thousands of Black slaves willingly volunteered to bear arms for the Confederacy, that is, to fight for their own continued enslavement. Without teaching our students how to discern truth from falsehood, we send them into the world as digital invalids, easy marks for every crank trolling the Internet. A generation ago, if we wanted to know whether Yorktown or Saratoga was the decisive battle in the Revolutionary War, we needed to have that information in memory – who, after all, could lug around a 1000-page textbook in their back pocket? But today our iPhone supplies that information in a split second. What our iPhones cannot do, however, is distinguish solid from spurious evidence, or discern cogent argument from a stupefying cloud of smoke and mirrors. For that, Nokes reminds us, our students must be *historically literate*. A historically-literate person knows how to evaluate the quality of information, rather than just regurgitate it on a test.

This book provides a road map for creating a generation of historically-literate students. Its chapters lay out in rich detail the many ways that forward-looking teachers are preparing students for the 21st century. It combines salt-of-the-earth wisdom with concrete examples from real schools and real teachers. It draws on insights from the latest research on historical thinking, but never loses sight of the fact that creative teachers must shape these insights to fit their own unique circumstances. Jeffery Nokes has performed a great service in writing this book. It is now our turn to put it into practice.

Sam Wineburg, Margaret Jacks Professor of Education
and (by courtesy) History, Stanford University
June 2012

PREFACE

"We can't trust Paul Revere as a source!" Manti shouted across the room. "We don't even know if he was there." My 8th Grade students were trying to decide what happened at the Boston Massacre. A colleague of mine had given me a collection of documents related to the event. Being a young teacher, I was happy to try just about anything that I was given. But even an inexperienced teacher could see that something special was taking place that day. The level of engagement was high as students argued about the relative value of the different accounts. Many students, like Manti, were passionate about their interpretations. Many were interested in the minute details of this historical event. The students' excitement in learning was something that I hadn't seen before in my classroom, which typically involved textbook reading, lectures, and documentary videos. My students learned a great deal through the activity, but I learned even more – I caught a glimpse of what a history classroom might be like.

Over the next several years I began to collect activities like this Boston Massacre analysis – activities during which students would sort through primary source documents and attempt to answer a historical question. My teacher instincts told me that this was good teaching. When I structured the activity correctly, with the right documents, handouts, and student groupings, engagement was high. And students learned the material better. However, in the days before the Internet, it was extremely time consuming to find primary sources and I, as a typical teacher, was expected to serve as a student government advisor, assistant basketball coach, mock trial team coordinator, and on multiple committees. Needless to say, most of my lessons followed a more traditional format – students listening to me lecture. But in my heart I understood that there was a better way to help students learn historical content. Over the years I shortened lectures and increased the frequency of activities during which students would construct their own interpretations based on documents and other historical evidence.

After a few years of teaching, while working on a master's degree, I stumbled, quite by accident, onto an article that changed the way I viewed history teaching. A content-area literacy professor assigned me to find a research article related to reading within my discipline. In one of the first journals I browsed, the *Journal of Educational Psychology*, I found an article that immediately caught my attention – it had the words "reading" and "historical text" in the title – just what I needed. What was even more appealing to me was that in the appendix there were eight documents related to the Battle of Lexington. Thrilled, I made a copy of the article and put the eight documents in my Revolutionary War file so that I could use them the following year.

But when I began to read the article I discovered two ideas that were worth much more than the eight documents. First, there is a purpose in teaching history even more important than building students' historical content knowledge, namely nurturing their historical thinking skills. By helping students read and reason like historians, history teachers could prepare them to survive and thrive as adults in an Information Age. The enhanced content knowledge that resulted from engagement in multiple text activities, which I had observed in my class-room, was an important by-product of this type of teaching. However, the real value of students' engagement in multiple text analyses was in their development of historical thinking skills. Second, there were individuals who systematically studied history teaching. These researchers, like Wineburg (1991), the author of the article in the *Journal of Educational Psychology*, were defining "historical literacies" and were experimenting with instructional strategies that helped students analyze texts with greater sophistication.

For the next few years I continued to add to my collection of historical literacy activities and found better ways to nurture students' historical thinking. And as I did, I gained increasing appreciation from students and growing attention from colleagues, parents, and community organizations. The students at Elk Ridge Middle School chose me as the "teacher of the year" the same year that the regional chapter of the Daughters of the American Revolution selected me as their outstanding history teacher. After 12 years in middle schools I moved to Bingham High School where, in my second year, I was named "most inspirational teacher" by the students, and the Utah High School history teacher of the year by Utah's chapter of the National Council for the Social Studies. I joked with my associates that the awards were a result of my being the only teacher in the building who wore a tie to school every day. But in the back of my mind I knew that a great deal of my popularity was a result of my efforts to engage students in multiple text activities.

I was on a constant lookout for new texts that I could incorporate in my classroom, and the harder I looked the more I discovered. For instance, one afternoon while reading the newspaper I found an obituary of a gentleman with a Japanese surname. Reading closer I found that he had been forced to relocate from California during the early years of World War II – sent to the internment camp at Topaz in central Utah. I cut out the obituary and took it to class the next day because it fit in with the lesson I was teaching. As students analyzed the obituary they made discoveries that went beyond what I had noticed. One student pointed out that the man's parents had traditional Japanese names, he had a traditional Japanese given name but an Americanized nickname, and his children had traditional American names. She had identified the process of assimilation in this family. Another student noticed that the obituary used active voice except for the line about him being sent to an internment camp. "It shows a spirit of forgiveness," Alicia pointed out. "It's like it happened but it wasn't really anyone's fault." This activity solidified a thought that had been growing in my mind for some time – my students had the ability to be not only consumers of historical knowledge, remembering things that others had figured out, but also they had the potential to be producers of original understandings, developing independent interpretations of historical events – interpretations that had significant value.

While teaching, I entered a Ph.D. program in "teaching and learning" with a focus on literacy. I discovered that research on building students' literacies had applications for helping students think historically. In my practice, research-based approaches to literacy instruction, such as explicit strategy instruction, helped me improve students' ability to engage in historical thinking. For my dissertation I systematically studied what I had observed repeatedly in my classroom. Eight colleagues agreed to teach lessons that I developed, including ten reading lessons that focused on either building content knowledge or building historical literacies using either textbooks or collections of primary sources. My research demonstrated that students learned better – both content knowledge and historical reasoning skills – with primary sources than they did with the textbook. Additionally, students showed significant improvement in their ability to use some of the historians' heuristics when they were given explicit strategy instruction (Nokes, Dole, & Hacker, 2005).

In 2006, after 15 years of teaching middle school and high school history, I became a history teacher educator at Brigham Young University. Since that time I have continued to study history teaching, with a specific focus on building secondary students' historical literacies. The most important insight I have gained is that research on literacy applies not only to written historical evidence, but to all types of historical resources, such as artifacts, photographs, architecture, and music. And looking back on my 15-year career, I always seemed to understand the value of helping students learn with multiple genres of evidence – I just never considered my efforts as building historical literacies, which I do now. Whether I was helping students use raw data from census records to discover trends in immigration, or helping students understand the symbols in a political cartoon, or helping them create a museum exhibit displaying their interpretation of a historical event of their own choosing, I was building students' historical literacies.

Thus, this book, written for prospective, new, and practicing history teachers, is a synthesis of the best of my teaching and current research on building historical literacies. I write it as a teacher turned teacher-educator and as a tinkerer turned researcher. The principles discussed in this book are grounded in my 15-year informal experimentation, current formal research on history pedagogy, and research on general and history-specific literacy instruction. The uniqueness of this book lies in its practical application of literacy research and history teaching research.

Each chapter in the book opens with a vignette. These vignettes, with few exceptions, are quasi-autobiographical in the same way that "fish stories" are. In each case there was a teaching moment that bears some resemblance to the vignette. But through the years, as I have told and retold my stories to students and fellow history teachers, my memories have become distorted, my successes exaggerated, and my failures forgotten. In the end, the vignettes represent case studies of how things might be rather than how things actually were. Admittedly, there is no guarantee that these vignettes would play out as narrated. In order to ease my conscience, I give the teachers in the vignettes the names of former students rather than take credit for doing things I mostly wish I would have done.

In the vignettes I try to capture the voice of students and teachers as they struggle together to think historically. I write the vignettes with rich detail, imagining the struggles of former students, and trying to create an image of history classrooms that, unfortunately, many prospective and in-service teachers have never observed. To help prospective teachers, I describe teachers' thinking through the planning stages of lessons. Additionally, I include dialogue with students in the vignettes because teaching moments come not only during the execution of a well-planned lesson, but in spontaneous interaction with young people. Some of my best historical thinking lessons were given to small groups of students or individual students when they raised their hands for help. I have tried to capture some of these moments in the vignettes. In some ways, building historical thinking is not as much about what the teacher says or does as it is about who the teacher is in his/her interaction with the students.

Part I includes four chapters that define historical literacies and discuss literacy instruction. Chapter 1 contrasts instruction that builds historical literacies with traditional history instruction. Chapter 2 further defines historical literacies, contrasting the reading of historians with the reading of history students. This chapter previews the texts, heuristics, and habits of mind that constitute historical literacies. Chapter 3 considers historical literacies within a context of general literacy, and outlines a theoretical framework for understanding literacy. This chapter establishes a pedagogical model for teaching historical literacies. Chapter 4 explores history as a discipline, suggesting that students must understand the nature of historical inquiry and historical knowledge before they will be able to develop historical literacies.

In Part II each chapter models and breaks down the teaching of a skill, heuristic, or habit of mind using a specific genre of historical text. The correlation between the processes described and the type of text, while not arbitrarily chosen, is not meant to indicate that certain aspects of historical thinking are used exclusively with certain genres. Instead, elements of historical thinking are presented as the warp and a wide array of texts is presented as the woof in weaving a classroom that builds historical literacies. Specifically, Chapter 5 discusses the use of historians' heuristics in working with primary sources. Chapter 6 focuses on making inferences with artifacts. Chapter 7 explores second order concepts or metaconcepts and the use of visual texts. Chapter 8 considers historical empathy and perspective taking with historical fiction. Chapter 9 promotes a healthy skepticism of textbooks. Chapter 10 considers reductionist traps and the use of audio and video texts. Chapter 11 addresses the important skill of argumentation, using quantitative historical data.

I conclude the book, in Part III, with two chapters that synthesize the strategies and texts described throughout the earlier chapters. Much of Chapter 12 focuses on critical intertextual analysis and the scaffolding that a teacher can build into lessons as students work through challenging historical reading and reasoning with multimodal texts. Chapter 13 draws upon the vignettes used throughout the book to present a template for creating powerful historical literacy lessons like those described in the book.

ACKNOWLEDGEMENTS

I acknowledge, with gratitude, the help that I have received throughout my career and on this project. I appreciate the professors during my undergraduate career who helped me develop some fundamental historical literacies, particularly Robert Kenzer. I appreciate the many mentors I have had throughout my teaching career, especially Scott Crump. Professors Jan Dole, Doug Hacker, Suzanne Wade, Kay Camperell, and Emily Swan patiently supported me throughout my graduate education, as my notions of teaching historical literacies took shape. Many others have been helpful in the completion of this project. I gratefully acknowledge the advice of Professors Sam Wineburg, Roni Jo Draper, and Brian Cannon, and a prospective history teacher, Lauren Angarola, who provided helpful feedback on early drafts of chapters. I have appreciated interaction with the Content Area Literacy Study Group at BYU, which has opened my eyes to new literacies and has given me critical feedback on my ideas about historical literacies. I'm particularly thankful for my wife, Gina, who has supported me throughout my career and the completion of this book. And I'm thankful for my good children who have been willing to allow me to test teaching ideas on them and who have been understanding of my investment in this project. While the ideas of many others have inspired my writing, I take sole responsibility for the content of this book.

PART I

Historical Literacies

A growing number of history teachers have a vision of a different kind of history classroom – a classroom that nurtures historical literacies. It makes sense that I start with an explanation of why something different is needed, and why a focus on building historical literacies fulfills this need. In the four chapters of this section, I will introduce you to four fictional history teachers. Mr. Rich, who is being observed by his principal during a historical literacy lesson, illustrates the contrast between traditional instruction and historical literacy instruction, the theme of the first chapter. In the second chapter, Mrs. Francis demonstrates the process of identifying an opportunity to nurture literacy using resources that aren't normally associated with reading or writing. Her planning and instruction model how historical literacies can be fostered with many types of texts and evidence. In Chapter 3, Mr. Nguyen, like Mrs. Francis, gives students an opportunity to read a non-traditional text, but unlike Mrs. Francis, does not build literacy instruction into his lesson plan. I use his frustrations, which I admit are autobiographical, as a springboard into a discussion of what it means to be literate, and how a teacher can provide historical literacy instruction. Finally, in Chapter 4, the students in Mrs. Hansen's classroom reveal a range of responses when called upon to read and reason like a historian. They illustrate the concept of epistemic stance – showing that students must have a basic understanding of the nature of history as a discipline before they can engage in the literate activities that I describe in Part II.

1

BUILDING HISTORICAL LITERACIES

Ms. Cordova, the principal at McArthur Middle School, walks down the hall of the social studies department during third period. She notices the lights are off in Mr. Hanks' classroom and, glancing in, observes that he is showing students a video. Most students are filling out a worksheet. Ms. Cordova is distracted by loud voices coming from the next classroom down the hall. As she approaches, she hears students reciting in unison the names of the Presidents of the United States in chronological order. Continuing down the hall, she hears the hum of voices coming from another classroom and peeks in to see students sitting in small groups studying passages on Greek city-states in their world history textbook. In the next classroom, she hears Mr. Adams, one of the most popular teachers, involved in an animated lecture on the causes of World War I. Students laugh at his exaggerated German accent. As she passes his door she sees that he is dressed in the uniform of a German officer. From the silence in the hall ahead, she wonders whether the next classroom is empty. But, looking in, she sees that it is full of students who sit quietly at their desks either reading their textbook and taking notes or snoozing.

Finally Ms. Cordova sees Mr. Rich's classroom, the class she has come to observe. As she enters, students' behavior appears somewhat chaotic. Some students sit in desks that are arranged in small groups. Other students huddle around Mr. Rich's computer browsing the Internet. A few students stand at the white board flipping through papers on a table and drawing some type of chart on the board. Mr. Rich is engaged with three students in one of the groups. As Ms. Cordova approaches, Mr. Rich nervously welcomes her, inviting her to join the students' discussion. Students pay little attention to her. They are looking at a black and white photograph of children working in a textile mill.

"I think it's fake," says Antonio. "It looks staged. The kids look like they're posing."

"Yeah!" Angie agrees. "Do we even know who took the picture? What was he trying to show? We need to know who he was and what his purpose was. Do you know, Mr. Rich?"

Mr. Rich knows, but pretends he doesn't. He explains that the students at his computer had the same question and are searching the Internet to see if they can find out who the photographer was. Angie stands up to go talk to them.

Mandy, disagreeing with the others, suggests that the picture is accurate because it shows the factory and workers exactly as she imagined them when reading an excerpt from the novel *Lyddie* (Paterson, 1991). She flips through a pile of papers on the desks until she finds the excerpt. "I think the picture is accurate because it matches with this book."

"That book is a novel. Do you know what that means?" Antonio criticizes. "It's made up. It's fake. We can't trust it as evidence."

"Yeah, but Paterson might have done research before she wrote it," Mandy retorts.

Ms. Cordova moves through other groups where students are engaged in similar conversations using the same collection of documents. A student explains to her that they are debating a question written on the whiteboard: "Was child labor in 19th century factories really worse than child labor on family-owned farms of earlier generations?" Ms. Cordova watches students rummage through graphs, political cartoons, a map, an excerpt from a historical novel, photographs, diary entries, letters, and song lyrics. She hears students using terms like *account*, *unreliable*, *accurate*, *evidence*, and *corroborate*. More interesting to her, she senses in these young people, not simply an ability to comprehend a wide variety of historical texts, but the disposition and ability to think critically about them.

Ms. Cordova likes the level of engagement in Mr. Rich's classroom. But what she does not recognize is the fundamental difference between the instructional methods in the other history classrooms and the way Mr. Rich teaches. Videos; memorization drills; lectures, no matter how entertaining; and textbook reading assignments, whether done individually or in groups, represent efforts to transmit to students a historical narrative that has been produced by others. Students' role in these activities is to receive, manage, remember, and repeat information. Lectures, videos, and textbooks simply represent different media through which information is conveyed. In Mr. Rich's classroom, on the other hand, students construct their own understanding of history using many of the same types of texts that historians use. Students' role in his class is to semi-independently solve historical problems, building their own understanding of the past in the process. Students in Mr. Rich's class are immersed in historical literacies.

Ms. Cordova does not recognize the effort, energy, and time that Mr. Rich and his students have invested to develop the ability to work with multiple types of documents with the fluency that they exhibit. She doesn't realize that Mr. Rich has dedicated time during most class sessions to helping students read, critique, and use historical texts, including the genres found in the collection of papers on students' desks the day of her visit. Impressed by the high level of engagement and students' fluency in talking about child labor in factories and on farms, she gives Mr. Rich a positive review at the end of her observation in spite of her superficial awareness of the purposes of this lesson.

Research on Traditional History Instruction

Much of my career has been spent working with colleagues like the hypothetical teachers in McArthur Middle School's Social Studies Department. Many have taught with impressive energy, passion, and humor, but most use traditional instructional methods. Research suggests that they are typical of history teachers across America: lecturing, showing documentaries, and assigning textbook reading (Lee & Weiss, 2007; Nokes, 2010a; Ravitch & Finn, 1987). Classrooms like Mr. Rich's are uncommon. However, an ever-increasing number of innovative teachers, like Mr. Rich, regularly engage students in historical reading and reasoning. In this chapter I consider the methods and materials of traditional classrooms and the results of traditional instruction. I introduce a redefined notion of history teaching, making a case for historical literacy instruction like that provided by Mr. Rich. I establish a definition of historical literacies that I use throughout the book.

Traditional Methods

In popular culture, the image of the history classroom includes a monotone teacher at the front of the room, lecturing to dozing teenagers about topics that they perceive to be irrelevant, like the Hawley Smoot Tariff (Chinich & Hughs, 1986). Many adults experienced history classrooms where days were spent "reading the chapter and answering the questions at the end." Adults remember history classrooms that were teacher centered – the teacher doing most of the talking, with the students being assessed on their ability to remember what the teacher told them. Students' involvement was limited to listening to the teacher, reading the textbook, taking notes, and, in the best cases, working together with peers to prepare for dreaded exams that would assess their ability to remember a wide range of historical facts – tidbits of information that would quickly be forgotten after the exam. These adults, looking back on their high school days, often summarize their experience thus: "I hated history in high school, but I really like it now." Does this image, presented in popular culture and in the collective memory of adults, reflect the reality of today's history classrooms?

Some of the best data on history classrooms of 25 years ago and today come from the National Assessment of Educational Progress (NAEP) (Lee & Weiss, 2007; Ravitch & Finn, 1987). As part of the 1987 assessment, nearly 8,000 seventeen-year-old students were asked how often they engaged in different activities in their history class. Seventy three percent of students reported that they "listen to the teacher explain a history lesson" daily, and almost 60% reported to read from their history textbook daily. In contrast, only 12% of students reported "analyzing historical events in small groups" daily. About twice as many claimed to "memorize information" every day. The report concludes that

> in the eyes of the students, the typical history classroom is one in which [students] listen to the teacher explain the day's lesson, use the textbook, and take tests. Occasionally they watch a movie. . . . They seldom work with other students, use original documents, write term papers, or discuss the significance of what they are studying.
>
> (Ravitch & Finn, 1987, 194)

Jumping ahead two decades, the 2006 NAEP survey of 4th, 8th, and 12th grade students showed few changes in instructional methods. The survey asked students how they studied history or social studies. It did not offer the response of "listening to the teacher," like the earlier survey did, but the most frequently selected option, reported to have been done daily by more than half of the secondary students, was the option most like it: "discussing the material studied." Additionally, 32% of 4th graders, 42% of 8th graders, and 34% of 12th graders reported to have read daily from a textbook. Although the percentage of students reporting daily textbook reading and discussions has declined, many history teachers continued to use these traditional activities (Lee & Weiss, 2007).

As part of my dissertation, a research assistant and I spent 72 hours observing eight high school history teachers for six consecutive class sessions over a three-week period. We found that these eight teachers lectured over 56% of the time, with more than half of the lectures involving little interaction with the students. In addition, students in these classrooms spent 23% of class time engaged in reading assignments that, in most cases, involved their textbook. The remaining time was divided relatively evenly between assessments and cooperative learning. Several teachers provided brief mini-lessons on skills such as how to make a poster, write a paper, or engage in a debate. However, these lessons occupied just a few minutes over the 72 hours of observations. In contrast, traditional notions of history instruction, lectures and textbook reading, occupied almost 80% of class time (Nokes, 2010a).

In summary, students' surveys and my experience and observational study suggest that traditional activities continue to have a prominent place in history classrooms. Certainly, the image of the boring history teacher portrayed in movies is exaggerated. However, the instructional methods used are fairly accurate. Through both lectures and textbook reading, teachers maintain control of the historical accounts students hear. Students' role in history classrooms is primarily to listen, manage information, record it in their notes, memorize it in preparation for exams, and report it back to the teacher during assessments. There is evidence to support the quintessential image of history class.

Traditional Materials

My observations also revealed patterns in the resources history teachers used with their students. The eight teachers we observed employed textbooks about five times as often as they used primary sources. Textbooks were used as expository or "informational texts," intended to transmit information. Students were not encouraged to critically evaluate or question the validity of textbook passages. Instead, they accepted the information in the textbooks without question, summarized textbook passages, and used textbooks to find answers to factual questions. Students watched documentary videos and listened to lectures for the same reason they read textbooks: to receive information. Many teachers that we observed did not expose students to primary source documents, artifacts, photographs, music, or other historical sources that a historian might use as evidence (Nokes, 2010a).

Both the 1987 and 2006 NAEP surveys corroborate the findings of these observations. In 1987, almost 60% of the students reported that they were exposed daily to textbooks. One third of students reported watching movies weekly. In contrast, only 12% reported using documents or other original sources at least once a week and 45% said that they never used primary source documents (Ravitch & Finn, 1987). Changes between the results of the 1987 NAEP survey and that conducted in 2006 cause some optimism. The more recent survey showed a significant drop in the percentage of students who reported using the textbook daily – from almost 60% in 1987 to about one third in 2006. The survey also showed an increase in the frequency of primary source use, particularly in middle and high schools. Still, 39% of 4th graders, 28% of 8th graders, and 20% of 11th graders claimed to have never used primary sources in their history classes (Lee & Weiss, 2007). And although primary sources may be increasingly common in history classrooms, my observational study found that when primary sources were used, the teacher typically read and explained the source to the students. Students listened and took notes on the information contained in the primary source, as they would have done during a lecture or when reading a textbook. Reisman (2012) observed primary sources being used in a similar manner – to reinforce information found in a textbook. During the three weeks of my observations I saw only one extended lesson and two brief activities that resembled the historical literacy activities that Mr. Rich conducted, where students were given multiple primary sources and were allowed to independently construct interpretations (Nokes, 2010a).

Results of Traditional Instruction

Traditional history instruction, in spite of its dullness, would be celebrated if it properly prepared students for college, careers, and a lifetime of informed civic engagement. However, this is not the case. One of America's favorite pastimes is to mock fellow Americans' ignorance of historical facts. For example, a 2011 issue of *Newsweek* asks in the headline, "How Dumb Are We?" (Romano, 2011). It reports that 38% of the 1,000 Americans given a U.S. citizenship test failed. The good news, if there is any to be found, is that Americans are not becoming much dumber: Romano cites studies that show that shifts in Americans' civic knowledge since the 1940s have averaged out to less than 1%. In other words, today's Americans have a similar grasp of history to that of their parents and grandparents – and on average their grasp of history is poor. Even older research suggests that Americans' struggles with remembering historical facts go back several generations earlier. For example, Bell and McCollum (1917) tested elementary students, high school students, normal school students, and university students on their basic knowledge of historical facts. Average scores for the different groups ranged from 16% to 49%. They concluded that "this does not show a very thorough mastery of basic historical facts" (274). Many history teachers, even those without an inclination to rethink their methods, are aware of the ineffectiveness of traditional instruction in promoting long-term learning. I've heard on many occasions comments similar to the following, made by a student teacher I was recently working with: "I need to give the test tomorrow [Friday] because the students will forget over the weekend everything we have been studying."

Struggles with learning history are not confined to remembering historical facts but include difficulties in processing historical information. For example, the 2010 NAEP assessment found that only 20% of 4th graders demonstrated proficiency in historical thinking and writing. Even more alarming, only 17% of 8th graders and 12% of 12th graders showed proficiency (National Center for Educational Statistics, 2011). Students' lack of skill in using historical evidence to solve simple historical problems mirrors their lack of content knowledge. Put bluntly, most students are not very good at remembering history or doing history.

To summarize, in spite of the efforts of history teachers, traditional instruction, consisting of lectures, videos, and textbook reading, does not yield significant long-term learning for most students. Historical content knowledge that students passively receive and rarely use is quickly forgotten. Within weeks of when facts are taught, students retain little beyond the simplistic and erroneous notions of pop-history that cultural immersion fosters with or without history classes (Wineburg, 2007). Further, students leave traditional history classrooms with little ability to engage in historical reading, reasoning, or writing because their time has been spent managing information rather than engaging in historical thinking. An honest appraisal of ongoing studies of general historical knowledge creates doubts about the value of traditional history instruction today, 50 years ago, or 100 years ago. Traditional instruction has apparently never worked very well for the majority of students.

Redefining History Instruction

Increasingly history educators are redefining the purpose of teaching history. Many question the value of traditional instruction that focuses exclusively on distributing historical information. Of what value, for example, are learning standards that require a future welder or waitress to memorize information about Mohenjo-Daro, the Zhou Dynasty, or Japan's Yamato period (Wineburg, 2005), particularly when unused factual knowledge isn't retained? History educators suggest – and this is the theme of this book – that instead, history teachers should focus on building students' historical literacies: students' ability to gather and weigh evidence from multiple sources, make informed decisions, solve problems using historical accounts, and persuasively defend their interpretations of the past. Instead of focusing solely on historical information, teachers have the potential to prepare students to survive and thrive for a lifetime in a world where texts must be evaluated, conflicting accounts must be weighed, and information must be questioned. Historical literacy is crucial for participation in a democratic and increasingly globally-linked world.

In addition to questioning the value of traditional instruction, some history educators have gone so far as to argue that what occurs in most history classrooms is not really history teaching. Bruce VanSledright, for example, makes a distinction between heritage teaching and history teaching. He claims that heritage teaching exposes students to a single historical narrative, carefully tailored to "create a sense of pleasure and joy in being who we are" (2002, 11) – or, more accurately, who some of us are, because this narrative rarely celebrates accomplishments outside of the male, Anglo-American realm. Students in heritage classrooms rehearse the "official history" as teachers and policy-makers revel in the notion of building little patriots. Instead, my goal has always been to develop *critical* patriots: young people who appreciate remarkable Americans and unique American institutions, but who also acknowledge the flaws that have tormented and continue to plague American society.

History teaching, with the express purpose of building historical literacy, is crucial in the development of critical patriotism. VanSledright contrasts heritage instruction, with its focus on a single narrative, with history teaching, which opens the past to continual inspection and revision. He encourages teachers to engage students in historical inquiry using the rigorous methods of historians, weighing evidence and understanding contexts before passing judgment. He concludes, ironically, that history teaching is rare in America's history classrooms, adding that much of society is completely satisfied with heritage teaching rather than history teaching.

Researchers raise other concerns about the teaching of a single historical narrative. Stahl and Shanahan (2004) suggest that traditional instruction causes students to view texts as bearers of information. Objective sounding history textbooks stand above criticism, unquestioned by student-readers (Paxton, 1999).

How different this is from historians' view of texts as "'speech acts' produced for particular purposes by particular persons, at particular times and places" (Stahl & Shanahan, 2004, 96). They suggest that history instruction should build students' disciplinary knowledge – students' ability to engage with texts using methods similar to those used by historians. The call for reform in history teaching celebrates efforts to improve students' ability to work with historical evidence and build students' historical literacies.

The call for reform is becoming more common in mainstream discussions about history teaching. For instance, the Common Core State Standards for History and Social Studies, adopted by most of the states in the United States, call for history teachers to expose students to multiple sources, help students consider the origins of documents, introduce students to the distinction between primary and secondary sources, teach students to use evidence to argue a claim, require students to synthesize information from different texts, and expect students to be fluent with various types of texts (Common Core State Standards, 2010). The Common Core State Standards echo the National Standards for Social Studies published by the National Council for the Social Studies (Nash & Crabtree, 1996). Increasingly, there is a vision of a future with teachers like Mr. Rich in every history classroom.

Making the Case for Historical Literacy Instruction

Mr. Rich is not an entirely fictional character. He represents a growing number of history teachers who make historical literacy instruction an integral and daily part of their classrooms. And researchers are investigating the results of innovative historical literacy instruction.

For example, Bruce VanSledright (2002), a teacher education professor, was convinced that elementary students would benefit by investigating evidence and independently developing historical understandings. He spent much of a school year helping 23 fifth-grade students study historical controversies, explore teacher-prepared "archives", produce document-based group presentations, and debate conflicting interpretations of historical events. He helped students "learn history by doing it" (196). His ambitions were confronted by three formidable challenges as students a) struggled to understand the difference between historical interpretation and the reality of the past, b) continued to search for the single "correct" historical narrative, and c) imposed present conditions, values, and standards on people and events of the past. In spite of these challenges he saw students "deeply drawn into the process of investigating the past" (150), taking "to the task of reading texts with considerable zeal" (152). His teaching methods were highly engaging.

Even more importantly, all eight of the students with whom VanSledright did follow-up interviews, had developed a more sophisticated understanding of the nature of historical inquiry. They understood and adopted the role of historian in interpreting evidence, recognizing bias, distinguishing between primary and secondary sources, and corroborating across texts. They became more willing to insert themselves into the historical discussion, one suggesting that he would rather rely on his interpretation of primary sources than on either of two contrasting interpretations made by other investigators. VanSledright tentatively celebrated the "conditional successes" of his work with the youngsters (134).

Other researchers have fostered historical disciplinary knowledge with middle school (Ashby, Lee, & Shemilt, 2005; De La Paz, 2005; Levstik & Barton, 2005), high school (Bain, 2005; Britt & Aglinskas, 2002; Lesh, 2011; Nokes, *et al.*, 2007; Reisman, 2012; Young & Leinhardt, 1998) and undergraduate students (Hynd, Holschuh, & Hubbard, 2004; Perfetti, Britt, & Georgi, 1995) with positive results. Student-participants in these studies developed a more sophisticated view of historical interpretation, improved in their historical reading and writing skills, used historians' strategies for working with texts, became more sensitive to perspective, and, as a by-product, increased in content knowledge.

For example, my dissertation studied the building of historical literacies in high school students in eight history classrooms (Nokes, *et al.*, 2007). Eight teachers taught a four-week unit on the 1920s and 1930s that I had planned. During the unit, all of the activities that students did in all of the classes were the same except for ten one-hour literacy lessons. During these lessons there were differences between what occurred in different classes. In two of the classes teachers conducted traditional reading activities – "read the textbook and answer these questions" about the historical content. In two other classes teachers continued to use the textbook, but they discussed and practised historians' strategies with students. Students were taught to read the textbook with a more critical eye. In two of the classes teachers used documents and other authentic historical texts and students answered questions about the historical content. In the last two classes students read the same collection of documents and received instruction on historians' reading and reasoning strategies. In this fourth treatment condition, students were taught to pay attention to perspective, to synthesize across texts, and to use other strategies. Students in the two treatment conditions that studied documents scored significantly higher than the students who studied textbooks on tests of their content knowledge, regardless of whether their lessons had focused on content or historians' strategies. However, only the students that were taught historians' strategies while working with primary sources showed significant growth in their ability to read and reason like historians. On post-tests, these students paid greater attention to the source of the document, they more skillfully compared and contrasted conflicting accounts, and in the end they wrote about historical controversy with greater sophistication. One important conclusion of my study, and others like it (Reisman, 2012), is that if a teacher focuses exclusively on content instruction, students are not likely to develop strategies for reading like a historian. If, on the other hand, a teacher spends a significant amount of time teaching historical literacies, students will start to use the strategies, will interact more deeply with texts, and, as a result, will learn the content better. Ironically, when some content instruction is replaced by literacy instruction, greater content knowledge is developed.

To summarize there are at least three research-based reasons why history teachers should build students' historical literacies. First, working with documents can be highly engaging for students – much more so than traditional instruction consisting of lectures and textbook reading. Second, students who actively piece together historical events from documents, learn historical content better. This shouldn't be surprising given current research on learning, which shows that individuals learn best when they are active, i.e. solving a historical mystery using documents, rather than passive, i.e. watching a documentary video (Bransford, Brown, & Cocking, 2000). Third, students who are taught to read and reason like historians exhibit more sophisticated critical reading and thinking skills. They develop historical literacies. And students who are skilled in constructing historical understanding are better prepared to be life-long learners of history. They are more likely to be able to know where to find reliable sources when they have questions about historical events. They are more likely to seek corroborating evidence rather than rely on a single source. Further, students who are historically literate are better prepared to survive and thrive in a democratic society during this Information Age. They are better prepared to be critical patriots, serving as informed voters or responsible jurors, roles that require an individual to sort through conflicting messages, pay attention to sources, and interpret evidence.

Defining "Historical Literacies"

The concept of literacy means different things in different settings, and is currently being defined and redefined in the research. There is a movement in education to make a distinction between "reading" and "literacy." Reading involves constructing meaning with traditional texts that include words, sentences, and paragraphs. Literacy, on the other hand, involves constructing meaning with a wider variety of sources including traditional texts but, in addition, including images, sounds, or other resources (Cope & Kalantzis, 2000). For instance, most propaganda posters from World War I combine words and images. The designers of posters use not only loaded language but also emotive colors and images to achieve a particular purpose. To effectively comprehend a poster and use it as evidence, a viewer must attend to not only the words but the images as well. Thus, literacy includes the ability to read in the traditional sense (i.e. words, sentences, and paragraphs) and the ability to construct meaning with non-traditional texts (i.e. colors, images, and sounds). In the vignette that opened this chapter, some of Mr. Rich's students debated the authenticity of a photograph of children factory workers. Their analysis incorporated both traditional texts (i.e. a historical novel excerpt) and non-traditional resources (i.e. exploring the Internet to find the source of the photograph). Because the study of history involves both traditional texts and non-traditional texts, this book focuses on building a wide range of literacies including, but not limited to, students' reading abilities.

Further, the term "literacy" denotes an individual's ability to construct meaning with some sort of resource – a text. Remaining true to the term's original denotation, then, literacy within a field (i.e. scientific literacy, or historical literacy) is defined as an individual's ability to interact appropriately with the texts that are valued within that discipline (Draper, Broomhead, Jensen, Nokes, & Siebert, 2010; Moje, 2008). In contrast, some current uses of the term literacy have drifted from its original meaning, suggesting that rich content knowledge within a field qualifies an individual as literate in that field. It should be noted that rich background knowledge often facilitates the comprehension of texts, but content knowledge may not be necessary on one hand or sufficient on the other. For example, research has shown that historians with expertise in one field, i.e. medieval China, are able to analyze historical texts from a different, unfamiliar field, i.e. the antebellum United States (Wineburg, 1998). In contrast, some individuals may know much historical information, but be unfamiliar with historical thinking processes (Wineburg, 1991). In spite of a wealth of historical knowledge, an individual remains historically illiterate when he/she does not know how to construct historical interpretations using evidence.

So historical literacy, as defined in this book, is the ability to appropriately negotiate and create the texts and resources that are valued within the discipline of history using methods approved by the community of historians. Historical literacies require a mature understanding of the nature of the discipline of history and the ability to approach a historical problem from an appropriate frame of mind. Historical literacies include the use of historians' strategies for comprehending and evaluating the vast array of artifacts and records that are useful in making inferences about the past.

Mr. Rich understands the importance of building students' historical literacies. But he faces a daunting challenge in trying to not only change the way his students work with texts, but the way they view history as a discipline. A large part of this challenge is due to the fact that during the prior school year most of his current students sat in a traditional history classroom passively listening, taking notes, memorizing, and regurgitating information during exams. Unfortunately, his students might be in another traditional class the year after leaving his. Except for those few who might go to graduate school and study history, they may never have another experience like the one they have in his history classroom. The work of building young peoples' historical literacies is not a task for a single history teacher to complete. Instead, it requires a multi-year, collaborative effort.

Chapter Summary

This book calls for a revolution in the way history teaching is perceived. This chapter calls on history teachers to face the harsh reality that traditional methods and materials do little to build long-term content knowledge or to promote critical thinking skills in students. I make the case for redefining history teaching by placing historical literacies at the center of instruction. When students assume the identity of historians and use historians' methods to study primary source materials, they become more active and engaged, learn historical content and critical thinking skills, and are better prepared for the adult world. This chapter defines historical literacy as the ability to negotiate and create texts that are authentic in historical inquiry. The chapter sets the stage for the further exploration of historical literacies in the chapters that follow.

2

DEFINING HISTORICAL LITERACIES

Mrs. Francis reads an article about how archeologists use a research method called dendrochronology to determine when cliff dwellings at Mesa Verde, Colorado, now abandoned and in ruins, were originally built. She discovers that the process involves taking a cross-section sample from timbers used in construction. Using the distance between tree rings, archeologists identify the climatic pattern in the years leading up to the time the tree was cut down, presumably for construction of the home. Comparing these tree ring patterns to core samples taken from living ancient trees located nearby, they search for a similar series of wet and dry years. Once they find a match they can state, with some authority, what year the tree that was used in the construction of the home was harvested and, by implication, the year the cliff dwelling was built.

While reading the article, Mrs. Francis has an epiphany. Her eyes are opened to the vast number of resources, like a log used in the construction of the cliff dwelling, that archeologists, historians, scientists, anthropologists, and others use to construct an understanding of the past. She also begins to consider the number of different skills required to become historically literate. She contemplates what it would take to introduce her 8th grade American History students to the process of dendrochronology and wonders about the value of doing so. She thinks that it might be worth exposing students to tree ring dating in order to show them how scientists, archeologists, and historians work together to construct an understanding of the distant past. Dendrochronology is a simple enough process that most students would be able to understand it and many might even be able to engage in it. She recognizes that the logs are only one of many pieces of evidence used to track the evolving culture of the Ancestral Pueblo people, and she determines to develop a pair of lessons – case studies of evidence of the Ancestral Pueblo culture – in order to reach the following objectives:

1. the students will consider the way geography and climate influence culture
2. the students will debate the causes of the changing culture of the Ancestral Pueblo people
3. the students will practice using observations from artifacts to make logical inferences about a prehistoric people, an important skill in archeology.

In the process, she hopes that students will appreciate the strong ties between historical thinking and archeological thinking.

On the first day of the lessons, Mrs. Francis briefly lectures, giving students background information on the Ancestral Pueblo who lived in the Southwest United States until about nine hundred years ago. Following the lecture she brings in the school's mobile computer lab and has students work on a National Park Service website that explains and gives them simple hands-on experience in dendrochronology (National Park Service, 2012). She then has them form small groups to see what they can infer about the Ancestral Pueblo based on observations made of their homes. Mrs. Francis creates images of tree ring core samples from logs used in construction and living trees. In addition to the tree ring samples, Mrs. Francis gathers pictures of the ruins of Ancestral Pueblo homes from a variety of locations. Using the tree ring samples, the groups of students rate each year as "d" for dry, "a" for average or "w" for wet, ending up with a letter series for a sample such as d,d,a,w,a,a,w,a,a,d,d,a,d,d,d. They then compare their sample with a sample given from the living tree. When they find a matching series they date the construction of the home. Doing so correctly helps the groups discover that the Ancestral Pueblo built homes on the plateau tops of Mesa Verde centuries before building homes in the cliffs. Rotating from group to group she helps students discover through tree rings that about the same time construction ended on the plateau tops, construction began in the cliffs. Coming to one of the groups that has just made this discovery, Mrs. Francis asks, "What logical inferences could be made based on where and when their homes were built?"

"Maybe things got too crowded on the mesa top and so they had to find a new place to live," Angela suggests.

"So you think some groups were building on the mesa tops and other groups in the cliffs?" Mrs. Francis probes.

"Yeah, I guess that's what I think."

"I don't think so," chimes in Demi. "I think that they all moved down into the cliffs from the mesa tops. They weren't building on the tops any more once they moved into the cliffs. I think there was something that was pushing them down into the cliffs. I think that they probably had wars or that enemies were raiding their villages so they moved down there for safety."

"Yeah. It would've been hard to attack them down in the cliffs," agrees Curtis.

"I think you're both wrong," Christie interrupts. "I think they moved down there because it was getting hotter and dryer. Look at all of the tree ring samples. Their climate was changing."

"Why would they just move to a place close by if the climate was changing? If it was dry on the mesa top it would be dry in the cliffs. Wouldn't they move far away if there was a drought?" Angela asks.

"Maybe eventually. Maybe that's why they disappeared from Mesa Verde altogether like Mrs. Francis told us. But first I think they moved down into the cliffs for the shade," Christie explains.

"But look at this picture (see Figure 2.1). It shows their homes in the sun," Curtis points out.

"Yeah, but that picture was taken in the winter time. See the source. Look at this picture of the same cliff dwelling in the summer time (see Figure 2.2). It's shaded," Christie observes.

"That's just a coincidence, isn't it Mrs. Francis?" Curtis asks.

"Actually, almost all of the cliff dwellings were built on south facing cliffs, so they are shaded in the summer and sunny in the winter. I doubt if it was a coincidence."

"Wow. Those people were pretty smart," Curtis concludes.

"See, I told you that they built their homes in the cliffs because the weather was getting hotter and dryer," Christie celebrates.

"I still think they built them down there to get away from enemies," argues Curtis.

Mrs. Francis has moved on to another group where a similar conversation is taking place. The last few minutes of class Mrs. Francis leads the entire class in a

FIGURE 2.1 A photograph of Cliff Palace taken during the winter months (Photograph printed with permission of Bruce Schundler).

FIGURE 2.2 A photograph of Cliff Palace taken during the summer months (Photograph printed with permission of Bruce Schundler).

discussion of what they could infer about the Ancestral Pueblo people from their homes. Students agree that there was a movement from the plateau top to the cliffs but they still disagree about why they moved into the cliffs.

"That's alright," Mrs. Francis assures the class. "Historians and archeologists disagree about why they moved as well. And it's certainly possible that there were several related causes for them moving down there. Maybe they moved because the climate was getting dryer *and* because enemies were threatening them."

"Maybe enemies were threatening them *because* the climate was getting dryer," Curtis suggests. "If there wasn't as much food, then people might have been fighting over it."

During the discussion Mrs. Francis emphasizes that the Ancestral Pueblo people went through cultural change over decades and centuries, and that a changing climate may have played a role in that change.

The next day, students again work in groups analyzing other replicas or photographs of Ancestral Pueblos artifacts. At the start of class Mrs. Francis tells them that during the last part of class they will write a brief introduction to the Ancestral Pueblo that could be placed on a virtual museum website that has links to artifacts. Their description should provide museum-goers with a basic understanding of who the Ancestral Pueblo were, prior to looking at their artifacts. Students will have most of the class to prepare by making inferences about the Ancestral Pueblo based on their artifacts – much like they did the day before with their homes. Students are given a worksheet (see Figure 2.3) on which they

Sketch of Artifact	Observations	Inferences

FIGURE 2.3 A graphic organizer designed to support students' work with artifacts.

sketch the artifact, list observations, and record inferences based on their observations. Photographs of artifacts show a mano and metate, baskets, pictographs, decayed sandals, a diagram of a kiva, clay pots, stone tools, stone weapons, and a small clay human figurine. Mrs. Francis circulates throughout the class, helping each group make discoveries such as that the Ancestral Pueblo were farmers who also hunted, they had religious beliefs, and they did not have metallurgy. She works to make sure that students can justify each inference using the evidence found in artifacts.

"How do you know that they hunted?" she asks Derrick.

"They draw a lot of mountain goats in their pictographs so I think that they were obsessed with them. I don't think they would have been so obsessed if they didn't hunt them," he explains.

The last few minutes of class she reminds students that they need to write a brief description of the Ancestral Pueblo that might be used on an introductory page for a virtual museum website that shows collections of their artifacts. "Keep it to less than 200 words," she explains, as students get out paper and start to write.

Historical Literacies

Some of my most engaging historical thinking lessons, like Mrs. Francis', involved students in an analysis of artifacts rather than written forms of historical evidence. You might react, "This isn't literacy! They aren't reading anything!" However, students engage in many of the processes used in traditional reading as they attempt to construct meaning with artifacts and other types of evidence. For instance, Mrs. Francis' students engage in historical literacies by conducting a form of "close reading," by making inferences, and by using evidence to support claims. Working with artifacts, students find that our understanding of the past is influenced significantly not only by historians, but by a host of other researchers.

The work of archeologists, historians, scientists, anthropologists, and others, whose intent is to describe and interpret the past, involves the construction of meaning with a wide variety of resources. Mrs. Francis realized that what a tourist at Mesa Verde might consider an old log becomes a "text" to be read by someone who knows how to make sense of its markings and skillfully interpret them. Architecture styles, trends in music, prehistoric garbage dumps, census numbers, family patterns in modern nomadic societies, ancient artifacts, modern artifacts, and written records – especially written records – are the building blocks with which history, the interpretation of the past, is constructed. The world abounds in print and non-print, visual and aural, natural and man-made "texts," useful in the study of history. But the usefulness of texts comes only when an individual knows how to read them. Historical literacy involves a search for data – evidence with which to build defensible interpretations of past events – from this vast array of texts. Using Mrs. Francis' classroom as an example, in this chapter I a) define the concept of historical literacy, b) consider historians as models of historical literacy, and c) demonstrate the need for secondary students to receive historical literacy instruction.

Defining the Concept of Historical Literacy

Historical literacy is the ability to construct meaning with multiple genres of print, non-print, visual, aural, video, audio, and multimodal historical texts; critically evaluate texts within the context of the work historians have previously done; use texts as evidence in the development of original interpretations of past events; and create multiple types of texts that meet discipline standards. As mentioned in Chapter 1, historical literacy is different than general historical knowledge. Historical literacy is not the possession of an encyclopedic knowledge of historical facts, but the ability to glean appropriate information about the past from resources of many genres. It is the ability to engage in historical processes – to not simply possess knowledge, but to know how to build it. Historical literacy connotes the ability to not only learn from the historical accounts that others have written, but to independently develop new interpretations of the past and to communicate them to others.

Mrs. Francis' lesson serves as a good model of historical literacy. She introduces and supports students' work with familiar and unfamiliar genres of texts, such as the cliff dwelling ruins, artifacts, and core samples used in dendrochronology. She provides students with some background knowledge prior to exposing them to the texts. In doing so, she helps students understand what archeologists and historians have hypothesized about the Ancestral Pueblo. The majority of time in her lesson is spent with students exploring evidence, developing hypotheses, and defending their ideas before their critical peers. In her interaction with students, she repeatedly pulls them back to the texts, asking them to justify their interpretations using evidence. In the end students produce an authentic text, the type of summary that a historian or archeologist might write.

Historians as Models of Historical Literacies

A description of historical literacy must begin with consideration of the literacies of historians. Specifically, I explore the following questions: Which texts are essential in historical inquiry? Which literacy skills do historians employ? And which habits of mind characterize historians' work?

Which Texts Are Essential in Historical Inquiry?

The work of historians primarily involves the study of written records, with artifacts, such as those in Mrs. Francis' lesson, supplementing the written record. Historians spend much of their research time in archives searching through collections of documents, such as old newspaper articles, trial transcripts, church records, journal entries, and letters, for sources of information related to their topic of interest. Historical literacy involves searching for materials, skimming, distinguishing relevant from irrelevant information, and judging the relative worth of sources. As a general rule, when working with written texts historians value primary sources, first-hand accounts, over other types of writing. They do so for much the same reason that those investigating a crime scene would value eyewitness testimony over hearsay accounts. Primary sources, although influenced by the writer's involvement in an event and his/her point of view, are not distorted by any other individuals' interpretations. In spite of their admitted imperfections, primary sources provide the purest evidence about the past. Historians seek out all possible primary sources related to their inquiry and construct an interpretation through a critical analysis and synthesis of primary source evidence. Historical literacy, then, includes the ability to gather sources, recognize and account for point of view, identify corroborating and conflicting evidence, and build logical and defensible interpretations.

It is rare that historians pioneer an entirely new topic of study; instead, their work is generally grounded within a field of research on similar topics. Thus historians must be aware of, and skillful in working with, secondary sources, second-hand accounts produced from primary sources. Historians must pay attention to other historians' interpretations of their topic. They must ask how other historians have dealt with evidence and whether flaws exist in the work of others. They must explore what others have omitted that is worthy of consideration and whether new evidence has been uncovered. Within the context of prior work, they consider how their new perspective leads to new and better interpretations of the past. Historians understand that secondary sources, like primary sources, reflect the values, interests, and interpretations of the individuals who produce them. Historical literacy involves the ability to distinguish primary from secondary sources, and to work with them in appropriate ways. It includes the ability to use source information, including the context of the document's creation, whether a primary or secondary source, to build meaning with it.

Along with written records, historians draw upon a number of scientific, oral, visual, numeric, and anthropologic sources and artifacts to construct interpretations of the past. For example, historians use the findings of anthropologists who study modern nomadic societies to make inferences about prehistoric nomadic groups who left behind no written records and few artifacts. Ice core samples give clues about climatic fluctuations – something that is absent in written records but has become a new lens through which to interpret historical events. Scientific fields of study, such as paleobotany, explore the prehistoric record found in evolving plant life, helping historians trace the origins and spread of agriculture. Census records capture patterns in immigration providing data to supplement the more personal records kept by some immigrant families. And historical archeology, the study of artifacts at historical sites (such as the slave quarters at Mount Vernon), corroborates or raises questions about interpretations that would otherwise be based solely on written records. From tree rings, to magazine ads that show the fashionable length of women's hair, historians draw from a wide range of resources to supplement written records. Thus Mrs. Francis' lessons, although devoid of written texts, included numerous sources that historians and archeologists would use as evidence to interpret the past.

Furthermore, historians produce a variety of texts, including monographs, journal articles, maps, cartograms, population pyramids, charts, graphs, and diagrams, intended to help others understand the past and to persuade others to accept their interpretations. These texts are used to convey historical ideas to fellow historians as well as to individuals who lack disciplinary expertise – students of history or newspaper readers, for example. Thus historians' literacies include not only the ability to read and critically analyze multiple genres but to produce multiple types of text.

In addition, the historical record includes public or popular histories produced as museum exhibits, historical novels, movies, and popular books. Although of less importance to historians, students must learn how to be wise consumers of these types of texts. Teachers must not underestimate the influence of popular culture and students' experiences on understandings of the past. For instance, researchers have found that students' conception of the Vietnam War era has been shaped significantly by the movie *Forrest Gump* (Wineburg, 2007). Ironically, the media that are the least helpful to historians (i.e. public and popular histories) are often the most influential in the lives of non-historians. Since most students will not be historians, it makes sense that history teachers spend time helping them think critically about popular histories, weighing them against other forms of historical evidence.

Expository texts, most notably history textbooks, complete the list of the types of texts that individuals might encounter when learning about history. Textbooks, encyclopedia articles, Wikipedia, and other expository texts represent, for the most part, tertiary sources – third-hand accounts of historical events, far removed from the primary sources that serve as evidence. Expository sources generally follow a traditional historical narrative including few explanations of how evidence was used, or how interpretations were made, and few explicit attempts to persuade the reader that their notions of historical events are reliable. Instead, expository texts, by their very nature, give the impression that they are above question or critique, simply providing facts (Paxton, 1999).

To simplify things for students, I categorize texts either as evidence, secondary sources, tertiary sources, or public/popular histories as shown in Figure 2.4. This figure illustrates for students that all historical interpretations should be based directly or indirectly on some form of historical evidence, though some public and popular histories, produced to entertain, have little or no evidence base. It should be noted that a text's placement in this categorization system is primarily based on the way a historian uses it. For instance, textbooks are normally tertiary sources, but to a historian who investigates the evolving portrayal of African Americans in the public school curriculum, textbooks become a primary source. The movie, *Birth of a Nation* (Griffith & Aitken, 1915) would serve as a tertiary source for a historian investigating the origins of the Ku Klux Klan, but as a primary source for a historian studying White southerners' perceptions in 1915, the time the movie was produced. With this understanding, the categorization system can help teachers and students remember the purposes for using different types of texts and identify the approaches most helpful in working with them.

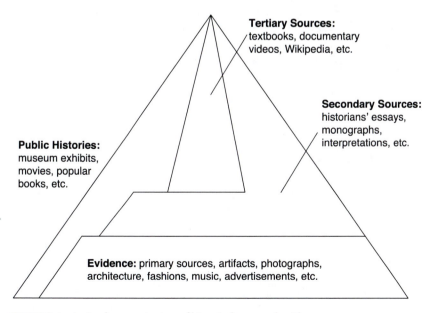

Tertiary Sources:
textbooks, documentary videos, Wikipedia, etc.

Secondary Sources:
historians' essays, monographs, interpretations, etc.

Public Histories:
museum exhibits, movies, popular books, etc.

Evidence: primary sources, artifacts, photographs, architecture, fashions, music, advertisements, etc.

FIGURE 2.4 A visual categorization of historical texts and evidence.

Which Literacy Skills do Historians Employ?

Perhaps more than any discipline area, researchers have explored the literacies used by historians as they construct meaning with historical texts. Researchers suggest that historians are extraordinarily active readers, comparing them to attorneys who interrogate evidence (Wineburg, 1991, 2001). Historians' work involves a balancing act between carefully examining evidence and trying to imagine what things were like in the past. Historians' literacy skills range from observation and reasoning to visualization and imagination. Historians do not view texts as conveyers of information, as students often do, but as the product of individuals with emotion, flawed perception, a particular point of view, conflicts of interest, and personal insights. Further, they acknowledge that texts can be interpreted in multiple ways, which opens the door for historical debates, continued investigation of old questions, and the regular rewriting of history. Thus, reading historical texts requires more than the comprehension of the meaning of words and sentences; it requires an understanding of the subtext – the context, audience, purposes, biases, and insights of the author (Lesh, 2011; Perfetti, *et al.*, 1999; Wineburg, 1994).

Historical literacy requires a critical analysis of evidence, always keeping the source in mind. Wineburg (1991) and other researchers identify this technique as "sourcing." Sourcing is a universal and instinctive heuristic employed by historians. When they pick up an unfamiliar text they look first at the author, consider the context of its creation, and begin to build expectations about its content even before reading (Wineburg, 1991). Texts are viewed as extensions of individuals. Historians' reading, then, is an exchange with people, separated by time and place, but connected through the writing/creation and reading/interpretation of texts.

Additionally, historians compare and contrast evidence from multiple sources, a strategy labeled "corroboration" (Wineburg, 1991). Corroboration involves checking and cross checking evidence (VanSledright, 2002). As historians encounter new information in a primary source, they search for verification in other sources, holding new interpretations as tentative until substantiating evidence can be found. They also pay attention to and account for conflicting evidence. Corroboration allows historians to evaluate the validity and reliability of various sources. Additionally, corroboration, when coupled with sourcing, allows historians to gain the advantage of having multiple perspectives of an event. For instance, if studying the Battle of Little Bighorn, historians would corroborate across oral histories from the Sioux and Cheyenne, written records from the U.S. Army, artifacts from the battle site, personal writings that provide insight on Native American and U.S. military leaders, and other sources (Lesh, 2011). Their interpretations are bolstered when multiple sources point to their conclusions.

One of the challenges of studying the past is that it is always done through the lens of the present. Today's values, attitudes, and environment differ from those of past generations. This explains why the actions of historical characters often seem odd to us today. It is difficult, particularly for students, to consider the past without making judgments based on modern standards. However historians attempt to do this – to understand the past on its own terms – in their investigation of historical texts. Researchers have labeled historians' efforts to understand the physical and cultural context of a text's creation as "contextualization" (Wineburg, 1991). Historians use their rich background knowledge, as well as clues in texts (Wineburg, 1998), to imagine the context of the document's creation. They attempt to construct meaning with the document with that context in mind, putting out of mind, as much as possible, the present.

Different aspects of the context can take on importance. The linguistic context is important in comprehending written texts because the meaning and use of words can change over time. For instance, during Shay's Rebellion, when George Washington wrote to General Benjamin Lincoln asking if the farmers of Massachusetts were "mad," he was not asking whether they were angry but if they were crazy (Washington, 1786). The physical context gains significance in working with artifacts. For instance, archeologists painstakingly document the precise location of artifacts in relation to other artifacts in an archeological dig. The physical context carries implications about the way an artifact may have been used. Further, the timing of a document's creation can influence its usefulness as a source. Individuals who write immediately after an event often remember details, but lack the perspective that time can give. For instance, when studying documents related to the battle of Lexington, one historian pointed out that an account had been written several years after the battle at the end of the Revolutionary War. Although the author was an eyewitness, because the account didn't match other eyewitness accounts, the historian concluded that the author might have confused events from later battles in his memory of events on Lexington Green years earlier (Wineburg, 1991).

Further, contextualization involves a consideration of the broad context of an event – the macro-context, as well as the immediate context – micro-context. The macro-context includes societal trends, the language of the time period, etiquette, common values, generally accepted theories, and familiar national and international events. The micro-context includes immediate factors that influence an event such as the weather, the day of week of the event, and whether the people involved in the event had had a good night's sleep. I've found that students can sometimes infer some elements of the micro-context from documents, but they have a more difficult time keeping in mind the macro-context.

A strategy similar to contextualization is historical empathy or perspective taking. Historical empathy replaces the deficit view of people in the past (i.e. the notion that people in the past were intellectually and culturally inferior to us) with the understanding that people's decisions generally make sense given their current knowledge, technologies, and values (Foster, 2001; Lee, 2005; Lesh, 2011). Historical empathy is the process of considering an individual's context in an effort to understand his/her actions. It is not purely an emotional process, like empathy in the traditional sense, but is a cognitive and logical process – an important part of understanding historical actions.

In addition to sourcing, corroboration, contextualization, and historical empathy, historians make inferences. Historians must "read between the lines" as they construct interpretations. VanSledright (2002) points out that often the greatest challenge historians face is not synthesizing information from conflicting sources, but filling in gaps when no evidence exists, a process also referred to as "historical imagination." Collingwood shows that what is inferred, is imagined (1993). Unlike pure imagination, historical imagination that is used in making inferences is constrained by evidence and reason (Collingwood, 1993; Levesque, 2008). The development of historical inferences and interpretations is the heart of historical literacy. It involves skillfully using evidence when it is available; employing sourcing, corroboration, and contextualization; and blending logic and imagination to fill in the gaps when the historical record is silent. As Collingwood described, history is "a web of imaginative construction stretched between certain fixed points provided by [critically analyzed evidence]" (1993, 242). Historians make inferences about historical motives, purposes, causes, or trends.

Which Habits of Mind Characterize Historians' Work?

In addition to the skills described above, there are several habits of mind that historians demonstrate, perspectives on working with evidence and developing interpretations, that influence their use of texts. Historians approach a historical question with a mature epistemic stance (Reddy & VanSledright 2010). They understand that history is not the past, but instead is a study of the past based on the incomplete and imperfect record that has been left behind. They acknowledge that there is not a single historical narrative but that multiple interpretations are possible. Further, they understand that not all interpretations are equally valid, making judgments based on the way evidence was used.

Additionally, historians maintain a healthy skepticism as they approach texts. They do not accept information in any text at face value but critically evaluate text content with the source in mind. Texts do not convey information but, instead, represent an individual's viewpoint, parts of which the historian may or may not accept as reliable based on a great number of factors. They maintain the power of the "line item veto" to discount any part of a text that they judge to be inaccurate (Wineburg, 1994).

Further, historians maintain an open mind, holding interpretations as tentative. They understand that new evidence, which regularly surfaces, or new ways of thinking about the past, lead to a constantly evolving understanding of history. Perfetti and his colleagues (1999) hypothesized that as historians engage in inquiry they not only construct an understanding of an event (labeled a "situation model" in literacy research), but they also construct alternative explanations (labeled "hypothetical situation models" by Perfetti). As more evidence is encountered, historians lean toward certain interpretations, but alternative interpretations are not completely dismissed. Thus, historians, though skeptical about all interpretations, remain open to new, evidence-based theories. Ironically, Wineburg (1991) found that students were much more confident in their naïve understanding of the past than were historians of their sophisticated interpretations.

Historians' habits of mind are based on their understanding of important concepts related to historical methodology and general historical thinking. Such concepts include evidence, accounts, change, continuity, time, and cause. A correct understanding of these concepts, sometimes labeled second order concepts or metaconcepts, is key to historians' work (Lee, 2005).

The Need for Secondary Students to Receive Historical Literacy Instruction

Historians' professional activities contrast sharply with traditional history teaching methods. I can think of no other discipline where the work of students differs more drastically from the work of professionals. In science, students do labs. In gym class, they play sports. In English class, they write poetry. In music class, they perform in ensembles. And in industrial arts they work with the same tools carpenters use. However, in history, students typically listen to lectures and memorize information, activities that do not reflect historical thinking. Students are so distanced from historical processes that they typically have no inkling of how historians go about their work. I recently interviewed 30 5th grade students, asking, among other things how they thought historians spent their time. Students confused the work of historians with paleontologists, history makers (such as explorers or pilgrims), or simply admitted they didn't know what historians did. They imagined them surfing Wikipedia, watching the history channel, or listening to lectures, all processes more closely associated with the way students learn history than with actual historical inquiry. Most students can't imagine the work of historians because they have never experienced anything like it.

Unfortunately, many people are satisfied with traditional history teaching. In fact, the teaching of historical literacies has been controversial in the past. For example, the United States educator and eventual president, Woodrow Wilson, was afraid that the complex cognitive processes of historical thinking exceeded students' abilities. He contended that "we must avoid introducing what is called scientific history in the schools for it is [a] history of doubt, criticism, examination of evidence. It tends to confuse young people" (VanSledright, 2002, vii).

Indeed, the confusion of young people in working with historical texts has been well documented. Without support, they struggle when exposed to historians' texts and when asked to engage in historians' literacies. For example, Sam Wineburg (1991) compared think aloud protocols of historians with the protocols of advanced high school students as they negotiated meaning with multiple texts related to the Battle of Lexington. He found that the students, unlike the historians, struggled with contradictions in the accounts, focused on remembering facts, and appreciated the straightforward, and what they perceived was objective, account in a textbook excerpt. The students misunderstood the nature of historical thinking, assuming that their purpose in reading was to remember information rather than to construct and interpret meaning. Other researchers have discovered similar types of challenges when students read multiple historical texts. Steve Stahl and his colleagues found that high school students focused on information that was repeated in multiple texts, but failed to notice, or chose to ignore, contradictions (Stahl, Hynd, Britton, McNish, & Bosquet, 1996). Bruce VanSledright (2002) suspected that the 5th grade students inappropriately applied background knowledge from Disney's movie, *Pocahontas,* in interpreting the causes of the "Starving Time" in Jamestown colony. In my research, I found that even after several lessons on the use of contextualization, students did not employ this heuristic on a post-test writing task (Nokes, *et al.*, 2007). And other studies further document students' struggles to engaging in historical reading and reasoning (Britt & Aglinskas, 2002; Seixas, 1993). How can teachers immerse students in historians' texts, literacies, and habits of mind without causing the confusion that Woodrow Wilson feared?

The success of Mrs. Francis' lesson is not imaginary. I experienced it often with both middle school and high school students. Mrs. Francis' lesson represents the growing movement among history teachers and researchers to engage students, as young as early elementary grades, in historical reading and thinking (Bain, 2005; Lee & Ashby, 2000; Levstick & Barton, 2005; Stahl & Shanahan, 2004; VanSledright, 2002). As described in Chapter 1, the National Standards of History Instruction encourage teachers to help students identify the source of documents, differentiate between facts and interpretations, consider multiple perspectives, hold interpretations as tentative, interrogate historical data, and marshal evidence to support interpretations (Nash & Crabtree, 1996). In other words, history teachers are encouraged to immerse students in the texts, literacies, and habits of mind of historians. But in the face of the research that shows that it is difficult for students to think like historians, does this kind of teaching produce results?

Indeed, several studies have shown that students begin to exhibit historical literacies when given many opportunities to work with primary source materials, particularly when combined with instruction on historical literacies and feedback on their historical thinking and writing. For example Young and Leinhardt (1998) found that repeated practice writing analytical essays, synthesizing evidence in multiple documents, led students to engage in more sophisticated historical writing. Britt and Aglinskas (2002) developed a computer program that students used to practice sourcing, which improved students' historical thinking. Ferretti, MacArthur, and Okolo (2001) experienced similar success teaching 5th graders to recognize bias in sources. My dissertation documented students' increased use of sourcing and corroboration after 10 literacy lessons (Nokes *et al.*, 2007). Hynd, Holschuh, and Hubbard (2004) found that asking a series of reflective questions improved undergraduate students' understanding of historical processes. Ashby, Lee, and Shemilt (2005) observed that 4th and 6th graders gained a better understanding of historical processes as they worked with multiple texts related to historical controversies. De La Paz (2005) discovered that integrating writing instruction with explanations of historical thinking improved 8th grade students' historical writing. And other innovative teachers provide anecdotal evidence that students begin to exhibit historical literacies when their teachers provide historical literacy instruction (Bain, 2005; Lesh, 2011).

The most comprehensive study of the building of historical literacies in high school students was conducted by Reisman (2012). She provided 83 "document-based lessons," which were flexibly executed by five teachers in five urban high schools over a 21-week period. Students in these classrooms were compared with students in five classrooms where traditional history teaching was the norm. Engagement in the document-based lessons, when carried out in their entirety, included brief lectures to build background knowledge, the posing of a historical dilemma, exposure to at least two primary sources that provided evidence about the dilemma, instruction on historians' inquiry methods, and a class discussion and debriefing. Students who engaged in the series of document-based lessons outperformed their peers from traditional classrooms on measures of historical content knowledge, historical thinking proficiency, application of historical thinking to current events, and, most surprisingly, general reading comprehension. Reisman's study, as well as the research cited above, documents the development of historical literacies by elementary through undergraduate students under the right conditions. I will explain and provide examples of these conditions throughout this book.

To summarize, students rarely spontaneously engage in historical reasoning even when given primary source documents – it is extremely challenging for them. But with instruction, students develop historians' literacies and habits of mind. They can overcome many of the challenges of historical thinking if teachers make historical literacy an explicit objective of their instruction.

Chapter Summary

Historical literacies include the ability to construct historical interpretations with primary and secondary sources, artifacts, scientific evidence and other sources as historians do – both consuming and producing texts of multiple genres. Historically literate individuals are strategic in working with texts, using sourcing, corroboration, and contextualization. They are able to make evidence-based inferences, like the students in Mrs. Francis' class. Historically literate individuals exhibit certain habits of mind such as skepticism and open-mindedness. On the other hand, students rarely demonstrate historical literacy unless they are taught to do so. But with such instruction, they begin to use historians' texts, literacies, and habits of mind with increasing sophistication.

3
TEACHING HISTORICAL LITERACIES

Mr. Ngyuen, a history teacher who usually relies on traditional instructional methods, is teaching a lesson on progressivism in his 8th grade U.S. history class. He wants to lecture on Theodore Roosevelt's trust busting policies, but he decides to start class by having students spend a few minutes analyzing a political cartoon from that era. He does some searching and finds the perfect political cartoon: an image painted in 1904 of an octopus-like monster, labeled "Standard Oil" with tentacles wrapped around a statehouse, other government buildings, and business executives (see Figure 3.1). The monster's eyes are fixed on the White House and a tentacle is reaching in that direction (Keppler, 1904). Mr. Ngyuen is excited by his discovery of this cartoon because it is a wonderful primary source that shows the fears of proponents of Theodore Roosevelt's trust busting. He hopes that during the analysis of the cartoon students will become curious about the conditions that existed at the time and will focus better during his lecture on Roosevelt and the Progressive Era.

When class starts Mr. Ngyuen displays the cartoon using a projector, asking the students to analyze it. There is a long silence, but since he knows the value of wait time, he waits. After a minute of quiet he calls on Joey to describe his analysis.

"I think it shows a monster trying to take over America," Joey answers.

"Would anyone like to elaborate on Joey's observation?" Mr. Ngyuen questions.

"Yeah, it's an octopus monster," adds Carly, "with mean looking eyes."

"Good observations. What do you think the message of this political cartoon is?" Mr. Nguyen tries to push the discussion into deeper analytical responses.

"Watch out for octopuses," replies Isaac.

"Actually, octopi are really not dangerous," Caleb offers, in correction.

Mr. Ngyuen attempts to refocus the discussion. "This painting is an example of a political cartoon. Does this help with your analysis? It was painted in 1904."

FIGURE 3.1 A political cartoon.
Source: Keppler (1904).

"I never understand those things," complains Carly. "My dad really likes them but I don't get 'em."

Joey jumps in to help. "Since the octopus has 'Standard Oil' written on it, I think it's supposed to represent 'Standard Oil' – so the message is that Standard Oil is attacking America. But I don't know what Standard Oil is."

"Standard Oil is destroying America. That's the message," agrees Mandy triumphantly.

"By polluting the oceans – ruining octopus habitat," Isaac adds.

"What leads you to think that the political cartoon is talking about the environment?" probes Mr. Nguyen.

"Standard Oil is an oil company and that's what oil companies do – destroy the environment," Isaac explains.

Already the discussion has taken longer than Mr. Ngyuen intended, cutting into his lecture time. "Well, not exactly. Let's back up a little. Joey was right. The octopus represents Standard Oil, which was a large and powerful oil company beginning in the late 1800s. The political cartoon shows Standard Oil Company reaching out toward the White House in an attempt to gain political control over the president. In the early 1900s . . ." Mr. Ngyuen continues to explain the political cartoon to the class and makes a transition into the lecture that will take the rest of the class period.

After class, Mr. Nguyen reflects on how poorly his introduction using the political cartoon went. He had found a great text, provided time for students to reflect, and asked open-ended questions. Why did Joey, Carly, and Isaac take the meaning of the cartoon so literally? Maybe the students just didn't have enough background knowledge. But he remembered that later Isaac used his background knowledge inappropriately – reading ideas about habitat destruction into the cartoon when there was no evidence to suggest that was its message. He wonders whether what Carly said is true: these students just can't read political cartoons. He comes up with a quick solution before his next class starts. "I will just explain it to them at the start of my lecture rather than waste the first part of class again."

Even if his students could "read" the political cartoon, there are other historical literacies that the class doesn't use. For example, why didn't any of the students ask who had produced the painting? They didn't seem to wonder much about the context of its creation, its intended audience, or its historical impact. They didn't ask about other documents or artifacts that might corroborate its message or ask to see contrasting opinions. In short, they weren't behaving much like historians. Neither Mr. Nguyen nor his students used the cartoon as historical evidence, but instead viewed it as a way to transmit or receive information. He wanted students to "read" it because it was part of the narrative he was going to give them during the lecture. There was no intent on his part to encourage students to question or critique the political cartoon, to consider its source, or to synthesize its message with other primary sources.

An observer of Mr. Nguyen's class would see that simply providing students with the right text, which Mr. Nguyen did, is not enough to build historical literacies. Students must be taught strategies for working with texts. And, more importantly, students need opportunities to independently develop evidence-based historical interpretations. They need to use historical texts and artifacts, like the political cartoon, not simply to gain information, but as one of multiple pieces of evidence to interpret historical controversies. Further, Mr. Nguyen's students did not know how to comprehend the cartoon, a prerequisite for analyzing it, and he didn't know how to help them comprehend or critique it. He didn't consider how to break down the process of analysis into simpler steps that his students could do. His troubles stemmed from the fact that he didn't think about methods of building his students' historical literacies. He, like me in my early years of teaching, resorted to reading the document to his students rather than helping them read it for themselves.

In this chapter I explore how research on reading and literacy and on teaching reading in the traditional sense (i.e. instruction on reading words, sentences, paragraphs, and books) can inform instruction on building students' historical literacies with both traditional and non-traditional texts. I consider a) general literacy strategies and historical literacies, b) a framework for understanding literate processes and historical literacies, c) two models of literacy instruction, and d) warnings about the potential misapplication of general reading research to building students' historical literacies.

General Literacy Strategies and Historical Literacies

Students have a difficult time working with texts as diverse as political cartoons, diary entries, textbooks, artifacts, or televised debates, unless they possess general comprehension skills in addition to historical literacies. History teachers can co-operate with language arts and other content-area teachers to build these general abilities. Often literacy strategies are useful in the reading of both traditional print texts and non-traditional texts, such as the political cartoon Mr. Nguyen used. There are several general skills and elements of general reading instruction that apply to building historical literacies. For instance, concepts such as close reading; metacognition, particularly the monitoring of one's comprehension; vocabulary instruction; and the categorization system of before, during, and after reading strategies apply to building historical literacies. I will introduce each of these four concepts.

Close Reading

Research on reading has shown that proficient readers purposefully vary their reading speed. When searching through large bodies of text, looking for relevant passages, they may simply skim. However, when encountering dense or complex texts, good readers slow down, pause and reflect while reading, annotate the text, think about the author, pay attention to details, reread passages, ask questions, and seek clarification from other sources – practices that have been labeled *close reading*. The ability to select an appropriate reading speed is important for historians, who are able to sift quickly through volumes of material in an archive, searching for documents that are relevant to their research project. Upon making a discovery, they might spend hours, days, or even a career carefully ana-lyzing a single text. History teachers should encourage students to be purposeful in choosing their reading speed, pointing out the appropriate conditions for skimming, close reading, or moderate reading speeds. Students are more likely to engage in close reading when teachers give them a manageable reading load – one or two short passages to be considered carefully, rather than a long reading selection.

Unlike some other general literacy strategies, experts on historical thinking value the strategy of close reading. For instance, Reisman included close reading as one of four historical reading strategies that she fostered (2012). Using his-torians as models, advocates of close reading encourage students to slow their pace, consider the source, ask questions about the text, and reflect deeply about the context surrounding its production. Embedded within the teacher resources of the Stanford History Education Group website are lessons on close reading, where teachers provide reminders and support to help students think deeply about the short passages they meticulously analyze (Stanford History Education Group, 2012).

Metacognition

Research on reading shows that good readers tend to be metacognitive or reflective on their reading and thinking processes (Baker, 1994). One of the key metacognitive practices is monitoring one's comprehension – paying attention to whether one understands what is read, and noticing when comprehension breaks down. Surprisingly, early research on reading suggests that many young readers don't pay attention to whether or not they understand what they are reading (Baker, 1984; Markham 1979). Once, when I asked a student to summarize what he had just read out loud to the class, he responded, "How am I supposed to know what it means? I just read it." In some students' way of thinking, reading consists of the correct pronunciation of words, unaware that reading really only occurs when one comprehends what is read. In historical literacy, as in general reading, students must be taught the importance of monitoring their comprehension and being aware when they don't understand, recognizing that this is a problem.

Additionally, metacognition includes an awareness of strategies that can be used when comprehension breaks down. Generally speaking, students can reread, ask questions, look for additional sources, or, when appropriate, skip a passage when they don't understand what they are reading. When working with artifacts or photographs, students might discuss observations with peers, focus on parts rather than the whole, or consider the context of the artifacts' discovery or the photographs' creation. Research on reading suggests that good readers are aware of a repertoire of strategies that they can employ to improve their comprehension and use of texts. Thus, metacognition requires a knowledge of oneself, including one's strengths and weaknesses as a reader or historian; a knowledge of the reading task at hand, including the texts, strategies, and processes involved in completing the task; and an awareness of how successfully the reading is proceeding (Baker, 2002). Students engaged in historical thinking should be aware of the task at hand, know the cognitive tools available to them, and should have a sense, throughout the process, of how they are doing.

Vocabulary and Literacy

The development of a rich vocabulary is a basic element of general literacy instruction. Students need knowledge of word meanings in order to read and write. Such is also the case when working with written historical texts – students must know the meaning of the words that they encounter. There is history-related vocabulary that history teachers might need to define for their students. Reading research supports the notion (Baumann, 2009) that there is no better way for students to learn history-related vocabulary than to be immersed in discussions that allow them to hear and use unfamiliar words in context. History teachers should consider students' vocabulary needs when selecting texts, and should provide vocabulary support when needed for students to comprehend and critique the texts they are using.

Before, During, and After Reading Strategies

Research on the practices used by effective readers often categorizes strategies as those used before reading, during reading, and after reading (Pearson & Dole, 1987). For instance, before good readers start to explore an unfamiliar text they might preview the text to get a feel for what it is about, activating their background knowledge (Langer, 1984). They establish a purpose for reading and may make predictions about what they will read. Thus, even before reading they take an active role in learning with the text (Ogle, 1986). During reading, good readers vary their reading speed, monitor their comprehension, summarize, make inferences, seek clarification when needed, ask questions and continue to make and verify predictions (Paris, Wasik, & Turner, 1991). They may use visualization to picture in their mind's eye the things they are reading. They make connections to other things that they have read, to world events, or to their personal experiences (Tovani, 2000). After reading, good readers summarize, continue to ask questions, seek out others who have read the same text, or who have not read the text, with whom they can discuss it (Paris, *et al.*, 1991).

Although some of these strategies might not apply directly to historical literacies, some certainly do, and the notion of before, during, and after reading strategies might be an effective way for a history teacher to discuss strategic reading with history students. For instance, before a historian reads a text or analyzes an artifact, he/she looks at the source (Wineburg, 1991). In addition, he/she approaches texts with the appropriate epistemic stance (VanSledright, 2002). During reading, a historian often goes back and forth between different texts, both mentally and physically, in the heuristic referred to as corroboration (Wineburg, 1991). After reading, a historian uses the text as evidence, citing or paraphrasing it in his/her writing. History teachers might find it convenient to teach students the before, during, and after reading framework to help students remember what they should be doing before, during, and after working with historical evidence. To summarize, reading research explores constructs such as close reading, metacognition, vocabulary instruction, and before, during, and after reading that are directly applicable in building historical literacies.

A Framework for Understanding Literate Processes and Historical Literacies

Further, research on literacy can provide a helpful framework for understanding the roles of students as readers of historical texts. One such framework, which I use throughout this book, is the four resources model, developed by literacy researchers, Freebody and Luke (1990). This model presents the reader as active throughout his/her interaction with a text, engaging in the four roles of code breaker, meaning maker, text user, and text critic. This book addresses students' historical literacy needs in terms of these four practices. I provide a general description of each followed by a synthesis of the four resources model of literacy as applied in developing students' historical literacies.

Code Breaker

The code breaker is able to effectively decipher a symbol system. In Freebody and Luke's (1990) model, the code breaker is able to interpret the meaning of letters in traditional print texts, recognize the sounds associated with letters, and use letters and the sounds they represent to form words and sentences both in reading and writing. Acknowledging a literate individual as a code breaker is important for history teachers for three reasons. First, history teachers must develop instructional accommodations for students who struggle with breaking the code in traditional writing – students who lack basic reading skills. History teachers can accommodate struggling readers by providing audio recordings of text, allowing parents to read with students on homework assignments, finding simple texts, or modifying complex texts into simpler language. Additionally, teachers must become involved in helping students resolve this serious threat to their academic and social wellbeing. Although it is not the primary responsibility of a history teacher to build students' ability to decode in the traditional sense, when he/she identifies a student who cannot read, the history teacher should seek the resources provided by the school, such as reading teachers, counselors, and special education departments, in order to help that student. The focus of this book is not on building students' ability to decode written text.

Second, traditional print texts sometimes contain unfamiliar conventions or symbols – codes to which history students have had no exposure. For example, the symbols BCE and CE are commonly used in place of the more familiar symbols BC and AD in working with dates. Students might need to be taught the meaning of these symbols. Similarly, students might be unfamiliar with other symbols in historical print texts, such as the "long s" symbol, commonly used in the 18th century, which looked like the letter f but represents the sound of the letter s. Further, old handwritten documents in cursive script can be hard for students to decode. When students can't decode, the teacher can either change the text, by transcribing or translating it, or change the students by teaching them new decoding strategies.

Third, when building historical literacies, the concept of code breaking must be projected onto the variety of sources used in historical inquiry, such as the ability to decode the symbolic images in a political cartoon. Much of Mr. Nguyen's frustration with students stemmed from their inability to decode the political cartoon and his failure to recognize their struggles as a decoding issue. Different formats of text, such as political cartoons, propaganda posters, artifacts, music, photographs, artwork, radio broadcasts, and debates, use different symbolic codes. When a history teacher exposes students to new sources, it is his/her responsibility to teach students to negotiate that unique symbol system. This process is part of building students' historical literacies.

To clarify, many historical sources use symbol systems that are unfamiliar to students, and, for that, to the language arts teacher and others outside of the discipline of history. For instance, a cartogram is a map with the relative size of states or nations distorted in order to represent a statistic other than land shape and size. A cartogram that represents world population expands China and India and shrinks Canada and Australia (see Figure 3.2). Someone unfamiliar with the structure of a cartogram might have difficulty decoding what the shapes and sizes mean. However, with brief decoding instruction, a cartogram becomes a valuable resource for learning history. Musicians, artists, political cartoonists, and others have unique symbol systems that require some decoding, and history teachers cannot assume that students have the skills needed to decode the multiple genres that are useful in studying history. Instead, a teacher should be sensitive to students' decoding needs and adjust instruction appropriately. Before history students can use historical texts as evidence, they must be able to decode the symbolic system associated with constructing meaning with that text.

Meaning Maker

The meaning maker constructs meaning with the code that has been broken. In traditional reading, the meaning maker can summarize a passage, demonstrating basic comprehension. Similarly, in working with non-traditional texts, such as a table or painting, the meaning maker can summarize the factual information

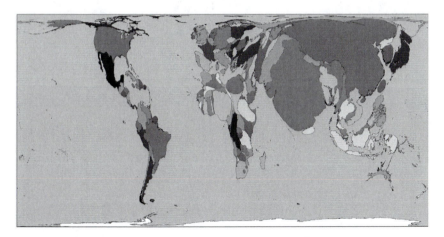

FIGURE 3.2 A cartogram illustrating relative population by nation (© Copyright SASI Group (University of Sheffield) and Mark Newman (University of Michigan)).

contained in the table or describe the subject of a painting. It should be noted that code breaking and meaning making go hand in hand. For example, as an individual attempts to break the code and find meaning in a table from an early 20th century census, he or she would have to identify the meaning of numbers located in columns and rows (see Figure 3.3). Doing so would involve some traditional decoding – reading the name of the country at the top of each column and the state listed to the left of each row; some numerical decoding – reading the numbers located in each cell; and some structural decoding – understanding the meaning of columns and rows. The ability to break this code allows individuals

	Table 33—Continued.										PERSO
							Northwestern Europe.				
	DIVISION OR STATE AND CENSUS YEAR.	Total foreign born.	Eng-land.	Scot-land.	Wales.	Ireland.	Ger-many.[1]	Nor-way.	Swe-den.	Den-mar
	MIDDLE ATLANTIC.										
	New York:										
1	1910	2,748,011	146,870	39,437	7,464	367,889	436,911	25,013	53,705	12,
2	1900	1,900,425	135,685	33,862	7,304	425,553	499,820	12,601	42,708	8,
3	1890	1,571,050	144,422	35,332	8,108	483,375	498,602	8,602	28,430	6,
	New Jersey:										
4	1910	660,788	50,375	17,512	1,202	82,758	122,880	5,351	10,547	5,
5	1900	431,884	45,428	14,211	1,195	94,844	121,414	2,296	7,337	3,
6	1890	328,975	43,785	13,163	1,069	101,059	106,181	1,317	4,159	2,
	Pennsylvania:										
7	1910	1,442,374	109,115	32,046	29,255	165,109	195,202	2,320	23,467	3,
8	1900	985,250	114,831	30,386	35,453	205,909	226,796	1,393	24,130	2,
9	1890	845,720	125,145	32,081	38,301	243,836	230,516	2,238	19,346	2,
	EAST NORTH CENTRAL.										
	Ohio:										
10	1910	598,374	43,347	10,705	9,377	40,062	175,095	1,110	5,522	1,
11	1900	458,734	44,745	9,327	11,481	55,018	212,829	639	3,951	1,
12	1890	459,293	51,027	10,275	12,905	70,127	235,668	511	2,742	
	Indiana:										
13	1910	159,663	9,783	3,419	1,498	11,266	62,179	531	5,081	
14	1900	142,121	10,874	2,805	2,083	16,306	77,811	384	4,673	
15	1890	146,205	11,200	2,948	888	20,819	84,900	285	4,512	
	Illinois:										
16	1910	1,205,314	60,363	20,755	4,091	93,455	319,199	32,913	115,424	17,
17	1900	966,747	64,390	20,021	4,364	114,563	369,660	29,979	109,147	15,
18	1890	842,347	70,510	20,465	4,138	124,498	338,382	30,339	86,514	12,
	Michigan:										
19	1910	597,550	42,737	9,952	786	20,434	131,586	7,638	26,374	6,
20	1900	541,653	43,839	10,343	838	29,182	145,292	7,582	26,956	6,
21	1890	543,880	55,388	12,068	769	39,065	135,509	7,795	27,366	6,
	Wisconsin:										
22	1910	512,865	13,959	3,885	2,507	14,049	233,384	57,000	25,739	16,
23	1900	515,971	17,995	4,569	3,356	23,544	268,384	61,575	26,196	16,
24	1890	519,199	23,633	5,494	4,297	33,306	259,819	65,696	20,157	13,
	WEST NORTH CENTRAL.										
	Minnesota:										
25	1910	543,595	12,139	4,373	1,023	15,859	109,628	105,303	122,428	16,
26	1900	505,318	12,022	4,810	1,288	22,428	125,191	104,895	115,476	16,
27	1890	467,356	14,745	5,315	1,470	28,011	116,955	101,169	99,913	14,
	Iowa:										
28	1910	273,765	16,788	5,162	2,434	17,756	98,759	21,924	26,763	17,
29	1900	305,920	21,027	6,425	3,091	28,321	123,277	25,634	29,875	17,

FIGURE 3.3 A portion of a table from the 1910 census.

Source: Durand & Harris (1913).

to then begin to construct meaning, discovering, for example, that there were thousands of immigrants from Sweden who settled in Minnesota in the mid 1800s (Durand & Harris, 1913).

It should be noted that sometimes the meaning that readers construct is highly subjective, such as in listening to a piece of music or viewing abstract art. In all cases, the making of meaning integrates both the readers' background knowledge and the content of the text being read. In some cases, two people from different backgrounds will comprehend the same text differently, a notion understood very well by historians. Even in cases where the construction of meaning is highly subjective, the teacher can discern comprehension problems. For example, struggling readers often rely heavily on background knowledge rather than the text during the meaning-making process, reaching conclusions that are unwarranted given the evidence in the text. Such was the case with Isaac, who thought the political cartoon made a statement about the impact of the oil industry on octopus habitat. Teachers can assess students' capabilities as code breakers and meaning makers by asking comprehension questions, such as "What is the main idea of this paragraph?" "What event does this painting depict?" "How many tons of steel were produced in Pittsburg in 1910?" When a teacher identifies comprehension problems he or she should provide instruction to address students' needs as code breakers and meaning makers.

Because historians, as seasoned readers, often engage in code breaking and meaning making without conscious effort, these two elements of literacy are often left out of the discussion of historical reasoning. However, code breaking and meaning making are not automatic with many students. Thus, it falls on the shoulders of history teachers to help their students with these two important elements of historical literacy, prerequisites for more sophisticated analyses. As is the case with code breaking, if students struggle with meaning making, the teacher can either alter the text, by providing a modified, simplified translation (as is done with most of the texts used in lessons on the Stanford History Education's website), or alter the reader, by fostering in him/her an improved ability to comprehend. The approach the teacher chooses should be based on his/her instructional objectives. As a student grows in historical literacy he or she becomes increasingly capable of constructing meaning (code breaking and meaning making) with an increasing number of text genres and increasingly complex texts.

It should be noted that historical meaning making can be tricky for students because historical questions require historians to seek for meaning that is often very different from the meaning intended by the writer. The historian's interest may not be in the message of the text, but in its subtext, and the message that it sends about the historical period in question. For example, the writer of a letter from colonial Massachusetts might have intended to give a description of the local native cultures to a friend in England. However, a historian might use such a document to construct meaning about the effects of Puritan religious doctrines on colonists' beliefs about Native Americans. As Lee states "historians can ask questions about historical sources that those sources were not designed to answer" (2005, 37). Thus students need to seek for the meaning in texts that answers historical questions rather than simply the literal meaning intended by the author. Students/historians, and not the text, are the meaning makers.

Text User

Freebody and Luke (1990) label the third role of the reader as that of a text user. After reading a novel, a text user wants to talk about it. Text users conduct Internet searches with a practical purpose in mind. They read textbook passages in order to prepare for an exam. They find in a table answers to questions that the teacher poses. Text users write with a purpose in mind, for example using digital media to remain in contact with friends. Good readers find ways to apply the understandings that they construct with texts, and quite often those applications involve authentic and self-initiated writing.

Historians provide an excellent model of professionals who use text. The work of historians is to gather and use evidence of a variety of genres to develop and support interpretations of the past. Historians' reading and writing is always purposeful. Early in their research, during archival work, historians search for texts that are relevant and useful. They evaluate evidence in terms of their purposes – does it support or conflict with their emerging interpretations? As historians gain confidence in their understandings, they reflect on how they will use the evidence to persuade others that their interpretations are sound. As they write, they quote or paraphrase texts as evidence. Thus, historians spend the bulk of their research time acknowledging a need for text, searching for appropriate text, and determining how they will use various texts. The work of historians revolves around the use of texts for particular, discipline-appropriate purposes.

Often, in history classrooms, students are asked to use texts in a manner that is irrelevant to them, uninteresting from their perspective, and only indirectly related to historical literacies. Answering the questions at the end of a chapter in a history textbook is certainly a way to require students to use text. Such an assignment might build students' general literacies, particularly the skills of skimming and summarizing. However, it does not require students to use texts as a historian would, and so, does not build students' historical literacies. One of the challenges and joys I experienced in teaching history was in developing activities that required students to engage in authentic historical inquiries – to use historical texts in discipline-appropriate ways. In the vignettes and chapters of this book, I describe ways students might use various texts to build historical interpretations.

Text Critic

Freebody and Luke (1990) further describe proficient readers as text critics, critically evaluating texts. Information Age technologies give individuals unprecedented access to ideas, information, and opinions. Good readers are able to screen incoming information in order to ascertain its relevance, accuracy, and usefulness. Researchers have found, however, that many students struggle to critically evaluate information, particularly when it is found online. For example, Leu and his colleagues (2007) discovered that 7th grade students accepted information on a bogus website about the Northwest Tree Octopus, a fictional species, because it was rich in details, interesting, and had colorful images (which had been digitally falsified). Even when directly confronted by a researcher and told that the site was inaccurate, some of the students continued to argue its reliability (Leu, *et al.*, 2007). One by-product of building students' historical literacies is increasing their ability to think critically about all of the texts to which they are exposed.

As described above, historians are, above all else, critical readers. They do not accept information found in texts at face value but they interpret it based on its source and how it relates to other texts. Because history requires this type of critical analysis of texts, history classrooms are an ideal location to nurture students' critical thinking. History teachers must encourage students to question every author (McKeown, Beck, & Worthy, 1993), including the textbook author; to recognize that history is always interpretive in nature, and thus open to revision; and to search for the voices of those silenced in the traditional historical narrative. Lee suggests that "Once students begin to operate with a concept of evidence as something inferential and see eyewitnesses not as handing down history but as providing evidence, history can resume once again; it becomes an intelligible, even powerful, way of thinking about the past" (2005, 37). Much of the basis for the difference between historians' reading and history students' reading is the lack of experience for most students in engaging as a text critic.

The Four Resources Model in Developing Students' Historical Literacies

The four resources model provides a suitable framework for considering historical literacy for several reasons. First, the four resources framework suggests that readers are active in the construction of meaning. Meaning does not reside on the page or in the picture, but is built in the mind of the reader/viewer as his/her background knowledge interacts with his/her experience with the text. History classrooms that promote historical literacy acknowledge students' active role in constructing understandings. They encourage students to construct independent and original historical interpretations rather than merely learn the history written by others. There is no expectation that every student in the class will develop the same interpretations. Nor are students evaluated by how closely their construction of an event matches that of the textbook narrative. Teachers that promote historical literacy invite students to discuss, disagree, and debate historical ideas, always demanding that students support their interpretations with evidence found in historical texts. The skillful use of texts requires students to actively break the symbolic code used in the creation of the text, actively construct meaning with the text, and critically evaluate and use texts as evidence. Additionally, students should be able to use texts to actively critique the historical interpretations forwarded by their peers, the teacher, textbook publishers, and even historians.

Second, in classrooms that are committed to building students' historical literacies, teachers must nurture students' ability to decode and construct meaning with a great variety of texts. Implied in this assumption is the notion that teachers expose students to a variety of genres, and devote class time to helping students learn various symbol systems. History teachers who are devoted to building students' historical literacies take the time to explicitly discuss with students the skills used in reading various texts. They do not simply read and explain texts to students, as the frustrated Mr. Nguyen eventually did. Instead, they discuss openly with the students how meaning is constructed and allow students to construct that meaning for themselves. Historically literate students are skillful in finding meaning in political cartoons, music, art, architecture, artifacts, documents, and other genres because their teachers help them learn how to do so.

Third, historically literate students are able to critically evaluate texts using the unique literacies of historians. They engage in sourcing, corroboration, and contextualization. They exhibit historians' habits of mind in withholding judgment, recognizing interpretations as tentative, and approaching all texts with a healthy skepticism. They use their imagination, fueled by text-based evidence, to produce reasoned speculation when the historical record is silent. They view texts not as conveyors of truth but as evidence. And they take an active role in sifting through the evidence, independently building historical interpretations.

Two Models of Literacy Instruction

General research on literacy provides not only a model for understanding the roles of readers, but also models of instruction designed to help teachers build students' literacies. The two models that are featured most prominently in this book are explicit strategy instruction and implicit strategy instruction. Both types of teaching are based on Vygotsky's theory of socio-cultural learning (1986). Vygotsky suggested that all learning is social in nature and that learning is facilitated when a more knowledgeable individual, such as a mother, a baseball coach, or a history teacher, designs appropriately challenging activities for the learner and provides temporary support, referred to as scaffolding, for the learner as he or she engages in the activity. As the learner becomes more able to engage in the activity independently, the teacher gradually removes the scaffolding. A key to Vygotsky's model is that activities must be designed at an appropriate level of difficulty, referred to as a Zone of Proximal Development (ZPD). The ZPD includes tasks that an individual cannot do independently, but can do with assistance. As the learner's skills grow, scaffolding is removed and the learner engages in the activity independently. Learning has occurred. A new task can then be assigned at a slightly higher level of difficulty (within a new ZPD) with the required scaffolding. In the vignette above, Mr. Nguyen provided too little scaffolding at first, and students floundered to make sense of the cartoon. After becoming frustrated he provided too much support, simply explaining the cartoon to the class, rather than helping them figure it out. Void of explicit or implicit strategy instruction, his lesson did little to improve students' ability to read political cartoons.

Explicit Strategy Instruction

Explicit strategy instruction is designed to provide training, practice, and support in doing activities that students could not do independently – activities that are within their ZPD. Explicit strategy instruction includes four stages: direct instruction of the strategy, modeling, guided practice, and independent practice (Nokes & Dole, 2005). During the first stage, direct instruction, the teacher openly discusses the strategy with students, naming it, describing the process, discussing the appropriate conditions for its use, and selling its effectiveness. For instance, instead of having students flounder in their attempts to make sense of the political cartoon, Mr. Nguyen might have introduced students to the strategy of "identifying the symbols" as a first step in reading a political cartoon. Further, during direct instruction, he could have described the process or sub-steps of "identifying the symbols" such as looking for labels on images, like "Standard Oil" written on the monster; identifying universal symbols, such as the White House; interpreting symbolic actions, such as extending a tentacle toward the White House; and attending to subtle symbols, such as the focus of the eyes of the monster on the White House. Thus, Mr. Nguyen would have named the strategy, "identifying the symbols," and described the steps involved in engaging in the strategy.

Following direct instruction on the strategy, the teacher models the strategy for students. The key element in modeling is thinking aloud for them. For instance, Mr. Nguyen might start by identifying the symbols that are labeled. He might say, "When I read a political cartoon, I start by identifying the symbols. It's easiest to identify the symbols that are labeled. I can see that 'Standard Oil' is written across the monster's body so that helps me identify the monster as a symbol representing Standard Oil, which was an oil company from the early 1900s. Next I look for universal symbols. This building looks like the White House, and I think the White House would be a universal symbol representing the president of the United States. This other building might represent a state government but I'm not really sure. I don't know whether that's really important at this point. But I will keep that in the back of my mind. Next, I want to look for symbolic actions. Do any of you see anything that the monster is doing that might be symbolic?" His question shifts the modeling from himself to the students. When a student offers a response, Mr. Nguyen might ask the student to explain his/her thinking to the class in order to have him/her model thought processes for peers.

It is important that during the modeling stage the teacher model processes rather than outcomes, a subtle but important distinction. In the vignette at the start of the chapter, Mr. Nguyen's interpretation of the political cartoon did not reflect the modeling of a strategy but rather demonstrating the outcome of his strategy use. He explained his interpretation of the cartoon rather than explaining the processes he used to figure out what the cartoon meant. In order for modeling to be effective the teacher must not simply give the answer, but reveal the normally hidden thought processes of those who engage with a strategy. Doing so models for students a strategic way to solve a problem.

Next comes a period of guided practice, during which students have an opportunity to engage in the strategy with scaffolding in place. Scaffolding might include such things as peer support, posted reminders about strategic processes, graphic organizers, the teacher or class completing some of the process together, working with simplified texts, or individualized help from the teacher. For example, after his lesson, Mr. Nguyen might have displayed a poster in his classroom listing the steps involved in reading a political cartoon (see Figure 3.4). After working together to make sense of the Standard Oil cartoon, he might have chosen a different political cartoon from the same era, perhaps showing a different perspective, giving the students the assignment to analyze in small groups. He could hang a poster with the steps used in analyzing political cartoons and provide one-on-one help as needed.

How to Analyze a Political Cartoon as a Historical Source

Step 1: Identify the symbols

- Look for labels
- Identify universal symbols
- Attend to subtle symbols
- Consider symbolic speech/captions
- Interpret symbolic actions

Step 2: Identify the relationship between symbols

- Attend to physical location of important symbols
- Interpret actions connecting symbols

Step 3: Interpret the author's methods and message

- Identify exaggerations
- Gather information about the artist
- Consider the artist as a source
- Summarize the artist's stance

Step 4: Critique the cartoon

- Identify your initial reaction
- Consider flaws in the artist's logic
- Consider information the artist has omitted
- Find contrasting opinions
- Offer your critique of the cartoon

FIGURE 3.4 A poster listing steps in analyzing a political cartoon.

The final stage of explicit strategy instruction is independent practice, during which the teacher assigns students to engage in the target activity without support. Independent practice allows the students and the teacher to assess their ability to engage in literate activities, providing important information about whether students are prepared to move on to more challenging tasks. In the case of Mr. Nguyen's class, he might assign students to find a current political cartoon at home and to prepare a written analysis.

Providing explicit strategy instruction requires a paradigm shift by history teachers like Mr. Nguyen. In contrast to exclusively content-focused lessons, explicit strategy instruction focuses on students' development of skills and literacies. Content knowledge becomes a by-product of students' work with texts like political cartoons. Admittedly, explicit strategy instruction takes time. Certainly Mr. Nguyen could cover more historical information if he didn't take the time to teach this skill. However, the trade off between the coverage of more information, information that 100 years of research shows is not likely to be retained, and the development of historical literacy skills that allow students to actively engage with content, is worthwhile.

Implicit Strategy Instruction

Another way that teachers can provide literacy instruction is through implicit strategy instruction (Dole, 2000). As mentioned, one of the drawbacks of explicit strategy instruction is the amount of time that is required to do it well. Another disadvantage is that some of the students may already possess the literacies that the teacher is targeting. For them, explicit instruction is frustratingly slow and tedious. Implicit strategy instruction, on the other hand, is a research-proven teaching alternative based on many of the same Vygotskyan notions. It engages students in a target literacy or strategy, but instead of speaking openly about the strategy with students and modeling the strategy, the teacher simply creates an assignment that requires students to engage in the strategy and then explains the assignment to the students. For instance, Mr. Nguyen might create a study guide for students to complete as they analyze the political cartoon. The study guide might give a brief description of the nature of political cartoons and ask students to list the images that are labeled, list the images that should be universally recognizable, list symbols that are hidden in some of the details, and identify symbols in speech/captions or actions. The study guide could walk students through each of the steps of analyzing the cartoon without explicitly discussing strategies.

Alternatively, Mr. Nguyen might design an activity where students are placed in a group where they follow written instructions that guide them through the process of identifying the symbols in the political cartoon. Students then switch to a new group where a new set of instructions walks them through the process of identifying the relationship between the symbols. Students would continue to regroup and move through each of the four steps of analyzing a political cartoon.

Regardless of the structure of the activity, the main idea of implicit strategy instruction is that the teacher designs activities that walk students through literate processes without taking a significant amount of class time to talk openly about the process. The hope is that with repeated exposure to implicit strategy instruction students will discover and begin to internalize literate processes.

There are several advantages and disadvantages of implicit strategy instruction. It takes considerably less class time, is often a more familiar teaching approach than explicit strategy instruction, and is faster paced and less tedious than explicit strategy instruction. On the other hand, it takes more exposures to target strategies before students discover and internalize them. And implicit strategy instruction can be more work for the teacher, who must break down literate processes into tasks that students can manage and then design activities that provide scaffolding. Implicit strategy instruction, unlike explicit strategy instruction, is difficult to provide "on the fly" as needs spontaneously arise. Most researchers suggest that a combination of explicit and implicit strategy instruction is the best approach to building students' literacies (Dole, 2000).

Potential Misapplication of General Literacy Research

Although research on literacy provides helpful suggestions for building historical literacies, care must be taken to not overgeneralize the applications. In particular there are issues with the notion of text in general reading research, strategies in general reading research, metacognition and strategy selection, and a focus on strategy use. I describe each of these four concerns below.

Texts in General Reading Research

Although there is a growing acceptance of alternative formats of text (Cope & Kalantsis, 2000; Draper, *et al.*, 2010), much of the research on reading focuses on traditional print text, i. e. words, sentences, and paragraphs. This narrow focus of reading research ignores the vast array of sources that historians use. Further, it gives little thought to the unique literacies needed to work with these diverse texts. Reading a propaganda poster is a different process than reading a textbook excerpt. History teachers should not feel limited to language-based texts in their search for appropriate sources to teach historical literacies. Instead, they should consider the wealth of sources available and carefully choose texts that will meet their objectives.

Additionally, history teachers need to be wary of the classifications of text in general literacy research. In some cases such classifications may impede historical literacies. For instance, one of the troubling trends in current literacy research, from a historical literacy perspective, is the classification of certain types of texts as "informational texts." The implication of this classification is that there are texts, such as textbooks, that transmit information to students. Well-intended literacy advocates might suggest reading strategies for working with informational texts that include finding the main idea or summarizing. The use of these strategies leads students to accept information found in "informational texts" at face value – an approach that hinders rather than promotes historical thinking. In contrast, historians do not recognize any texts as informational texts – this is one of the traits that make them gifted readers. Instead, historians view texts as *accounts* or *evidence*, second order concepts that will be discussed more thoroughly in Chapter 7. Students have a tendency to consider texts as conveyors of information, and the classification of some texts as "informational text" might reinforce this worldview, impeding historical literacies.

Strategies in General Reading Research

In some cases, strategies suggested in general reading research, such as inference making, carry over into work with historical resources. However, in some cases, general reading strategies conflict with historical thinking. For example, text-to-self connections, the personal connections that an individual makes with a text, conflict with the strategy of contextualization that historians use. When text-to-self connections are made in the reading of historical texts, students impose their personal experiences, including modern perspectives and values, on historical people and events. Thus, what might be considered good reading is bad history. The responsibility for building students' historical literacies cannot be passed off to language arts teachers. Historical literacies represent a unique skill set that includes some general literacy skills, excludes other general literacy skills, and includes some skills unique to historical inquiry. As stewards of the discipline, history teachers must make sure that school-wide literacy programs, such as the expectation to read and summarize textbook passages as "informational texts," do not interfere with historical literacies.

Metacognition and Strategy Selection

General literacy research suggests that during reading things often proceed without problems that would require conscious strategy use. Often comprehension occurs nearly automatically. Good readers constantly monitor their reading and when they experience a comprehension problem they employ a strategy, such as visualization, looking up challenging vocabulary, asking a question, or rereading, in order to restore it. The strategies used to restore comprehension are sometimes referred to as "fix up strategies." Historical literacies should not be considered fix up strategies. They are not employed only when naturally proceeding comprehension breaks down. But, they must be employed constantly and consistently throughout every historical reading task. For instance, a student should not be taught to attempt to read a diary entry and if it doesn't make sense use the sourcing strategy by looking at the source. Instead students need to understand that the source always matters and that the comprehension, critique, and use of historical texts is impossible without sourcing. Thus the strategies used in historical inquiry are not selectively chosen "fix up" strategies, but they must be in constant use when working with historical evidence.

The Focus on Strategy Use

Some advocates of reading strategy instruction have been criticized because in their efforts to promote literacy strategies, they lose focus on what really matters: building students' ability to comprehend and use texts. The historical literacy strategies featured in this book must be considered tools to achieve the end of fostering in students the ability to read and reason with historical texts and resources. Certainly creative teachers can find other ways to achieve these same ends. However, consider how sad it would be for history teachers to focus on building students' ability to use a handful of strategies without promoting historical thinking, historical problem solving, or historical writing.

Chapter Summary

General research on both literacy and teaching literacy has numerous implications for history teachers who desire to build students' historical literacies. There are some direct applications of literacy research such as with close reading, metacognition – particularly monitoring one's comprehension, vocabulary instruction, and the categorization system of before, during, and after reading strategies. Mr. Nguyen's frustration with students' inability to read the political cartoon serves as a reminder that readers of all texts, including historical texts, should take active roles as code breakers, meaning makers, text users, and text critics. Teachers can improve students' ability to engage in historical reading and reasoning through explicit and/or implicit strategy instruction. In spite of the numerous applications of general literacy research to historical literacy, there are enough differences in texts and literacies that history teachers are cautioned not to inappropriately apply teaching practices associated with general literacy instruction.

4

DEVELOPING AN APPROPRIATE EPISTEMIC STANCE FOR WORKING WITH MULTIPLE TEXTS

During a unit on the Middle Ages in her 10th grade world history class, Mrs. Hansen decides to conduct a historical literacy activity during students' study of the Crusades. She determines to give them excerpts from multiple primary and secondary sources showing Muslim, Christian, Jewish, and historians' perspectives. She selects a historical question that she feels is simple enough for her students to understand, but complex enough to allow for different opinions: "Were the Crusades primarily motivated by religious factors?" (Mitchell & Mitchell, 2002). She hopes that her class will be unable to reach a consensus on this "yes" or "no" question, and that a debate, properly structured, will help them become more skillful at using historical evidence. She wants students to develop a more mature understanding of the nature of knowing and learning history, recognizing that historical understanding is open to multiple interpretations, but that through the skillful use of evidence, learners of history can make defensible claims.

Mrs. Hansen searches online and through several anthologies of world history primary sources and finds a number of texts that she decides to use. She discovers several versions of Pope Urban II's speech at the Council of Clermont in 1095 (Halsall, 2011). She chooses one recorded by Fulcher of Chartres, which she anticipates will sway students toward the notion that the Crusades were religiously motivated. Continuing her search, she finds an account by a Jewish witness, Ibn al Athir, of the Christian conquest of Jerusalem and the subsequent looting (Reilly, 2007). She is confident that this will sway students toward the notion that the Crusades were motivated by greed. She finds a letter written by Stephen of Blois which includes mixed evidence including quotes that suggest a materialistic purpose: "You may know for certain, my beloved, that of gold, silver, and many other kinds of riches, I now have twice as much as you, my love, supposed me to have when I left you;" juxtaposed with claims that he was "prepared to die for

Christ" (Perry & Xue, 2001). Wanting to include Muslim sources, she finds online a passage written by Beha ed-Din who describes the carnage of a massacre during the Third Crusade (Richard The Lionheart Massacres The Saracens 1191, 2001). Turning to secondary sources she finds two opposing historians' perspectives in an anthology on opposing viewpoints in world history (Mitchell & Mitchell, 2002). She continues to search for a balance of texts that she feels will allow the class to develop mixed opinions and to have a healthy debate on the topic. By the day of the Crusades activity she has gathered eight sources, which she edits to manageable lengths, copies, and places in folders for ten groups.

Mrs. Hansen has had to lay the groundwork for this lesson since the first day of the school year. Her lesson on the Crusades is just one of a series of lessons designed to help students develop a more mature understanding of the way historians view historical knowledge. She believes, for several reasons, that the Crusades activity will allow students to practice constructing and defending evidence-based historical interpretations. First, she has chosen a question and texts that are likely to foster alternative interpretations among her students – revealing to them that multiple interpretations are possible. Second, she has chosen texts that are packed with quotes and explicit references that support alternative interpretations, allowing students to cite concrete evidence from multiple sources. She has made certain that the evidence is fairly simple to find within these texts. Third, she has previously taught students strategies for working with historical evidence, such as sourcing, corroboration, and contextualization. Fourth, she has created a safe classroom environment where students have been encouraged to test historical ideas with their peers – a classroom where all ideas are subject to an open-minded critique.

The 90-minute class period at Mrs. Hansen's school requires some creative lesson planning on her part. She determines to follow the format of the "Document-Based Lesson" (Reisman, 2012). She intends to start class with a mini-lecture to build background knowledge, followed by explicit strategy instruction on the use of evidence to support an interpretation. When students are adequately prepared, she will provide a document analysis activity that will take up the bulk of the class period. During this activity students will explore in small groups the packets of documents she has collected. She intends to end the period with a debriefing on the activity, during which she can talk about the way historians view historical knowledge.

On the day of the lesson, Mrs. Hansen begins class by asking the central question – were the Crusades primarily motivated by religious factors? She points out that this is a question that is still debated by historians. She suggests to students that before they start to explore this question on their own, she gives the class some basic facts about the Crusades and the crusaders – general information that most historians agree on. She progresses into a short lecture during which she introduces students to concepts, background information, and vocabulary that will help them understand the documents they read. This lecture is not simply intended to give students information that they will be tested on, but to give them information that they will use as they work with the documents. She ends the lecture by paraphrasing two historians. The first, Mayer (2002), contends that European crusaders were drawn to Jerusalem because it was the place where Jesus had lived, "the center of a spiritual world," and the thought of it being under the "yoke of heathen domination" was unbearable (156). The second, Finucane (2002), argues that "the crusaders, then, were aided not only by their own religious zeal, cupidity, curiosity, and many other motives that pushed them eastward, but also by the turmoil and rivalries among the Moslems themselves" (165). For the first historian, the simple answer to the central question is "yes, the crusaders were primarily motivated by religious factor.s" For the second historian, the answer is "no."

Next, Mrs. Hansen previews for the class the documents that students will work with. She reminds them about the distinction between primary and secondary sources and encourages them to pay attention to whether each source is Christian, Muslim, Jewish, and/or modern. She also points out that these sources come from a variety of time periods, reminding them about the strategies of sourcing and contextualization, both strategies that she has taught before. Modeling the use of evidence, she asks, "What things in the sources might indicate religious motivation for the Crusaders? What would you expect them to write if they were motivated primarily by religion?"

Students hesitate to answer, unsure of what they might find without having looked at any of the texts. Mrs. Hansen rephrases the question, "So one of the documents is a letter that a crusader is sending home to his wife. What might he say that shows that he believes he is fighting for a religious cause?"

"He might say things like 'god helped us', or 'god was on our side'," suggests Alex.

"Absolutely," Mrs. Hansen responds. "So this is the kind of evidence you should be searching for. Little quotes and things that allow you to enter the minds of the crusaders so you can figure out what they were thinking. Motivation is kind of a hidden thing. We can see what people do, but we have to try to figure out why they do it. What things might they write that show that they were motivated by materialistic factors?"

Carson raises his hand. "They might talk about the money they were getting by looting."

"That's right," Mrs. Hansen confirms. "Now I do want to caution you about working with evidence like this. You shouldn't simply count how many times they talk about god and how many times they talk about money and base your answer to the question on what they talked about more often. You have to remember the source, the context, and the subtext, like we have talked about before. In some contexts a person would be more likely to talk about religious things, even if they were motivated by other factors. And in speaking or writing to some audiences there would have been more reason to talk about worldly things. This isn't an easy assignment. You're going to have to do a lot of good thinking, but you can work in groups to bounce ideas off of each other."

Mrs. Hansen explains that in a few minutes students are going to get into groups of three or four and receive a text set that includes excerpts from eight primary and secondary sources. Along with the texts, she will give each student a graphic organizer that provides a place for them to record information about the source and context, a place to cite evidence that crusaders were religiously motivated and to cite evidence that crusaders were motivated by other factors, and a place to corroborate across sources (see Figure 4.1). "Let me show you one

Crusades Documents Analysis Guide

Doc.	Source and context	Evidence of religious motivation	Evidence of other motivation	Similarities and differences from other texts
1				
2				
3				
4				
5				
6				
7				
8				

FIGURE 4.1 A graphic organizer designed to support students' work with Crusades documents.

of the texts that will be in your text set and show you how I would analyze it. You can follow along with me on your graphic organizer," she adds as she starts to pass them out.

Continuing her modeling, she projects on the screen Fulcher of Chartres' record of the speech made by Pope Urban II. "The introduction to this document helps me understand the source. This is a speech the Pope made in 1095 that marks the start of the Crusades. However, I know that at that time they didn't have audio or video recorders so I wonder how someone recorded this speech. The Pope might have read the speech and we might get the record from his notes or written text, but it looks like in this case we find out about the speech from one of the listeners – this is Fulcher of Chartres' record. I wonder how soon after the speech was made that he wrote this down, because I know that over time he might have forgotten exactly what was said. If I had more time to study this, I would probably look to see whether there were other recordings of this speech, or even if the Pope's record exists somewhere, but for now I will trust that it is a decent summary of the speech but might not be word for word the way it was given." She pauses and asks the students, "What was I doing right then?"

Several of the students call out, "Sourcing."

"Yeah. I'm also thinking about the context," Mrs. Hansen responds. "Now I can see on my graphic organizer that there is a place to record source information so I would write ..." She continues to model how to use the graphic organizer, as she fills out the source information and begins to read the text, which is full of religious references. She writes on the whiteboard several specific quotes that she recommends that students write on their graphic organizer under the heading "evidence of religious motivation." She also includes a few quotes that she suggests the students write in the column for "evidence of other motivation." As she finishes reading the first document she points out that there appears to be more evidence on the side of the argument that they were fighting for religious reasons. "Does this mean that we have found our answer?"

Several of the students who apprehend the direction she is going blurt out, "No."

"Why not?" she asks.

"Because there are still other sources," Theresa suggests.

"Because this was the Pope talking, or at least what one person said the Pope said, and so you would expect it to have more religious stuff," Jim offers.

"What was Jim doing just now?" Mrs. Hansen asks. "Do you notice how he was considering the subtext of the document? Well done Jim! And what is Theresa asking to do? She wants other texts to corroborate what this first document says. Do you see how sourcing, corroboration, and contextualization are important in using these texts as evidence?"

When Mrs. Hansen is certain that students understand how to complete the assignment, they form groups and she distributes the text sets. She circulates during the activity providing suggestions, prompting strategy use, modeling historical thinking, and complimenting students on their use of documents. When there are 15 minutes left in the class, she asks students to break up their groups and return to their seats so that they can talk about what they discovered. She starts the debriefing by asking students their answers to the central question. She finds that most students think that religious motives were the primary cause, but that other factors played a role. Mrs. Hansen decides to draw on the board a continuum with "religious factors" written on one side and "other factors" written on the other side (see Figure 4.2). Students are then allowed to quickly come to the board and plot their opinion on the spectrum. After they finish, she starts the discussion again. "Why do you think there is such a broad range of interpretations? We were all using the same evidence, weren't we?"

Jim raises his hand and Mrs. Hansen calls on him. "Sure, but there are a lot of different ways to interpret the evidence. Some people probably trusted one of the sources more and some people probably trusted a different source more."

"That's true. Is there a correct answer to this question?" Mrs. Hansen asks.

"I don't think so," says Theresa. "You could have any opinion on the question."

"But is one interpretation better than another?"

"No. How can there be a wrong answer. Since we can't know the answer for sure, then it shouldn't really matter what answer we come up with," Theresa continues.

"What if my interpretation was that the primary motivation for the crusaders was to escape an increasingly cold climate in Europe? Would that be a good interpretation – as good as any other opinion?" Mrs. Hansen probes.

"Sure," Theresa says. "Why wouldn't it be? Everybody is welcome to their own opinion."

"I don't think so," Alex interrupts. "There wasn't anything in the documents that said anything about the climate getting colder."

"So can we agree that although many different interpretations are possible, all interpretations are not equally strong? One of the criteria for a valid interpretation is that is must be based on the evidence. And the more skillfully and thoroughly we consider the evidence, the more valid our interpretation," Mrs. Hansen concludes. "As we've talked about before, studying history is kind of like solving a crime, and no detective would simply say 'go ahead and prosecute whomever' because we can't reach an agreement. Instead, the detective would search through

Spectrum Survey on Crusaders' Motives

exclusively religious factors	primarily religious factors	religious and non-religious factors	primarily non-religious factors	exclusively non-religious factors

FIGURE 4.2 An instrument for recording students' opinions on the causes of the Crusades.

every clue until he or she could say with confidence, 'This is the person that committed the crime, and these are the reasons I think so.'"

The discussion continues until the bell rings, signaling the end of class. Students leave the classroom continuing to argue their opinion and the evidence that they found most compelling.

Developing an Appropriate Epistemic Stance for Working with Multiple Texts

Mrs. Hansen didn't use the terminology with her students, but one of her primary objectives with this, and several other similarly structured lessons across the school year, is to help students develop a more sophisticated epistemic stance in order to improve their ability to work with historical texts. Epistemic stance, as it applies to history, is defined as an individual's understanding of the nature of historical knowledge, where historical knowledge comes from, and how it is developed. I begin this chapter by considering the nature of historical knowledge, what history is, and how historians learn history. I next explain and explore the concept of epistemic stance, with a focus on two immature stances common among students: objectivism and subjectivism, followed by the sophisticated stance typically taken by historians: criterialism (Reddy & VanSledright, 2010). Next, I consider instructional methods, like Mrs. Hansen's, using multiple historical texts, that are intended to help students develop a more mature epistemic position. I conclude with a consideration of methods for assessing students' epistemic stance.

Historical Knowledge

The past, as it was, is lost to us. We don't know what Stephen of Blois or other crusaders were thinking or feeling as they gathered their gear and began their trek to Jerusalem. And we can't ask them. Without the means to travel back in time, we are left with only the remnants of the past – artifacts and writings – to try to make sense of it. The crusaders left a scattered trail of evidence about their experiences, some of which has survived until today and been discovered by individuals interested in trying to comprehend their actions. Historians' work involves sifting through spotty evidence, searching for clues, interpreting the meaning of those clues, and reconstructing stories about the past. They attempt to write not only interesting stories, but stories that can be justified, given the existing evidence, and are fair to the characters of their stories – individuals who lived under circumstances often very different from our own. History, then, is not "what happened" but is a study of the past, filled with inferences, decisions about significance, interpretations, inclusions and omissions, generally accepted facts, and even speculations.

In spite of historians' efforts to avoid imposing themselves on their understanding of the past, they cannot evade doing so. VanSledright admits that "We imbue scattered artifacts and historical residue with meaning, and in the process –

despite heroic efforts to do otherwise – we concoct more or less evidence-based fictions" (2002, 144). Collingwood argues that "the past is … in every detail an imaginary picture" (1993, 245). Levesque (2008) agrees that some element of "historical imagination" is necessary as historians reconstruct, reenact, and rethink the states of minds of historical actors. However, VanSledright, Collingwood, and Levesque all acknowledge the role of evidence in tempering historians' imaginations. For instance, Levesque makes a distinction between historical imagination and pure imagination, arguing that historical imagination is exercised within the parameters of evidence and reality (2008). Historians understand that historical knowledge is influenced by the available evidence; by their colleagues' attachments and interests; by limited human perception, both of the producers and the analyzers of evidence; and by disciplinary norms. It is impossible to reconstruct things as they really were or to "nail down that one story," a naive but common notion held by those who don't understand the nature of historical knowledge. The manner that history is taught in schools perpetuates misconceptions about historical knowledge.

Students' Epistemic Stance

In contrast to historians, students often approach history classes with the idea that history is the past – it's simply what happened (VanSledright, 2002). And what happened is irrefutable, indisputable, and unquestioned. For instance, there is little doubt that the Pope called for a mission against the Muslims in 1095, that Christian crusaders gained control of Jerusalem in 1099, or that Muslims regained the city shortly thereafter, resulting in a series of crusades over centuries. For students, the whole of history is this type of string of unquestioned events. This way of thinking about historical understanding, the notion that history is simply what happened, is referred to as *objectivism* because students believe that learning history is a matter of gaining information about an objective reality, uncolored by human perception or interpretation. For them, learning history means accumulating information about what happened. They believe that any two individuals studying the same historical topic will eventually arrive at the same narrative. Differences in understandings or interpretations of historical events stem from someone not knowing the facts.

Where do students' ideas about the nature of historical understanding come from? VanSledright suggests that the importance of literal comprehension during the early years of learning to read creates the impression for young students that meaning resides in the text itself (2002). He suggests that by focusing nearly exclusively on skills such as summarizing, retelling, and finding the main idea, students are implicitly taught to uncritically accept the information in texts. As children grow, history teachers, by the methods they use, reinforce an objectivist epistemic stance. When children encounter history textbooks, with their omniscient, voiceless tone, the "reality effect" is strengthened. Students accept that " all the words in the text map directly onto what's real" (2002, 145). Additionally, when teachers exclusively assess students' factual knowledge rather than their ability to think historically, students continue to view learning history as a matter of remembering what the textbook or teacher told them. They believe that there is a single narrative and that their role is to remember the narrative long enough to answer questions about it on the test.

One of Mrs. Hansen's objectives for the school year is to help students begin to view historical understanding in more sophisticated ways – to help students reposition themselves epistemologically. In the activity that she has designed on the Crusades she asks students an interpretive question, the kind of question a historian would ask, and gives them conflicting evidence, the types of resources historians would use. She wants students to recognize that history is not simply facts about the past, but includes interpretations, opinions, and disputations.

Mrs. Hansen is aware of research that shows that students exposed to conflicting historical accounts often begin to reposition themselves, taking a *subjectivist* epistemic stance (Reddy & VanSledright, 2010). Students who view historical understanding from a subjectivist position recognize that there are multiple ways of interpreting past events. They understand that historical sources are extensions of imperfect individuals who have limited perspectives, and biases. Because historical interpretation comes from imperfect sources, and multiple opinions about historical events are possible, students who approach history from a subjectivist stance not only tolerate diverse opinions, but accept any historical interpretation as equally plausible. Since it is impossible to know what happened for certain, any version of the past is as good as any other. History becomes an unsubstantiated guess (Ashby, *et al.*, 2005). This way of viewing the past has also been referred to as naïve or vicious relativism (Lee, 2005).

The problems associated with subjectivism stem from students' inability to effectively cope with conflicting evidence – from their lack of any "criteria for managing bias" (Reddy & VanSledright, 2010, 2–3). It stems from their inability to use and make judgments about historical evidence. Research has shown that students have a difficult time distinguishing between more and less reliable sources (Ashby, *et al.*, 2005; Wineburg, 1991). Because they have a difficult time evaluating sources, generally accepting all information at face value, they experience frustration when exposed to conflicting accounts (Wineburg, 1991). A typical reaction to this frustration is to uncritically accept one of the accounts and accuse the others of lying (Ashby, *et al.*, 2005). When pressed to justify their interpretation over others, they cannot satisfactorily do so. Aware of their precarious position, they cannot critique interpretations that differ from theirs. They conclude that historical interpretations are simply subjective, with no way to judge between alternative claims.

With repeated exposure to multiple text activities and with instruction on how to evaluate and use evidence, like Mrs. Hansen provided, students emerge from a subjectivist epistemic stance. However, even as students begin to mature in their historical thinking, they typically use unsophisticated strategies for defending historical interpretations. For instance, Mrs. Hansen warned her class about one way young students handle conflicting accounts: tallying the evidence for different interpretations and choosing the interpretation that has quantifiably more support (Ashby, *et al.*, 2005). What is lacking in this approach is a critique of the sources. Historians know that the evidence found in a single good source outweighs a great deal of evidence from questionable sources. Although students' score keeping strategy is flawed, it demonstrates that students are beginning to recognize that there are certain criteria by which an historical interpretation can be evaluated. Given practice and strategy instruction on historians' heuristics, they are poised to assume a *criterialist* epistemic stance – that of historians.

Historians' Epistemic Stance

Historians understand that the instant pen strikes paper, historical writing is interpretive. Historians commence their research by making interpretive decisions about what is significant enough to study. They understand that there is no single, objective, agreed upon historical narrative that captures the whole of the past. Certainly there are widely accepted historical facts, but much of our historical understanding is a work in progress, undergoing continuous reinterpretation and revision based on new evidence, new ways of considering old evidence, and new interests. Further, historians do not accept all interpretations as equally valid. Much of historical writing is argumentation, explaining and justifying how evidence has been used to reach conclusions. Historians know that there are generally accepted criteria that can be used to evaluate interpretations. They approach historical study with a *criterialist* epistemic stance, judging evidence and interpretations using standards of evaluation – criteria – established by the community of historians. For instance, a historian would consider whether all available evidence was used to develop an interpretation. Was evidence used appropriately? How were conflicting evidence and alternative interpretations dealt with? How is an interpretation original yet grounded in prior historical research? Historians' heuristics of sourcing, corroboration, and contextualization are keys to answering these questions satisfactorily and to meet the criteria required for establishing a valid and valued interpretation. When standards are met, one interpretation is judged as superior to alternatives.

Using Multiple Text Activities to Foster a Mature Epistemic Stance

Traditional history instruction does little to foster in students a mature epistemic stance. Overreliance on lectures and textbook reading promotes an objectivist stance. Mrs. Hansen knew that for students to develop a criterialist epistemic stance she had to engage them in non-traditional activities. Several features of her Crusades activity were designed to foster a criterialist stance. First, to show students that there are often multiple ways to perceive past events, she asked a question that could be answered in multiple ways. Second, she carefully selected the texts that contained disagreements, contradictions, and evidence that could be used to support either side of an argument. Her purpose in doing so was to create cognitive dissonance – a feeling of tension or uneasiness that exists when unresolved conflicting ideas are held simultaneously. The texts that she provided demonstrate that there is no simple textbook answer to her question. Further, she chose texts that came from multiple perspectives, including Christian, Muslim, Jewish, and historian points of view, helping students see the effect of perspective on the content of a text.

Third, knowing that the conflicting evidence might cause some students, like Theresa, to adopt a subjectivist stance, Mrs. Hansen chose texts with easily recognizable evidence. She understood that one form of scaffolding is to simplify some aspects of an activity in order to allow deeper thinking about other aspects of the activity. She chose texts where the evidence practically leapt off the page at students. Additionally, during the lesson she gave an example of an inappropriate interpretation, that climate change had prompted the Crusades. Doing so illustrated the need for evidence to support a claim. Guessing simply is not enough. Criteria exist for judging interpretations and claims. Thus, the activity was designed to help students recognize that although multiple interpretations are possible, not all interpretations are equally valid. Historians must use evidence to judge between opposing claims.

Fourth, the class discussion was laced with mini-lessons on appropriate ways of working with evidence. For instance, after modeling sourcing, Mrs. Hansen paused and asked them to identify what she had done. This brief foray into metacognition allowed students to identify appropriate methods of thinking about evidence. Similarly, when Jim and Theresa modeled effective thinking, she asked students to reflect on their thought processes. Students are unable to take a criterialist stance if they do not understand historians' heuristics, and Mrs. Hansen's mini-lessons were designed to teach, reteach, model, and practice historians' ways of thinking about evidence.

Teaching Students Explicitly about Epistemology

Students have a difficult time engaging in historical thinking activities when they do not take an appropriate epistemic stance. However, I've found that it's difficult to discuss with students the idea of epistemology – it takes a great deal of time with limited productivity. However, I also found that there are other, fairly simple, means for helping students approach the learning of history from a criterialist stance. For instance, students are often familiar with the work of detectives, attempting to piece together the bits of evidence in solving a mystery. They have typically had enough exposure to detective work to assume an epistemic stance appropriate for solving a crime. By framing an activity as a historical mystery and positioning students as history detectives, they can, with relative ease, adopt an epistemic stance that more closely approximates that of a historian. Similarly, teachers can position students as jurors who interact with evidence about a historical situation in order to render a justifiable verdict (Kuhn, Weinstock, & Flaton, 1994). In both of these cases, however, the students may approximate the thinking that historians use, but they still might be searching for that single narrative that reflects reality. After all, television shows always end with detectives or jurors reaching the only correct conclusion.

A history teacher might instead encourage students to assume a historian's identity. This would first entail helping students understand the work of historians, what they do, how they search for evidence, and how they use it once they find it. When students understand the basics of how historians search, analyze, and write, they can be encouraged to work with evidence like historians. I've found that even elementary age students begin to identify the need for primary source evidence in judging between alternative interpretations when they have been taught to assume a historians' identity.

Whether history teachers use the analogy of the detective, the juror, or the historian, the key elements for promoting a mature epistemic stance must be that students a) are active in the process of historical thinking; b) are allowed to construct their own independent interpretation of the historical event that might be different from that of their peers; c) are aware of strategies that they can use to effectively weigh the evidence; d) are expected to base claims on evidence; e) are supported throughout the process by interaction with peers and the teacher, by graphic organizers, by teacher and peer modeling, and/or by checklists to remind them of effective processes; f) have regular opportunities to engage in historical thinking; g) are not overexposed to textbook accounts; and h) are assessed in a manner that values unique defensible interpretations and not just knowledge of historical facts.

Teachers need to be aware that students may move back and forth between epistemic stances, particularly students who are adept at playing the game of school. During a lecture, they might assume a more objectivist stance, accepting without question the information presented by the teacher. During a subsequent multiple text activity they might assume a subjectivist or criterialist stance. Students should be taught that history is always interpretive in nature, whether the resources used to learn it are primary sources, the textbook, or the teacher's lecture. After all, as soon as a teacher begins to lecture he/she makes decisions about significance, tone, and perspective.

Assessing Students' Epistemic Stance

Teachers can assess students' epistemic stance along with their content knowledge and historical thinking skills. Wineburg and his colleagues (in press) created a simple assessment, asking students to evaluate how helpful a painting of the first

Thanksgiving, produced in 1932, would be in understanding what happened at the first Thanksgiving. Students who approach the problem from an objectivist stance value the painting and the details that it provides about the event. They view the painting as a conveyor of information about the event, ignoring the context of its creation. Students who approach the question from a more mature epistemic stance recognize that the source reveals little about the original event, instead giving clues about the way the event was viewed when the painting was made. They understand that it says more about the artist's purpose in creating the painting, and the artistic styles of that later age. Without some background knowledge of the artist, his/her research, sources, purposes, and audience, the learner of history does not know how useful the image is in understanding the original event (Wineburg, Smith, & Breakstone, in press).

Ongoing, less formal assessments of students' epistemic stance can occur during multiple text activities as the teacher listens to and interacts with groups of students. Symptoms of an objectivist stance include: looking for the one right answer or story; uncritically accepting the information presented in the sources at face value; experiencing frustration when dealing with contradictory sources; focusing cognitive resources on summarizing, finding the main ideas, gathering facts, and remembering information; and expecting classmates to arrive at the same conclusions. Students approaching multiple text activities with a subjectivist stance expend little energy in constructing or defending their interpretation; care little if others' interpretations differ from their own; fail to justify their interpretation using evidence; discount evidence without valid reason simply because it disagrees with their ideas; change their mind with little resistance if peers suggest an alternative explanation; and wonder how their work with the documents will be assessed, failing to recognize that all interpretations are not equal in quality. In the vignette, Mrs. Hansen could see that Theresa approached the question on the crusaders from a subjectivist stance when she suggested "there isn't a wrong answer." On the other hand, students who take a criterialist stance will think deeply about the central question they are asked; spend significant time evaluating each source; use historians' heuristics such as sourcing, corroboration, and contextualization to weigh evidence; defend their interpretations citing specific evidence; change their mind when a peer persuades them using evidence; appropriately discount unreliable information contained in the documents; and engage in historical writing that mirrors that of historians – blending narration, description, and argumentation.

Chapter Summary

A prerequisite for students' historical literacies is to approach the historical thinking task from the appropriate epistemic stance. The objectivist stance positions a learner to expect a single, objective, agreed-upon historical narrative. Elementary reading instruction, with its focus on the literal comprehension of texts, and traditional history instruction, with its focus on lectures and textbook reading, foster an objectivist stance. The subjectivist stance positions the learner to accept any interpretation as valid, unable to evaluate evidence or claims. Exposure to multiple interpretations of historical events can lead students to assume a subjectivist stance. The criterialist stance, the epistemic stance of historians, positions a learner to recognize that multiple accounts are possible but that the skillful use of evidence allows one to judge between accounts. Frequently assigning multiple text activities, providing historians' tools for sifting through evidence, and creating a setting where students can begin to develop a historian's identity help them develop a criterialist stance. Teachers can and should assess students' epistemic stance in order to customize historical literacy lessons.

PART II

Fluency with Strategies and Evidence

Collingwood contends that anything that can be perceived could potentially be used as historical evidence, given the right question (1993). There is a world of texts and resources that could be brought into history classrooms, to be used by students as evidence. This section of the book explores a small sample of the types of texts a history teacher might use. Additionally, historians employ various strategies and habits of mind for reading, reasoning, and writing with this assortment of texts. This section explores methods of teaching these strategies to students.

In this section, I take the reader into the classroom of seven fictional history teachers who model the planning and execution of lessons associated with seven types of texts and seven historical literacies. Mr. Dunn conducts a case study of a Native American, John White, using various primary sources. He teaches students historians' heuristics for working with primary sources. Mrs. Dahl uses bas-relief sculptures from the World War II memorial, modern artifacts, to review a unit on World War II. She teaches students how to make appropriate inferences while working with artifacts. Ms. Jensen helps students use propaganda posters to explore home front trends during World War I. Her lesson is designed to help students develop metaconceptual understanding, with a focus on the concept of evidence, using visual evidence. Miss Anderson's lessons are intended to help students learn the historical context of the Civil Rights Movement. She uses a historical novel to help students develop historical empathy toward both African American and White southerners in the years leading up to the Civil Rights Movement. Mr. Johnson's lesson on the Mongols uses a mix of primary sources with the textbook. His intent is to have students approach textbooks, and all historical accounts, with a healthy skepticism. Ms. Chavez uses jazz music to get students thinking about the clash between tradition and change during the 1920s. Her objective is to have students become more fluent in working with music, an oral text, while warning about the tendency toward reductionist thinking. And finally, Mr. Erikson provides an opportunity for students to explore immigration trends using census records. His purpose is to help students use quantitative data in building an argument.

The reader is encouraged to think of the historical literacy strategies as the warp, and the various types of evidence as the woof in weaving together a comprehensive historical literacy program. Students with historical literacies are confident in working with a wide array of historical texts because they understand the nature of historical thinking, possess strategies for working with evidence, and are capable of thinking complex thoughts about history. This section is designed to explore the texts and ways of thinking about texts that will foster this literacy.

5

USING HISTORIANS' HEURISTICS FOR WORKING WITH PRIMARY SOURCES

Mr. Dunn is teaching a unit on the European colonization of North America in an 11th grade U.S. history course. He wants to show students the way many cultures from Europe, America, and Africa blended in the colonies. He thinks that students have misconceptions about the relationship between individuals from the three continents. He wants students to understand that Europeans, Native Americans, and Africans were all active agents of change. He thinks about the best possible texts that he might use. He could show a clip from the Disney movie *Pocahontas* to illustrate the interaction, but he is afraid that it might reinforce stereotypes and misunderstandings. The textbook has a long section about the English colonies but it doesn't portray Native Americans or Africans as meaningful contributors to colonial life, but merely as victims. He wonders whether there are primary sources that students could access that illustrate the complex relationships. He researches online and discovers John White, a Nipmuck Indian, who died in London, England in 1679 (Pulsipher, 2003). He decides that John White, formerly known as John Wampus, has an interesting story that is intertwined with major colonial events such as King Philip's War. He finds relevant, interesting primary and secondary sources on John White and determines that White's story will provide an engaging case study through which students can explore Native American and English relationships in the early colonies.

Mr. Dunn establishes the following objectives for a pair of lessons on John White and Native American/English relations in the British colonies:

1. Students will explore the complex, continuously changing relationship between Native Americans and European colonists in North America, considering examples of both cooperation and conflict and viewing both groups as active agents of change.

2. Students will differentiate between primary and secondary historical sources and develop strategies, including sourcing and corroboration, which are associated with effectively using historical evidence.

Mr. Dunn prepares a collection of documents that includes several primary and secondary sources including records of court proceedings, a petition by a Native American group, a letter written by King Charles II, and carefully selected excerpts from a historian's analysis of John White's life. He creates a legible transcript of one document that is particularly challenging to read. He notices the difficult vocabulary in another, defining unfamiliar terms in the margins of the text. He rewrites a third document, simplifying the language so that students will be able to comprehend it.

Mr. Dunn spends two days investigating this topic with his students. On the first day, he assesses students' prior knowledge. He begins class by engaging students in a short discussion of the Native Americans and English settlements of New England. During the discussion he asks students to think about the possible ways that Native Americans might have reacted to the arrival of colonists.

"If I would have been there I would have got all the Native Americans together and killed all of the Europeans while we still had them outnumbered," Jordan suggests.

"Yeah, but they couldn't see the future," Amber responds. "How were they supposed to know that they would be outnumbered back when there were only a few colonists here?"

Mr. Dunn makes a mental note of students' inability to comprehend the historical context of colonization or to view events from a historical perspective. He notes, for instance, that Jordan projects his understanding, in hindsight, onto Native Americans. Further, neither Jordan nor Amber appears to understand the rivalries that existed between Native American groups at the time of the colonists' arrival. He uses the discussion to discover students' background knowledge, their misconceptions, and their ideas about the 17th century American colonial frontier.

Once he has a sense of students' background knowledge, Mr. Dunn lectures for several minutes on the human and physical geography of colonial New England. He points out, for example, that there were many different Indian nations living in the region, some of them allied with each other and some of them enemies. He also teaches that tribes varied in size and strength, with some posing a grave threat to colonial settlements and others more vulnerable to the whims of colonists and rival tribes. He reminds students that there were different reactions within Native American groups to the arrival of the colonists, just as there were differences in opinion among the colonists on the best ways to interact with Native Americans. As his lecture ends, he informs students that they are going to do a case study of one Nipmuck Indian who viewed the arrival of the colonists as an opportunity to build his own personal wealth, adopting a dual Native American/English identity to negotiate the sale of much Native American land to English colonists. In the end he was viewed as a traitor by both groups.

Mr. Dunn introduces students to John White, by giving some basic facts and by revealing a few puzzling pieces of historical evidence that directly confront students' misconceptions. Students are told, for instance, that his original name was John Wampus (sometimes spelled Wompowess or Wompas) but it was later fully anglicized to John White. Students are surprised to hear that the he attended Harvard and later resided in a house in Boston. Mr. Dunn clarifies that a handful of Native Americans were admitted into Harvard in the 1660s and 1670s in hopes that they would become Christian ministers who would convert their people to both Christianity and to English culture. Mr. Dunn tells students about one of John White's schoolbooks from Harvard, now lost, but described in the historical record. The inscription "John Wompowess his booke" appeared on the front inside cover. On the opposite page near a sketch of a meetinghouse in different handwriting was written, "John Savage his meetinghouse the king of it I say." Mr. Dunn explains, "You probably thought vandalizing textbooks was a new activity, but it appears that it has been going on for a long time. It looks like John White wrote his name in his book, and someone else wrote an insult on the opposite page. There's a story in these two sentences that might help us to understand John White's life within the context of Native American and colonist interaction." He asks students, "Who might have written this insult and what did they mean by calling John Wampus 'John Savage?'"

"I'll bet it was written by a White person who was trying to put him back in his place as a 'savage' so that the Whites could feel superior," argues Jordan.

"I think it was another Native American who didn't like John Wampus acting like a White man. He refers to him as John 'Savage' to remind him who he really was," suggests Anthony.

A few other students voice their opinions. Mr. Dunn leaves the question unanswered, though acknowledging that either explanation is possible. He explains that students will look at evidence to reconstruct a better picture of John White, his life, and his context. As Mr. Dunn lectures, he continues to ask questions. "Why might a Native American have taken an English name? How did he gain admission to Harvard? Why was he in London at the time of his death? Why did his own people, in 1677, petition the Massachusetts magistrates not to allow him to represent them in future land dealings? What did his life suggest about general trends in Native American/English relations?" Students add to the list of questions – "Did other Native Americans feel like he was selling out his people? How did the White people feel about Native Americans like him, who adopted English lifestyles? Did they welcome them into their society? Did the English ever marry Native Americans?" As students speak, Mr. Dunn writes their questions on the board. After creating a good list of questions, Mr. Dunn announces that he has gathered documents that they will use to answer their questions.

"But before I give you the text set, I want to take a few minutes to help you be smarter in the way you work with the documents," he explains. "Imagine that you observed a traffic accident on your way home from school today, and police officers took your name and phone number and said they might call later to find out exactly what happened. Imagine that you went home from school and told your mother about the accident. Later, a police officer calls your home. Would the officer want to talk to you or your mother?"

In the discussion that follows Mr. Dunn helps students distinguish between primary and secondary sources. He introduces students to bias by asking, "What if one of your friends was the driver of one of the cars involved in the accident. Would the police officer want to talk with you or your mother? Does the source of the information matter?"

Mr. Dunn makes a connection between investigating an accident and investigating historical controversies. He points out that in both cases the investigator must sift through evidence that might be incomplete or contain contradictions. He asks students what an investigator might do when faced with contradictory evidence.

"Look at which side has more pieces of evidence," Connie recommends.

"That's one way to work with evidence, but what might be a problem with simply keeping score of the number of pieces of evidence?" Mr. Dunn probes.

"One really good piece of evidence might outweigh lots of other evidence so you can't just count how much there is on each side," Connie admits.

Mr. Dunn agrees and explains, "Historians definitely have to distinguish between weightier and less weighty, reliable and unreliable evidence. I want to tell you about two things that historians always do when they are working with evidence."

He continues talking explicitly about historians' strategies of sourcing and corroboration. After discussing each strategy briefly, he passes out the text sets and says, "Let me show you what I mean. Take a look at the first document. Historians always start by looking at the source. It's called sourcing. Down at the bottom of the first page I can see that it was written by Jenny Pulsipher in 2003. What do I know about it immediately?"

When students flounder a little, he restates the question, "Is this a primary or a secondary source?"

Students acknowledge that it is a secondary source. Edgar suggests that it must not be very reliable, reminding Mr. Dunn that the police officers wouldn't want to talk to his mother to find out about the accident. Mr. Dunn agrees that primary sources have some advantages over secondary sources, but suggests that secondary sources might also be of value.

"How can we find out about this source? Can we trust that she is an expert?" he asks. Eventually, with Mr. Dunn's guidance, the students decide to do an Internet search to find out about Jenny Pulsipher. They discover that she is a history professor who specializes in English/Native American relations during colonial times, recently publishing a book on the topic.

"She sounds like a reliable source," Dillon concludes.

"But I thought secondary sources weren't as reliable as primary sources," Shelby expresses with frustration. "You're confusing us, Mr. Dunn."

Mr. Dunn laughs. "This is a messy process, Shelby. You can probably start to understand why history books sometimes disagree with each other. Doing history involves a great deal of interpretation even after careful investigation. We've discovered that this text comes from a professor with a good reputation as a scholar. What else can we do to evaluate this secondary source?" he asks, getting back to the original issue. "Would a police officer simply talk to one witness and then think he/she had all the evidence?"

"We can see how it matches the other evidence, especially the primary sources," Shelby concludes.

"That's a great idea, Shelby. This is a strategy that historians call corroboration. Historians compare documents for similarities and differences. Corroboration goes together with sourcing to help us judge how reliable a documents is."

Mr. Dunn passes out a graphic organizer that he designed that has a place to record source information, a brief summary of the source, and how the source compares to other sources students have investigated (see Figure 5.1). He encourages students to make notes in the cells related to the first text and to continue filling it out as they evaluate the other texts. He points out that also included in the graphic organizer is a place to take notes on evidence as it relates to their original research questions, and space to record new questions that arise as the sources are explored.

"Let's look at one more text together before the bell rings," Mr. Dunn suggests. They examine a petition written by John Wampus to Charles II, King of England, explaining his plight. "What do we do before reading the letter?" he asks.

"We look at the source," several students call out simultaneously.

Mr. Dunn spends the rest of class considering the source, corroborating the story it tells with the first text they read, and reflecting on the context. As the bell rings he collects the text sets and dismisses the class.

The next day Mr. Dunn forms students into small groups and assigns them to take most of the class exploring their text set, which includes a variety of primary sources and carefully selected excerpts from secondary sources. He reminds them to use sourcing and corroboration to make sense of the texts. While students work, he circulates, listens to their discussions, makes suggestions, and asks questions.

With about ten minutes left in class, he reminds students about some of their misconceptions from the beginning of the day before. "Yesterday, someone suggested that the Native Americans should kill all of the colonists. What are your thoughts on this idea now?"

Research questions:

Source	Source analysis	Summary of content	Similarities to other texts	Differences from other texts	Other notes
Text 1					
Text 2					
Text 3					
Text 4					
Text 5					

Evidence that helps answer your research questions:

New questions that you have as you read the documents:
1.

2.

3.

FIGURE 5.1 A graphic organizer for supporting students' work with primary sources.

"Well, it sounds like some of the Native Americans, like John White, were glad the colonists were there and used them to make a lot of money. It might have been hard to unite a tribe to fight against them," Sandra suggests.

"Yeah, and you said that the different tribes were sometimes enemies – so that would have made it even harder to fight them," Jordan elaborates.

After a brief discussion of their misconceptions, he allows each group to report on what they found about one of their original research questions. As the bell rings, students leave class with a more sophisticated understanding of Native

American/White colonial relations, and they have had an opportunity to evaluate primary and secondary sources using historians' strategies of sourcing and corroboration. Mr. Dunn understands that this is just a beginning, and that he will need to continue to remind students about these important historical literacies and provide opportunities to practice throughout the school year.

Helping Students Learn with Primary Sources

As described in the introductory chapters of this book, written records provide the foundation of historical inquiry, and primary sources, such as those gathered by Mr. Dunn, are historians' preferred format of written record. However, as also reported in previous chapters, students have a difficult time working with primary sources the way historians do. They typically view texts – all texts, of any format – as conveyors of information. Their focus is on reading, remembering, and regurgitating. In contrast, Mr. Dunn wanted students to adopt a criterialist epistemic stance, using documents as evidence in building historical understanding. Mr. Dunn knows that familiarity with historians' heuristics would give students the tools needed to evaluate documents as evidence. This chapter discusses a) historians' heuristics of sourcing, corroboration, and contextualization, and how they can be taught; b) helping students read primary sources; c) how a teacher can help students critique and use primary sources to construct historical interpretations; d) ideas for selecting appropriate primary sources; and e) allowing students to produce primary sources.

Historians' Heuristics of Sourcing, Corroboration, and Contextualization

Even in the proper classroom setting, students are not likely to be able to work well with primary sources unless they have the tools to do so. I found that fostering debate and discussion without giving students tools for working with evidence created a potentially chaotic environment where unsubstantiated claims, voiced with passion, could win out over reasoned, evidence-based interpretations, presented with less gusto. In Chapter 2, I introduced historians' strategies and habits of mind for working with historical sources. As described there, historians' approach all sources with skepticism, consider the source of each text, determine the reliability of various sources through corroboration, maintain an openness to alternative interpretations, place themselves in the physical and social context of the document's creation, and fill in gaps in the evidence with reasoned speculation. Mr. Dunn's lessons included instruction on two of these heuristics: sourcing, and corroboration, which, when added to contextualization, make up the three most basic of historians' heuristics (Wineburg, 1991).

Sourcing

Students must be taught that when they begin to explore an unfamiliar text they must look first at its source. A reader cannot comprehend, critique, or use a text as historical evidence without establishing where it came from. When sourcing, students should identify the type of document they are working with and adjust their reading accordingly. For instance, after identifying a document as a letter a student should attend to the signature, to identify who wrote it; the greeting, to identify the recipient; and the date, to see when it was written. Other types of texts elicit different reading procedures. Students should always consider whether the author had first-hand knowledge of the event. Further, if investigating an event that pits two sides against each other, such as a battle, a political campaign, a sporting event, or a trial, the position of the author is important. The author's social standing, educational background, and even physical location during an event can influence the content and value of an account. For example, a person holding public office may have more to gain or lose by the way an event is portrayed. Students should think about the intended audience and its impact on a text. For instance, the tone of John Wampus' letter to King Charles II is obviously very different from the tone of the graffiti in the textbook. Much of this difference is a result of the intended audience. Students should consider the purpose of a text and look at the timing of its creation. Was it produced immediately following an experience, or years later, when some of the details might have been forgotten but a broader perspective of the event might have been gained?

When considering the source, there are few absolute rules that can be taught to students. The value of the record is based on the questions being asked, the range of sources available, and the content of the text. At times private writing, such as journal entries, is more valued than public records, such as sworn depositions, and sometimes it is not. At times, close personal involvement in an event yields the richest resources, and sometimes distance creates a more valuable perspective. In spite of the flexibility required in sourcing, all historians demonstrate that the use of any evidence should begin by a consideration of the source (Wineburg, 1991). Mr. Dunn recognizes the challenges of sourcing for young students. Whereas the students want firm rules, i.e. primary sources are always more reliable than secondary sources, he suggests that the evaluation of multiple texts is a messy business and that multiple strategies must be used together.

Corroboration

The graphic organizer that Mr. Dunn prepared reminds students to pay attention to the source of the text and encourages them to use corroboration across texts. Corroboration helps students determine the validity and reliability of sources. Texts with descriptions that are substantiated by other sources are deemed more reliable. Texts with content that is contradicted by other sources present a greater challenge to students. Differences between texts might include omissions of specific details by one or more source, unique inclusions, or outright disagreement on basic facts. Students must be taught to notice and seek explanations for discrepancies, which can often be accomplished through sourcing. There might be a simple explanation for discrepancies, such as the different physical location of eyewitnesses. In such cases, two divergent accounts might both be judged reliable. At times the differences between accounts might require students to make judgments between opposed texts. In such cases corroboration, sourcing, and other heuristics can help. Mr. Dunn's graphic organizer is intended to help students corroborate by asking them to record similarities and differences between texts.

Contextualization

Students must learn to use the physical and social context of a document's creation to help them comprehend, critique, and use it as evidence. This heuristic of placing oneself in a historical setting has been labeled *contextualization*. Important things to be kept in mind in contextualization include an awareness of the geography surrounding an event; the time of day or year that the event occurred; the cultural and social setting of the event, such as traditions or etiquette; a biographical awareness of participants, such as the tendencies of a general or politician; a linguistic awareness of the changing meaning of words across time; and a historiographic awareness of how an event has been perceived by historians. It's not surprising that students' lack of background knowledge makes contextualization difficult for them. In fact, there is some indication that students have a harder time using contextualization than they do sourcing or corroboration (Nokes *et al.*, 2007; Reisman, 2012). Not wanting to overwhelm students with too many new ideas in a single day, Mr. Dunn did not provide explicit instruction on the strategy of contextualization during this lesson. However, he used the story of John White to help his students understand the complex social context of Native American/colonist interaction. He will spend time explicitly teaching about contextualization later in the school year.

Teaching Historians' Heuristics

In spite of historians' nearly universal use of these three heuristics, Mr. Dunn understands that history students do not instinctively engage in sourcing, corroboration, or contextualization. It is up to him to help them develop these historical literacies as part of his overall goal of helping them learn to read like historians. He understands that teachers can increase students' ability to work well with primary sources by explicitly teaching these strategies (Nokes, *et al.*, 2007), so he builds historical literacy mini-lessons into his curriculum.

Mr. Dunn provided explicit strategy instruction on sourcing and corroboration. He openly discussed the heuristics with students, naming the heuristics, elaborating on the processes used in implementing them, and suggesting why the heuristics were effective and important. He modeled both sourcing and corroboration for the students. He thought aloud as he questioned one of the sources in the text set – pointing out that it was a secondary source. He walked them through the process of researching the authority of a source through the Internet. He also modeled how two heuristics, sourcing and corroboration, could be used together. Additionally, he provided a setting where students could practice these heuristics with support. The graphic organizer provided a gentle reminder that students needed to pay attention to the source and how the documents compared and contrasted with each other. The graphic organizer facilitated corroboration by easing the process of making direct comparisons across texts. It provided a place to summarize the content of each text in order to create a record that students could cross check against other sources as they were analyzed. Further, working in groups allowed students to think aloud, to get feedback on their ideas, and to observe others use heuristics. His circulating during group work allowed him to support the use of heuristics, to further use the language of the heuristics, and to offer praise when students used the heuristics appropriately.

In addition to explicit instruction on sourcing and corroboration, Mr. Dunn provided implicit strategy instruction on contextualization. Though not mentioning the strategy by name, his questioning prompted students to immerse themselves in the context of the time and his short lecture gave students background knowledge that was useful in doing so.

Helping Students Read Primary Sources

When working with primary sources, students often need support in each of their four roles as readers: code breakers, meaning makers, text users, and text critics described in Chapter 3. These roles suggest that working with texts is an active process. Teachers can further promote students' active engagement by encouraging them to ask questions and seek plausible interpretations using primary sources. Additionally, they can help students view primary sources as evidence rather than as conveyors of information. I consider each of these notions in this section.

Code Breakers and Meaning Makers of Primary Sources

Before students can adopt the role of historian and reason with historical evidence, they must be able to decode and construct meaning with primary sources – to "read" them. Teachers should be aware that basic comprehension of primary sources can present challenges for students for a number of reasons. First, decoding is difficult when texts are age-worn or written in illegible handwriting, as primary sources often are. The reading of old texts can be such a challenge that among historians there are specialists, palaeographers, who focus on the decoding of old handwriting. Students who must work hard to decode a text (i.e. read it) have fewer remaining cognitive resources with which to conduct an analysis (Nokes, 2011). Mr. Dunn compensated for this challenge by preparing a transcript of one document, which he presented beside the original so that students could use both. Second, comprehension is difficult when texts are written using challenging language, unfamiliar vocabulary, or terms that have a different historical meaning. Mr. Dunn addressed this problem by choosing some simple texts, one being only a single sentence in length, and by defining difficult vocabulary in the margins of another text. Researchers have suggested that teachers also help students understand the evolving or contextualized meaning of some words and in some cases even translate documents into simpler language that students can comprehend (Stanford History Education Group, 2012). Additionally, allowing students to work as a class or in small groups to read texts, as Mr. Dunn did, can provide scaffolding for students. The graphic organizer he prepared had a place for students to summarize their understanding of each text – allowing Mr. Dunn to assess their comprehension of the documents and providing them a place to refer back to when corroborating across texts. In summary, students cannot engage in the analysis of documents that they cannot comprehend. Mr. Dunn took measures to help students decode and comprehend the primary source materials he provided.

Critiquing and Using Primary Sources

Mr. Dunn is trying to create a classroom where students are expected to evaluate texts and use them as evidence to answer questions related to historical dilemmas. He has carefully structured his classroom to promote historical literacies. He uses the analogy of a witness at an accident scene to help students understand their identity as investigators of the past and the role of accounts as evidence. The purpose of his lecture is not simply to transmit information but to help students understand the context of historical questions. The explicit instruction that he provides is intended to help students evaluate texts as historians do, using sourcing, corroboration, and contextualization. The structure of his activities promotes questioning, a search for answers to questions, and further questioning. His assessment, in this case the graphic organizer, is meant to evaluate students' ability to engage in historical thinking processes, rather than their arrival at a predetermined conclusion. Thus, Mr. Dunn's lesson plans facilitate the critique and use of documents in authentic ways by creating an environment where students ask questions and seek plausible interpretations using documents as evidence.

Asking Questions and Seeking Plausible Interpretations

Mr. Dunn has found puzzling resources, the types of texts that historians would use, in order to promote students' spontaneous and authentic questioning. He poses questions that allow multiple interpretations. But more importantly, classroom activities revolve around not only his questions, but authentic questions that students develop under his guidance. At the outset of the case study on John White, Mr. Dunn is uncertain how students will interpret the texts or which questions they will consider. He is quite confident, though, that he has selected resources that will promote students' learning of concepts that are central to the required curriculum – Native American and White relations.

It is possible for teachers to use primary sources without promoting historical literacies. As I mentioned in a previous chapter, when I observed several history lessons, the most common way teachers used primary sources was to present short, one- or two-line quotes in order to illustrate a point made during a lecture. The teachers typically read and explained the primary source to students with few opportunities for students to interpret (Nokes, 2010a). In the worst cases, the primary sources were used for the same purpose that textbooks and lectures are typically used – to convey information to students. In the best cases, teachers used primary sources as evidence of a point they were trying to make. But even when primary sources were used under these circumstances, there was no explicit discussion of strategies like sourcing or corroboration, no explicit distinction made between primary and secondary sources, and no critique or questioning of the source.

Thus, exposure to primary sources does not build students' historical literacies unless teachers create the appropriate conditions. These conditions include introducing historical controversies or mysteries without an agreed upon interpretation; allowing students to semi-independently develop original interpretations based on the evidence; bringing in multiple contradictory texts that provide room for differences of opinion; permitting students to disagree with their peers, the teacher, textbooks, and even historians; and encouraging students to explore their own interests using both teacher-provided text sets and their own independent research. There is little opportunity for historical thinking when teachers simply offer, as factual, their interpretations of primary sources, expecting students to remember rather than to question and seek plausible alternative interpretations. On the other hand, in classrooms that not only tolerate but appreciate diverse opinions, students feel safe in positioning themselves in historical debates. I have found that students in settings that appreciate independent questioning and allow alternative evidence-based interpretations are more likely to work with primary sources in a discipline-appropriate manner.

Viewing Primary Sources as Evidence

As part of the process of helping students understand the nature of history and the role of historians, students must consider documents evidence rather than repositories of facts or conveyors of information. The graffiti in the textbook is not comprehended literally – suggesting that John Wampus was the king of his own meetinghouse. Instead, Mr. Dunn's students use it as evidence of the attitudes of others toward an Anglicized Native American. In the process of working with historical evidence, students must acknowledge that primary sources were typically not written for the purpose they are now being used. As a result, the author may assume background knowledge that students and historians lack. Some knowledge of the historic and geographic context may be necessary to comprehend the text. Aware of this, Mr. Dunn lectured briefly on the human and physical geography of New England in order to build the necessary background knowledge before expecting students to comprehend and evaluate the texts as evidence.

To illustrate further, I sometimes use a note Eisenhower wrote prior to the D-Day invasion to teach students that victory in World War II was not inevitable, to help students understand the risk of the attack, to help them understand the personality of Eisenhower, and to help them comprehend the nature of historical evidence (see Figure 5.2 and Figure 5.3). If students read the text with the attitude

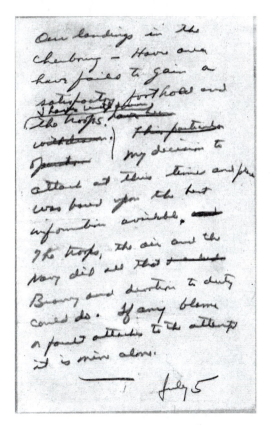

FIGURE 5.2 Eisenhower's unreleased press release of the Normandy Invasion (Courtesy of the Dwight D. Eisenhower Presidential Library, National Archives and Records Administration, Abilene, Kansas).

Our landings in the Cherbourg-Havre
area have failed to gain a
satisfactory foothold and ^I have
withdrawn the troops. ~~have been~~
~~withdrawn. This particular operation~~
My decision to attack at this time and
place was based upon the best
information available. The troops, the
air and the navy did all that
~~(undecipherable)~~ bravery and
devotion to duty could do. If any
blame or fault attaches to the attempt
it is mine alone.

July 5

FIGURE 5.3 A transcript of Eisenhower's unreleased press release of the Normandy Invasion.

that they are gathering information, they would learn that D-Day was an American failure, that the Allies fell short in their attempt to establish a foothold in France, and that the attack occurred in early July. All of these "facts" that could be gathered from the document are untrue. In order to learn with this text, students must understand the context and purpose of its creation: that it was written as a potential press release that could be used in case the invasion failed, that Eisenhower had written an incorrect date on the note, that he discarded the note after the invasion succeeded, and that an aid had retrieved the note from the trash as a relic. Students' purpose in reading this document is drastically different than Eisenhower's purpose in creating it. Students use it to answer questions *they* have developed – what kind of a man was Eisenhower, for example – and not simply to gather facts about D-Day. Thus, in the use of documents as evidence, the student/historian determines how the document is most useful.

Selecting Appropriate Primary Sources

As we help students adopt the role of historians, in addition to creating an investigative classroom climate and teaching historians' literacy strategies, we must choose appropriate primary sources. Mr. Dunn's careful selection of texts is an important factor in the success of his activity. There are several criteria that he used. First, the content should be appropriate for the age and maturity of the students. Violent or otherwise questionable content in some documents, particularly informal, private writing, may be inappropriate in some educational contexts. Second, as much as teachers would like students to analyze some difficult texts, the fact remains that if a student can't read it, they can't reason with it. Thus, teachers should choose primary sources that are at or below students' reading ability, or adjust instruction or modify texts in order to facilitate students' comprehension. Third, selected primary sources should promote instructional objectives. Mr. Dunn's lesson planning began with a consideration of objectives, for which appropriate texts were uncovered. With the nearly inexhaustible supply of texts available, including primary sources, teachers should ask themselves, "Is this the best possible text to use to reach my instructional objectives?"

Teachers should be purposeful in their selection of texts for document-based activities. Students are more likely to engage in sourcing when there is variety in the perspectives of the sources. When possible, text sets should contain documents with both contradictions and similarities in order to promote corroboration. And texts should vary in their reliability so that students can begin to distinguish between more and less trustworthy sources. Additionally, providing texts that represent multiple points of view can expose students to alternatives to the canonized historical narrative to which they have become accustomed. Further, texts from a non-majority perspective may carry greater appeal with minority students. I found that students were not as likely to engage in sourcing or corroboration or to question the reliability of texts if they were given only one text or multiple texts with a common point of view and similar content.

Mr. Dunn intentionally chose a wide variety of genres for students to evaluate. Doing so allowed students to practice recognizing the subtle differences, strengths, and weaknesses of various forms of evidence. Without exposure to various text types such as diaries, written on a daily basis, and memoirs, written after a lifetime of experiences, students might fail to acknowledge the subtle differences between genres. However, as students work with new genres of historical evidence they have the opportunity to discover the unique characteristics of each. Mr. Dunn provided students with both primary sources and a secondary source including a petition, graffiti, court proceedings, a letter, and excerpts from a journal article.

The following is a list of some written primary source documents that I have used with students. Creative teachers will be able to create an endless list of useful texts for historians and, thus, for students:

- Letters, notes, and emails (both informal, private letters and more formal, public letters)
- Official government documents such as laws, state constitutions, or treaties
- Speech transcripts
- Diaries, memoirs, personal histories, and autobiographies
- Newspaper articles, obituaries, want ads, and letters to the editor
- Accounts written by contemporary non-witnesses

- Historic local phone books
- Court records including indictments, transcripts, and depositions
- Historical magazine articles and advertisements
- Vandalism/graffiti/defacing
- Reports from medical examiners
- Novels written in historic settings (such as a novel written in 1920 used as evidence about life in 1920)
- Ship passenger logs
- Family histories and genealogical records
- Manuscript census records
- Transcripts of oral histories
- Property inventories, deeds, wills, or other personal documents.

These types of resources are increasingly available through the World Wide Web.

In addition to choosing a variety of genres, teachers should select texts with particular appeal to students. The adolescents that I worked with were drawn to issues of oppression, particularly the oppression of groups with which they felt some association (young people, minorities, women). Primary sources that include surprising content create curiosity and stimulate research questions. Texts that are shocking or disgusting are appealing to students. The tender relationships that are often revealed in primary sources, particularly letters, can be especially appealing to young people. And, humor and satire are often engaging for students – particularly when historical humor continues to be appreciated as funny. In the vignette, Mr. Dunn's selection of texts included some that were intended to catch students' attention by providing unexpected and puzzling content.

Helping Students Create Primary Sources

In addition to working with primary sources, students can learn about the nature of history by creating primary sources themselves. Students' personal reflections on national, world, or even personal events, written in a history class, create a source that can be used by future historians, or by the students themselves, as they learn how to do history. For example, Bain (2005) had his students write about their experiences on the first day of school. In a subsequent class session he asked students to analyze the various diverse accounts of that day. As students analyzed the accounts they had created, they recognized the profound effect of point of view on the content of primary sources. Additionally, students, realizing the impossibility of constructing a complete record of the first day of school, gained a better understanding of the work of historians in determining what to include and what to omit in their determination of historical significance.

When historical events occur during the course of a school year, such as the inauguration of a president or a national emergency, teachers can have students write descriptions and reactions to the events in order to create a historical record. Students' records can be compiled into a book or on a web page documenting important events and providing a record for future historians. Production of such records puts students on the other side of history – a perspective that can improve their understanding of the work of historians who interpret the past based on the types of records students will have produced. Students can also create oral histories by interviewing individuals with connections to historical events such as the Civil Rights Movement or the Vietnam War. Additionally, some history teachers assign students to build time capsules with written records and artifacts for a similar purpose – to create a record that individuals might use at some future date to understand current conditions. By carefully selecting items for inclusion, students gain a different perspective on the role of evidence, particularly primary sources, in the construction of understandings about the past.

Chapter Summary

Primary sources provide a foundation upon which the discipline of history is built. However students face several challenges in working with primary sources. Teachers, like Mr. Dunn, help students overcome these challenges by supporting their comprehension of texts by creating transcripts of hard-to-read documents and by simplifying the language in primary sources. Teachers help students adopt the role of a historian by teaching them historians' strategies for interrogating primary sources – particularly sourcing, corroboration, and contextualization. History teachers promote the effective analysis of primary sources by creating safe classrooms that honor questioning, by encouraging students to view documents as evidence, and providing them with regular opportunities to semi-independently develop original interpretations of historical events throughout the school year. Producing primary sources helps students understand the nature of evidence in the study of history.

6

HELPING STUDENTS MAKE
INFERENCES WITH ARTIFACTS

Mrs. Dahl is planning a unit on World War II for her 10th grade U.S. history classes. She recently visited Washington, DC and was moved by the National World War II Memorial that was constructed in 2004. She contemplates how she might have her students analyze the memorial as part of their study of the war. In her reflection she realizes that a memorial is an unusual type of artifact, and not only because of its enormous size. Most artifacts are not created to be a source of historical information for future generations. They are often intentionally discarded, such as a flawed brick or broken piece of pottery thrown into a garbage dump; are lost by accident, such as a coin or an arrowhead; or abandoned for various reasons, such as the ruins of an ancient village. Their use as historical evidence was not intended in their production or placement. A memorial, on the other hand, is built for the express purpose of helping future generations remember a historical character, event, or accomplishment. Memorials are artifacts that are produced as historical sources to help future generations remember or learn about the past. As such, they, like written or musical tributes to past events, are a source for learning not only about the event they celebrate, but about the people who produced them.

Mrs. Dahl considers how the National World War II Memorial represents not only the events of World War II, but it shows how modern society chooses to remember or forget those events. The various quotes, sculptures, symbols, and reflecting pool provide numerous resources that she could draw from to support students' learning about the war. She decides to use photographs of a series of bas-relief sculptures at the memorial, created by Ray Kaskey, that depict different events of the war, such as shipping war materials to Great Britain following the Lend Lease Act (see Figure 6.1). She remembers that there are 24 bas-reliefs, 12 depicting events associated with the war in the Pacific and 12 representing events from the war in the Atlantic. She decides to have students either individually or with a partner analyze one of the sculptures and report on their analysis to the class. She will have them make inferences about the way events of the war are remembered, and the way we would like future generations to remember them. She decides to use these sculptures toward the end of the unit as a review, allowing students to draw upon and apply background knowledge they have developed during the unit.

Additionally, she recognizes an opportunity to have students review the important events that they studied that are not depicted in the sculptures, and to consider why some things were chosen for inclusion on the monument and why other things were not. The more she thinks about it, the more she likes the idea – not only will students review the important events of World War II, but they will become more skilled in making inferences, will practice sourcing, and will become more literate in constructing historical interpretations with artifacts like this memorial. As she researches, she finds an interview conducted of the artist, which will help students understand the process of selecting, designing, and creating the monument, including the bas-reliefs (Gurney, 2004).

To introduce her students to the process of analyzing a sculpture, she models her thinking in an analysis of the bas-relief that depicts the Lend Lease Act (see Figure 6.1). Her modeling of her analysis of one will leave 23 other sculptures for the students to analyze and report on. She spends a few minutes thinking aloud in front of the students, considering the source, making observations and inferences about the story shown in the sculpture, and making inferences about the artist's message and what it says about the people who designed the monument. Projecting a picture of the sculpture in front of the class, she begins the lesson by thinking out loud to the students, helping them see code breaking and meaning making processes in action.

"Like with all other historical sources I want to start by thinking about the source. The article we read last night helped me learn about the artist, Ray Kaskey,

FIGURE 6.1 A photograph of the *Lend Lease Act*, a sculpture on the National World War II Memorial (Photograph printed with permission of Matthew Richardson). *Source:* Kaskey (2004).

and I know that the monument was constructed in 2004. I know who the intended audience is: the American people and others who might visit the nation's capital. I was there a few months ago so I know the physical context: it sits between the Lincoln Memorial and the Washington Monument near the Vietnam War Memorial on the national mall. I know that the purpose of these monuments is to celebrate great accomplishments and to remember those who made sacrifices, sometimes even their lives, to win the war. I know that the monuments are visited by individuals, families, and school children who often have an emotional or even religious experience while there. I know that the memorial has been built at a time when the generation of Americans who fought in World War II is growing old and passing away. I wonder whether it was created when it was in order to honor that generation before they're all gone."

"What was I just doing?" Mrs. Dahl asks the class.

"I don't know," answers Tanner. "You weren't talking at all about what's on the sculpture up there," he adds, pointing to the image projected in front of the class. "You were just talking about your trip to DC again."

Cindy raises her hand and Mrs. Dahl calls on her. "I think you're doing the same thing that you taught us to do when we look at a document. Before we start to read it you always tell us to think about the source and context. You're doing that with the monument – thinking about who made it, who it was made for, and where and when and why it was made."

"That's right, Cindy," Mrs. Dahl agrees. "It doesn't matter what type of historical evidence we're using – documents, artifacts, music, a building, or a monument like this – we always want to consider its source and context."

After modeling sourcing, Mrs. Dahl thinks aloud through an analysis of the content of the sculpture depicting the Lend Lease Act. "I can tell right away that this doesn't look like a scene from a war, except there is an army jeep. This must show something important happening on the home front. Sometimes it's hard to catch the details if I just look at the whole thing at once so I am going to start on the left side and move slowly toward the right. On the left I see a man. What jumps out at me about him is his hand stretched out toward a boy. I can't really tell what he is doing but he looks like he is holding something small. His other hand is in his pocket."

"I think he's buying a newspaper," Jonas interrupts. "See? He's looking for change in his pocket to buy a newspaper and the boy is pulling out a paper to give him."

"Oh yeah," Mrs. Dahl agrees, continuing her modeling. "It looks like the newspaper headline says something about Germany, but I can't read the second word. Maybe it says 'declares.' I can't tell for sure. Now, looking behind the man and boy I see boxes marked 'Great Britain.' Now I think I know what is happening – this must be at a shipyard. The boxes and the jeep are being sent to Great Britain. There is a man sitting on the boxes with a newspaper in one hand with his other hand at his face. He seems to be in deep thought. I wonder what he is thinking about – maybe he wonders what the future will bring or whether the United States is making the right choice shipping these things to Great Britain. Now I'm starting to make a connection to one of the things we studied in class, the Lend Lease Act, when the U.S. became involved in the war by sending war supplies to Great Britain. How do I know what's in the boxes? That's an inference. I have to read between the lines using my background knowledge of the war and the evidence on the sculpture."

Mrs. Dahl pauses to allow students to think about what she has done. "Do you see how I worked to comprehend this sculpture? I looked over the whole thing first, and then began looking at details, focusing on small parts of the sculpture. I didn't know what it was showing at first, but gradually, I started to piece together what it represented using the background knowledge that I had about the war. You're going to have to go through this same process with your assigned sculpture to try to figure out what it's showing. Once I have a feel for the basic representation I can begin to think more deeply about the artist, Ray Kaskey's intended message. For example, I notice that there is one man who appears to be an African American and the others appear to be White. I wonder what kind of meaning Mr. Kaskey intended with that. Looking at the whole sculpture I think that he is trying to show that Americans were working together to support the Lend Lease Act, represented by the African American and White workers lifting together. Now I'm noticing that the man sitting and thinking and staring off into the distance is a young man. I think he's probably thinking about his future – another inference. I see this as a tribute to the young men who ended up fighting in the war. I think Mr. Kaskey is trying to show the nervousness of an uncertain future. Now the final question for us to think about has to do with how this event is remembered by us today. In the sculpture it appears that most people, Black and White, were united behind the Lend Lease Act. Does this match what we learned about it in class?"

Derek raises his hand, "No. We talked about how lots of Americans like Charles Lindberg opposed the Lend Lease Act. I think this sculpture oversimplifies the issue. Making it look like everyone was happily working together to help ship stuff to Great Britain."

"It also doesn't show that we were sending supplies to other places too, like the Soviet Union," Lisa adds.

"Do you think that the people that designed the monument planned it that way or is it just a coincidence?" Mrs. Dahl questions.

Lisa continues, "Yes, I think they designed the memorial to celebrate American unity in winning the war. They didn't want to include controversy here."

"Yes," Mrs. Dahl agrees. "I think it makes sense for a memorial like this to celebrate unity and cooperation rather than to reflect the reality of the time when the Lend Lease Act was being debated. It would help it fit in with the context of the national mall and the other memorials."

The discussion of this representation of the Lend Lease Act continues for a few more minutes, then Mrs. Dahl has students draw numbers for their assigned sculptures. "When it's time for you to present, I'll project an image of the sculpture for the class and you'll need to describe what's going on in it. Be sure to include details in the sculpture that agree with and disagree with things we studied in class. You won't need to model all of your thinking with the class, like I just did, but you should explain what some of the details in the sculpture mean. You'll only have a few minutes for your presentation so start preparing by talking about what the sculpture shows, what event or events it represents, and how it represents it. Then talk about what Mr. Kaskey's message was and what it shows about how we remember or want to remember that aspect of the war. You'll only have about 15 minutes to prepare, so you'll have to work quickly. I've created a worksheet (see Figure 6.2) to help you analyze your sculpture and to keep a record of the other sculptures during the group presentations. During your preparation time you should complete numbers one through five on the back of the study guide. During the presentations you'll complete the front. After the presentations we'll work together as a class on numbers six through nine. You can use a textbook, your notes from class, or my computer to help you prepare."

Mrs. Dahl passes out the study guide and circulates as the students work. Most of them work on their own, but she assigns pairs of students to some of the more challenging sculptures. As she approaches Brad and Julio, Brad whines, "How are we supposed to know which battle this shows?"

"Which sculpture were you assigned?" Mrs. Dahl asks.

"Well it's labeled 'Jungle Warfare' but how are we supposed to know which battle it was?" Brad repeats.

"Does it matter?" Mrs. Dahl asks. "Is there a reason that the sculpture is vague enough that it could be from a great number of places?"

Julio and Brad both think for a minute and then Julio speaks up. "Maybe because this is a memorial for the whole war they wanted it to represent all of the jungle warfare rather than one battle," he suggests.

"I think you're probably right, Julio. So which of the battles *could* this represent?" she asks.

"It's listed on the Pacific side of the study guide so it must have been somewhere in the Pacific. Do the Philippines look like this? With palm trees and jungle?" Brad thinks aloud.

"Yeah," Julio responds. "This could be from the Philippines or from any of the islands." He opens up his notebook and looks through his papers from the unit. "It could be from Guadalcanal or Okinawa or another island. I think it represents all of the jungle warfare on all of the islands during the island hopping campaign."

"What evidence on the sculpture leads you to this inference?" Mrs. Dahl asks.

"The tropical trees are the strongest evidence. Plus the fact that this sculpture is on the Pacific side of the monument," Julio explains.

"I think you're on the right track with this," Mrs. Dahl compliments as she starts to walk away. "You're already using evidence from the sculpture to make inferences. Now start on one side of the sculpture and pay attention to the details as you move across. Then see if you can come up with Mr. Kaskey's message and what it tells us about how we want to remember the war."

As she walks away she hears Julio suggest to Brad, "Hey! Maybe that guy on the radio is a Navajo Code Talker."

Mrs. Dahl circulates, helping other groups. When she can tell that some of the groups are satisfied with their analysis she warns, "In two minutes we are going to start the presentations."

The quality of students' presentations varies significantly. Most of them capture the main idea of what the sculpture represents. Some of them do an excellent job of considering what the message of the sculptor was and some even talk about what it suggests about the way we want to remember the war. Kalli and James point out, for instance, that the beach at Normandy is pretty clean.

"There is only one man who looks dead and his face is hidden and his body is in one piece. He isn't twisted or gross like the dead bodies in some of the photographs of Normandy I've seen. And the soldier who's injured is being helped by another guy. It's kind of a pretty picture of what was an ugly event. I think it means we prefer to think about the terrible events of the war in a good way today."

The richest discussion of the day takes place after all of the groups have presented. Mrs. Dahl works with the students to answer the questions on their study guides. Reading number six, she asks, "What patterns do you see across the panels?"

Jenna answers first, "I was surprised how many of them had to do with the home front. I think at least eight or nine of them show scenes at home. I mean, there is even one that shows farmers out in the field working."

"Why do you think they included so many non-combat scenes?" Mrs. Dahl asks. "This is a *war* memorial, after all, isn't it?"

"It's like we talked about in class," Julio responds. "This war was about industries and farming and buying bonds and everybody helping. Plus, it makes people who visit the memorial feel good about what their grandma or grandpa did to help, even if they weren't on the battlefield. I think this memorial tries to say that everybody sacrificed to help us win."

Mrs. Dahl responds, "That's a good point, Julio. This memorial is an account of the war and they chose to include certain things for a reason. This brings us to the next question on the study guide: what events are missing from these panels? What did they choose to leave out of this account? Go ahead on your own and make a list on the study guide of important events of the war that are not shown." After a few minutes Mrs. Dahl calls on students to report what they wrote.

Analysis of the bas-relief sculptures on the National World War II Memorial.

Complete this chart as the class reports on the 24 bas-relief sculptures depicting events from World War II. After hearing all of the reports complete questions 5–7 on the back of this paper.

Atlantic Panels	Description of panel	How we remember	Pacific Panels	Description of panel	How we remember
Lend Lease			Pearl Harbor		
Bond Drive			Enlistment		
Women in military			Embarkation		
Rosie the Riveter			Shipbuilding		
Battle of the Atlantic			Agriculture		
Air war/B-17			Submarine warfare		
Paratroopers			Navy in action		
Normandy Beach landing			Amphibious landing		
Tanks in combat			Jungle warfare		
Medics in the field			Field burial		
Battle of the Bulge			Liberation		
Russians meet Americans			V-J Day		

Complete the following to prepare to report to the class:

1. Summarize the things shown on your assigned panel.

2. What are some of the interesting details shown on your panel? What is the significance of their inclusion?

3. What, if anything, is missing from the way your sculpture depicts the event?

FIGURE 6.2 A graphic organizer and worksheet for supporting students' work with World War II Memorial sculptures.

4. What was Mr. Kaskey's message in creating the panel?

5. What does the panel suggest about the way we remember World War II?

Complete the following after listening to all of the presentations:

6. What patterns do you see across the panels?

7. What events are missing from these panels?

8. Why do you think these events were not included in the memorial?

9. What do these omissions suggest about the way we would like to remember World War II?

FIGURE 6.2 *(continued)*

"The atomic bomb is one big thing," Kristin explains. "I think it's funny that the panels go from jungle warfare to V-J Day without any hint of the bomb."

"Why do you think the dropping of the atomic bomb is left out of these panels? Don't you think it would be important to include it?"

"Well, it's like the Normandy panel. They had to keep the memorial appropriate for children. Some mom doesn't want to have to explain to her little kid about the atomic bomb killing civilians and kids."

"Do you think they left that out in order to protect innocent children, or do you think that we, as a nation, want to forget some parts of the war? That's what number seven on your study guide is asking. What else did you notice was missing?"

"There was nothing related to the internment of Japanese Americans or the Holocaust," Brittani answers.

The discussion continues as students use the account shown in the bas-reliefs of the memorial to make inferences about how Americans want to remember World War II. In the process, students review the major events of the war, and analyze the memorial as an artifact created for the unique purpose of remembering a historical event.

Helping Students Make Inferences with Artifacts

The memorial that Mrs. Dahl's students studied represents only one of a wide array of types of artifacts that might be used to study history. Archeologists and historians more commonly use items produced *by* the people they intend to study rather than produced *about* the people they study, such as the World War II memorial. Still, many of the strategies that Mrs. Dahl taught her students reflect tools archeologists use to learn about people of the past. Although archeology is often associated with the study of prehistoric people who had no written records, historical archeologists study the material remnants of societies that also produced written records. In historical archeology the material record is used as corroborating evidence for the written record, or to study those groups within a historical society that left few written records, such as the lower classes and enslaved individuals. Thus archeology and history provide two lenses for understanding the past, each considering unique types of evidence. In this chapter I explore the use of archeological evidence in history classrooms to foster historical thinking in general and inference making specifically. I consider inference making, including the role of inferring in historical thinking, the sister strategies of observing and inferring, the role of background knowledge in inference making, and criteria for judging inferences. I also consider the use of artifacts in secondary classrooms, including the challenges students have in working with artifacts, and support teachers can provide to help students use artifacts as evidence. The chapter concludes with practical advice about bringing artifacts or virtual artifacts into classrooms.

Inference Making and Historical Thinking

To infer is to use evidence to reach a probable, but uncertain conclusion. Inference making has been described as "reading between the lines," using what *is* in the text to construct what *is not* there. Whether working with primary source documents, secondary sources, or artifacts, historians' work requires them to make inferences. For example, inference making is involved in historians' heuristics of sourcing, corroboration, and contextualization. When considering the source of a document, for instance, the historian might infer the author's intent in producing the document using knowledge of the author, the historical context, and the intended audience. When working with artifacts, the archeologist or historian might infer the purpose of an artifact based on its shape, the location where it was found, and the artifacts that were found around it. Historians use anthropological work on the culture of modern hunter gathering societies to make inferences about prehistoric societies who left behind no written records and few material remains. And inferences are used to explore causation, such as when scientific research dates climate change at the same time that a society experienced cultural change. There is no literacy strategy that cuts across more elements of historical thinking than inferring.

Inference making is a general literacy strategy that is not exclusive to historical thinking, and a great deal has been written about helping students improve their inference making abilities. In many texts, the ability to make inferences is essential in comprehension. In fact, in their review of reading comprehension research, Afflerbach and Cho list "attempting to infer information not explicitly stated in a text when the information is critical to comprehension of the text" as one of 15 essential strategies for reading traditional texts (2009, 77). In addition, they list inferring as one of a handful of strategies necessary for reading multiple texts and Internet hypertexts. Across genres and content areas, including history, the ability to make inferences is essential in literate activity. Literacy research makes it clear that appropriate instruction can improve students' ability to make inferences (Paris & Hamilton, 2009). Further, literacy research provides specific guidelines that are useful for fostering inference making in historical thinking, including the connection between observing and inferring, the connection between background knowledge and inferring, and criteria for judging inferences.

Observing and Inferring

Good inferences must be based on evidence, and an effective evaluation of archeological evidence begins with careful observation. Observation includes collecting information through the five senses. Scientific instruments, like microscopes or thermometers, increase what humans can observe. Since observation revolves around the use of senses, some students think that it is easy and automatic. However, not all individuals are equally adept in their ability to observe, with those who are unusually gifted at observing being labeled "observant." Teachers can help students become more observant. Mrs. Dahl understood that before students could analyze the sculptures they had to look at them carefully, making observations. In order to help her students become more observant, she gave them a specific strategy, recommended starting at one side of the sculpture and moving slowly across it, thinking out loud about what they observed. In addition, she recommended looking at the sculpture holistically in order to observe the relationship between its different parts. She understood that collaboration with peers would increase the number and quality of observations, so she assigned teams of students to work together with the difficult sculptures.

Background Knowledge and Inferring

In addition to evidence, inferences are based on the reader's background knowledge. Research on literacy has shown that students' ability to make inferences increases when they or their teachers "make a conscious effort to draw relationships between text content and background knowledge" (Pearson, 2009, 16). Mrs. Dahl knew that the best time to engage students in the analysis of the bas-relief sculptures was at the end of the unit after they had deeper knowledge of the war.

She knew that rich background knowledge improves the quality and quantity of inferences. Further, as she modeled the desired thought processes, she made explicit to the students that she was drawing upon her background knowledge of the war to construct understanding. She was implicitly teaching the students that a thorough review of the evidence combined with rich background knowledge leads to plausible inferences.

I should give a warning about students' use of background knowledge in making inferences. Researchers have found that poor readers rely too much on background knowledge and not enough on the evidence in a text when making inferences. It's easy to understand why. Students who lack basic decoding and comprehension skills cannot access the evidence in the text. In the absence of evidence they are left with their background knowledge alone, leading them to inferences that are unwarranted given the textual evidence. Overreliance on background knowledge may serve as an indication to a teacher of a student's struggles to access written or physical evidence.

The opposite problem also occurs in history classrooms. Given an artifact or document, students who lack historical background knowledge are unable to stray far from the evidence. Their analysis often represents a summary of what the document says with little contextualization, sourcing, or other acts of "reading between the lines." Teachers can improve students' ability to make inferences by building their background knowledge prior to having them engage in historical thinking activities. Lectures take on a different tone when the purpose is not simply to transmit information to students so that they can regurgitate it on a test, but so that they can apply it while working with historical evidence. For instance, acknowledging the role of background knowledge in historical thinking, each lesson developed by the Stanford History Education Group (2012) dedicates a short amount of time to build students' background knowledge before conducting the historical thinking activity (Wineburg, Martin, & Monte-Sano, 2011).

Evaluating Inferences

It has been established that good inferences are a synthesis of background knowledge and evidence. Teachers can improve students' ability to infer by reflecting with them on their inference-making processes. Questions such as, "What evidence is there in the text that leads to that inference?" require students to think about and justify their inferences. Further, asking students to review the specific background knowledge that led to a conclusion enhances their ability to judge inferences. Simply put, students' misconceptions of history can lead to poor inferences. Further, good inferences generally follow the principle of parsimony, which contends that the hypothesis that requires the fewest assumptions is usually correct. Stated plainly, the simplest explanation is usually best. Inferring that the crates stamped for shipment to Great Britain contained war goods is easier to explain than the inference that they contained bananas. Good inferences account for background knowledge, all text-based evidence, and do so in logical and simple terms.

Teaching with Artifacts

There is something about artifacts, particularly ancient and strange items, that sparks curiosity. Who made this? Why did he or she make it? What does it represent? Which parts possess important meaning? How was it used? Many artifacts carry with them engaging mysteries that students enjoy considering. Artifacts produced more recently, such as items found in grandparents' attics or collectors' driveways, also provide evidence about the culture and values of the people who produced, consumed, and preserved them. Countless artifacts exist that a history teacher might use as evidence to ponder historical questions. Working with artifacts can provide students with opportunities to think historically, consider historical contexts, corroborate interpretations across artifacts and texts, and contemplate the role of evidence in the construction of historical interpretations. Because students who struggle with traditional reading may excel in their ability to make observations and inferences with artifacts, the use of artifacts can bring struggling readers into conversations about evidence. Artifacts represent an important genre of historical "texts," requiring students to use historical literacies.

Mrs. Dahl's lesson shows that artifacts provide clues about the people who produced them, whether they were made a few years ago or thousands of years ago, and whether they were intentionally buried or placed where millions would see them. Further, her lesson shows that the literacies useful in constructing meaning with artifacts include a range of strategies such as observation, inference making, sourcing, corroboration, and contextualization. And as in working with other forms of historical evidence, students must engage in the four roles of a reader, acting as a code breaker, meaning maker, text user, and text critic. Mrs. Dahl modeled each of these roles, showing students both how she decoded and comprehended the symbols in the sculpture and how she thought critically about its source and context, making inferences about the society that produced the monument. The study guide she created provided additional scaffolding as students worked through all four roles. She knew that helping students engage in these roles required special measures, because reading artifacts presents unique challenges for students.

Challenges in Working with Artifacts

The most obvious challenge, perhaps, in engaging students with artifacts is finding them and bringing them into the classroom. Certainly any human-produced item, from a cave painting of Lascaux, France to a modern tool, is an artifact, useful in discerning the values and cultures of the people who produced it. Any classroom is full of modern artifacts. However, artifacts associated with an historical era under investigation, such as Classical Greece, or the Trail of Tears, might be difficult to procure. Further, many of the most insightful observations require instruments that are unavailable to students or that require specialized training that students and history teachers lack. For instance, in looking through a microscope at bones that were stirred in rough stoneware pots, archeologists have detected a trait they call pot polishing. Rubbing against the rough edges of the pot smoothed the exposed edges of bones. Based on pot polishing, archeologists are able to establish the meats, including at times human, that prehistoric people stirred in pots and presumably ate. Pot polishing is an observation that students, without scientific training and tools, are unable to make. In other cases, DNA testing has revealed traces of blood or flesh of a variety of species of megafauna, such as mammoths and giant camels, on the same hunting implements, allowing archeologists to make numerous inferences about the culture of prehistoric Americans. Obviously, students do not have opportunities to engage in DNA testing or other advanced scientific analysis of evidence.

Additionally, students face epistemic issues when working with artifacts. Historians readily admit that constructing an historical understanding from artifacts requires some speculation, particularly when there is little written evidence to corroborate interpretations. For instance, in the first chapter of a popular college world history textbook describing Ice Age societies, of whom there is but scanty artifactual evidence, there are over a dozen admissions of uncertainty (Armesto, 2010). Armesto acknowledges "perplexing problems," "puzzling" bits of evidence, and at one point admits "we have no idea – beyond guesswork" about the most ancient migration patterns (12–13). Although students can gain insight on historical processes, and, perhaps, develop a more mature epistemic stance from such admissions, there is also a risk that students will think that artifacts invite wild speculation. They might assume that any artifact-based interpretation is as speculative or impossible to support as any other. By admitting that we don't know *everything* about the origins or meaning of certain artifacts, some students might incorrectly assume that we can't know *anything* for certain about the cultures that produced them.

Supporting Students' Use of Artifacts as Evidence

As with all other historical literacies, experience working with artifacts in a simplified context is valuable for students. For instance, in order to expose students to the types of thinking needed in interpreting artifactual evidence, a teacher might bring in several items from his/her own garbage can, such as empty pizza boxes, packaging from a new purchase, or a discarded toy that is broken or no longer used. Students could then be asked to list what they can infer about the teacher based on these "artifacts." Within this context the teacher could help students explore the process they use to make observations and inferences. Further, the teacher might introduce the concept of parsimony by pointing out outrageous explanations for why an item might be in his/her garbage can and allowing students to think about why some inferences are better than others. If a teacher wanted to introduce the idea of corroborating artifactual and written evidence, he/she might introduce a grocery store receipt or some other piece of garbage with writing on it. Students could explore the relationship between history and archeology by analyzing this combination of evidence. It is helpful for students to practice the literacies of working with artifacts within a context that is familiar, and for which they have rich background knowledge, before engaging with artifacts from unfamiliar eras.

Mrs. Dahl's lesson included several measures designed to improve students' analysis of the monument. As mentioned, she knew that students would have a difficult time analyzing the sculptures until they had rich background knowledge of the war. History teachers can facilitate students' analysis of artifacts by building students background knowledge prior to exposing them to the artifacts. She gave students explicit instruction on observing, pointing out that she liked to start at the left and work her way slowly to the right focusing on the details of the artifact. She pointed out that good observations also required a holistic look at the artifact, paying attention to the relationship between the different parts. In addition to explicit instruction on observations, she modeled inference making for the students. Further, during group work she asked students to justify their interpretations, requiring students to engage in metacognition and to make explicit their thought processes for themselves and their peers. Explicit and implicit strategy instruction, teacher and peer modeling, and metacognitive interactions nurture students' ability to work with artifacts and other types of historical evidence.

Nurturing students' ability to think creatively and critically using artifacts as evidence requires multiple exposures to them. As with working with primary sources or any other type of evidence, students need opportunities to practice in a variety of contexts, with different research questions, and with a range of types of artifacts. For instance, the curriculum of most history classes includes opportunities to engage with both prehistoric artifacts from people who produced no written records, and historic artifacts from people who had writing. In lessons dealing with prehistoric people, students can use corroboration across artifacts to test and retest their hypotheses. In lessons dealing with historic people, students can similarly corroborate across artifacts and written records. With repeated exposure to artifacts, teachers can reduce the amount of time dedicated to explicitly teaching literacy strategies, such as observing and inferring, and increase the amount of time students are actively engaged with texts and artifacts.

One key element of students' development of skills in working with artifacts and other types of historical evidence is teachers giving them room to develop their own interpretations, which can and should be subject to peer and teacher critique. As explained in Chapter 1, history classrooms are often places where students simply listen to others' interpretations of the evidence, stated in unquestionable terms. In traditional classrooms, teachers introduce students to historical evidence, but it is usually done simply to bolster the material presented during a lecture (Nokes, 2010a). Instead, teachers can provide students with multiple artifacts, and give them room to construct, test, revise, and share their independent interpretations. This involves some measure of creative thinking, as students discover unique interpretations of evidence. It further involves critical thinking as students test and revise their interpretations based on corroborating evidence. Further, as students share their insights with peers, their ideas are subject to peer review. Students who have been taught explicitly the elements of effective inferences are more able to critique their peers' ideas. They might be prompted to ask questions such as, "What evidence do you base this interpretation on?" or "What background knowledge helped you develop this interpretation?" or "Is this interpretation the simplest explanation that accounts for all of the evidence?" Developing independent interpretations and engaging in the critique of interpretations made by others provides students with opportunities to engage in historical thinking.

As part of efforts to teach students to work with artifacts, history teachers might allow students to observe the work of archeologists as they engage with artifacts. This can be done by bringing in an archeologist to describe his or her work to the students, showing a video clip that describes an archeologist's work with evidence, or exploring websites that show archeologists working at excavations or in artifact labs. Observing the work of archeologists provides a model for students to emulate as they work with artifacts in the classroom.

Bringing Artifacts Into the Classroom

As mentioned, one of the challenges of having students work with artifacts is procuring them for the classroom. Teachers have limited access to traveling exhibits and few resources for field trips to archeological sites, artifact labs, or museums. However, with the advent of the Internet, all types of historical evidence, including artifacts, have become increasingly accessible. Often, photographs of artifacts, easily available online, are sufficient to allow students to make inferences about a culture. Teachers might prepare digital or physical folders containing photographs depicting different aspects of a society, such as homes, tools, art, toys, weapons, and floral and faunal remains. Small groups of students can work together to make observations and inferences about a culture based upon an artifact folder made up of photographs of one type of artifact. Their inferences can then be tested and expanded as different artifact folders are circulated between groups.

Further, some websites provide an opportunity for students to engage in a virtual archeological dig or to observe the evidence in an artifact lab. Virtual field trips to museums offer additional online access to artifacts. Although not as intimate as holding the artifact in one's hand, I have found that online resources provide enough engagement with artifacts to allow teachers to involve students in artifact-related historical literacies.

Questions about the more recent past can be considered by having students collect everyday artifacts at home and bring them to class. For instance, students in a U.S. or local history class might address the question, "What did young people do for fun before television?" Investigating such a question might involve a number of historical literacies as students gather and analyze historical evidence. For instance, students might interview grandparents or elderly neighbors, creating a historical record. In addition, they might be asked to bring to class artifacts, or photographs of artifacts, that could be analyzed to corroborate the historical evidence they collect.

Chapter Summary

Mrs. Dahl's review of the World War II unit involved students working with sculptures representing historical events. In a way, the images that the students studied as evidence are not very different from prehistoric pictographs that celebrated a successful hunt or other event. In both cases the art was created to memorialize an important event. Artifacts, ancient and modern, are a valuable source of evidence about the past. Working with artifacts requires students to make inferences about the people who produced them. Good inferences are simple and are based on evidence merged with background knowledge. Explicit instruction on inference making, and repeated practice in settings that allow independent interpretations, builds students' ability to work with artifacts. And the Internet makes artifacts increasingly accessible to history classrooms.

7

DEVELOPING METACONCEPTUAL UNDERSTANDING WITH VISUAL TEXTS

Ms. Jensen, an 11th grade U.S. History teacher, is planning for a lesson on the home front during World War I. She wants students to learn about such trends as shortages, voluntary rationing, the sale of war bonds, and the general war hysteria that engulfed the nation during the war. She brainstorms, producing a list of texts that might be used to teach these concepts: there might be transcribed oral histories of individuals from the local community; the textbook chapter has a section that gives an overview of life on the home front; and the school has in its collection a video series on World War I, which certainly includes appropriate clips. When she asks other U.S. History teachers at the school what they use, Mrs. Wade tells her that she uses propaganda posters produced by the U.S. government. Ms. Jensen researches and finds propaganda posters used to advertise war bonds, to encourage home production, to promote enlistment, to encourage conservation, and to vilify the enemy. She decides that propaganda posters are good evidence that students can use to study home front trends. She goes to work planning her lessons.

Ms. Jensen understands that using propaganda posters as historical evidence will require her students to have specialized literacies including the ability to identify propaganda in its various formats; the disposition to consider the sources of propaganda; and skills in analyzing the use of color, visual imagery, and language that is intended to produce emotional responses. Further, she wants students to recognize the role of propaganda in moving people from an attitudinal state to a behavioral state. She wants them to assess the effectiveness of propaganda posters from World War I. She sees this as an opportunity to review the concept of "evidence," an important element of historical thinking. In the process of working with the posters, she wants students to be immersed in home front issues during the war.

Ms. Jensen decides to dedicate one class period to working with propaganda posters. She intends to teach explicitly about the purpose of propaganda, and have students explore the characteristics of visual-oriented propaganda, using the posters as evidence to identify home front trends. Ms. Jensen goes back to the Internet and finds numerous examples of propaganda posters from World War I. She chooses several examples that are associated with trends, such as the selling of war bonds, enlistment drives, and home food production and preservation, and creates PowerPoint slides to display them. She prepares a graphic organizer to structure the class discussion, with a place for students to sketch the poster, identify the emotion being manipulated, describe characteristics that intensify the emotion, and summarize what the poster suggests about life on the home front (see Figure 7.1).

During the first part of class, Ms. Jensen projects the image of a propaganda poster from the war (see Figure 7.2). She asks Spencer to come up to the whiteboard and record students' observations, then she calls on students to list things they see on the poster. At first, they describe the most obvious items.

"I see a gorilla monster," calls out Andrea.

"He's holding a partly naked woman," adds Thomas.

"You would notice that," blurts out Andrea.

"He's holding a club that says something on it," Maria adds.

Students continue to call out what they see as Spencer records their comments on the board. Eventually they begin to notice more subtle elements of the propaganda.

"His helmet has a weird spike on it. Why does his helmet have that?" Jasmine asks.

"German helmets had those types of spikes during World War I," explains Ms. Jensen.

#	Sketch	Target emotion and elements of the propaganda that intensify it	What the poster suggests about life on the home front
1			
2			

FIGURE 7.1 The top two rows of a graphic organizer for supporting students' work with propaganda posters.

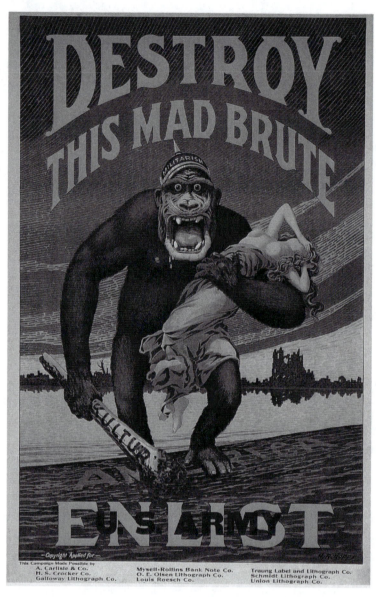

FIGURE 7.2 A World War I propaganda poster.

Source: Hopps (1917).

"It looks like he's standing on some letters. What does it say?" asks Anthony.

"It says 'America,' I think," Andrea responds. "Yeah, it says 'America.'"

After a few minutes, Ms. Jensen interrupts the class and asks students to interpret what the poster is trying to say.

"Well, the ape monster must stand for the Germans because of the helmet, and this poster is saying that the Germans are going to invade America if Americans don't enlist in the army and go fight them," summarizes Anthony.

"Good thinking, Anthony. Any other ideas about what it's saying?"

"I think that it's saying that the Germans are monsters because they left Europe in ruins behind them and they were beating up a poor defenseless woman in America," adds Samantha.

"Yes, Samantha. Now let's think about who might have created a poster like this and why they might have produced it. Any ideas?"

"It must've been made by the government to try to get soldiers," explains Thomas.

"How did you figure that out?" asks Mrs. Jensen.

"I think the picture is meant to make people mad, like they want to do something to help the poor woman, and then the bottom tells them to 'enlist' which means to join the army," he explains.

"Do you think it worked? If you had been alive at the time would you have become mad enough to run out and enlist?" Mrs. Jensen wonders.

Landon raises his hand, "I think if I really believed that Germany was threatening the United States I might have."

Other students make comments agreeing or disagreeing with Landon. Eventually Ms. Jensen gives the class a brief explanation of propaganda.

"This poster is an example of propaganda," she begins. "Propaganda is designed to motivate people to take some type of action. Propaganda is intended to intensify a target emotion and promote an active response. In other words, it makes you feel so angry, sad, proud, or guilty that you'll run out and do something. Thomas identified the target emotion for this poster as anger. And we can see what the hoped-for response is – 'enlist,' like Landon said. It's written on the bottom of the poster. Propaganda is generally not intended to change a person's mind, but to intensify what someone is already feeling in order to get the person to do something. If your cousin lived in Germany, and millions of Americans did immigrate to America from Germany and still had family and friends there in 1917, this poster would probably not convince you that the Germans were evil monsters. But if you were already inclined to think of Germans as monsters, it might motivate you to enlist. So propaganda posters are good evidence about what many people were thinking about and feeling at the time they were created."

Ms. Jensen continues by reminding students about the concept of *evidence*, something that has been discussed on occasion throughout the school year. "Your assignment is to use a series of posters as evidence of what people were feeling on the home front during World War I. Who remembers what evidence is?"

Several students raise their hands and Ms. Jensen calls on Camille.

"It's a clue that helps us figure things out, like a detective trying to solve a crime. He looks for evidence and then decides what it's telling him."

"Well said," responds Ms. Jensen. "I especially like your idea that *you* are in charge of figuring things out. The propaganda posters that you look at are not primarily to give you information. We can't take what they say literally. The poster we just looked at doesn't tell you what was happening. Germany had not invaded America and Germans were not ape-like monsters. The way we want to use the propaganda posters is to try to interpret the attitudes of Americans on the home front, assuming that the posters play on common opinions, which is usually the case with propaganda. So what does this poster suggest about Americans on the home front?"

Students offer many suggestions: "They didn't like Germany." "They were afraid the Germans might invade America." "They thought Germany was strong and threatening." "They were more afraid of what Germany might do to America than they were about what Germany was doing in Europe." "They questioned the morality of the Germans." "They thought Germans threatened our liberty." In the end, the class concludes that the poster is primarily playing on a fear that many Americans had of the threat of a German invasion.

Ms. Jensen wants to review for students the cognitive processes they used as they evaluated the poster as evidence. "Do you see how we used the poster as evidence of what people were feeling on the home front? The poster wasn't made for this purpose, and it doesn't just give us information, but we are using it to answer a question that *we* came up with. This is the way historians work. They ask questions and then seek out evidence to answer their questions. These propaganda posters give us clues about what Americans were feeling during a particular part of World War I. They serve as evidence."

Ms. Jensen passes out the graphic organizer (Figure 7.1) and helps the class members fill out the first row related to the poster they have just analyzed. She then projects a second propaganda poster and asks students to go through the same process with a partner, using the poster as evidence about life on the home front. The remainder of the class period, Ms. Jensen alternates between partnered work and whole-class discussions analyzing each of the posters she projects. Students complete their graphic organizers as they work. At the end of class, Ms. Jensen conducts a short debriefing. "How might the propaganda posters serve as evidence to help us answer other historical questions?" she asks.

"I wonder whether other countries made propaganda posters that made Americans look like monsters," Spencer asks.

"That's a great question," Ms. Jensen responds. "Are there common elements of propaganda posters that cut across different cultures? Do they all make the enemy look like a brute? Any other questions?"

"I wonder how effective the posters were," Landon answers. "Can't people see right through propaganda? Don't they feel tricked by it? I'm not sure the posters would be enough to get me to enlist in the army."

"Great question. What other clues would we need to figure out how effective the posters were? If you were a detective trying to solve this mystery on the effectiveness of propaganda posters, what other historical evidence could you use?"

"Maybe someone wrote in a letter or their diary that they joined the army after seeing a poster," Maria suggests.

"Do they have recruitment numbers that show how many people were volunteering for the army at different times. I wonder whether the numbers went up after a certain propaganda poster came out," answers David.

As the bell rings ending class, Ms. Jensen commends the students for their good thinking. Most of them seem to grasp the concept of evidence, which she was trying to teach. They have also been active in identifying home front trends – she thinks that the visual images of the posters will help them understand what was going on at home. And she is quite confident that students have a better understanding of the nature of propaganda.

Metaconcepts and Visual Evidence

In this chapter I explore two elements of Ms. Jensen's lesson. First, I consider important historical metaconcepts, such as *evidence*. I define "metaconcept" and list and describe several historical metaconcepts. In the next section, I discuss the use of visual texts, like the propaganda posters in Ms. Jensen's lesson.

Metaconcepts

Metaconcepts, also known as second order concepts, are ideas, notions, or tools that are related to the methods historians use to study the past. Lee (2005) lists the following metaconcepts, the understanding of which is essential to historians' work: *time, change, empathy, cause, evidence,* and *accounts.* Limón (2002) describes additional metaconcepts such as *explanation, space, source, fact, description,* and *narration.* Other metaconcepts include *significance* and *context.* Metaconceptual understanding is vital to the work of historians – they understand the nature of historical accounts as evidence, for instance. To write effectively they must understand the difference between description, explanation, and narration, and know when to employ each. However, because historians use metaconceptual understanding with little conscious thought, a shroud of mystery hides metaconceptual knowledge and use. As Gaddis explains, "Our reluctance to reveal our own [structures] ... too often confuses our students – even, at times, ourselves – as to just what it is we do" (2002, XI). History teachers rarely devote class time to building students' metaconceptual awareness.

Metaconcepts should not be confused with *substantive concepts,* the structures, phenomena, persons, and periods of history (Lee, 2005; van Drie & van Boxtel, 2008). Substantive concepts have been categorized as *inclusive concepts,* concepts that transcend any given historical period or topic, such as depression, democracy, or compromise; *unique concepts,* concepts that describe a specific person, place, or event, such as Franklin D. Roosevelt, Athens, and Gettysburg; and *colligatory concepts*, hierarchical classifications that bring order to history such as Persian Empire, Progressive Movement, or Great Awakening (van Drie & van Boxtel, 2008). Most history instruction revolves around substantive concepts, both unique and colligatory. However, without metaconceptual understanding of ideas like *change* and *time* students might fail to understand the subtleties of substantive concepts. For instance, without a correct understanding of the concept of change, a student might think that the concept of "king," an inclusive concept, remains stagnant throughout history, when, in fact, a 15th century king was very different from an 18th century king which is very different from a 21st century king (Lee, 2005). It is rare for teachers to address metaconcepts, the subject of this chapter. Without an understanding of key metaconcepts, historical literacy is impossible. To illustrate the importance, I will consider several metaconcepts.

Evidence

Because history is the evidence-based study of the past, without evidence there is no history. Most history students spend little time considering how we know what we know about the past. As described in earlier chapters, they typically accept the authoritative historical narrative they receive from the textbook and teacher without question. However, students who understand the metaconcept of evidence have a different understanding of their role in learning history. They accept the task of semi-independently constructing their own understanding of historical events using texts as evidence. Ms. Jensen wants students to consider how a researcher might know what people on the home front were thinking and feeling during World War I. The propaganda posters serve as evidence through which they answer this question. In Ms. Jensen's class the posters serve as clues about the past rather than as conveyers of information. Students, with the continual prodding of Ms. Jensen, view them as evidence.

Accounts

An account is a historical narrative. Each account represents a particular point of view, with contents that are filtered through the author's decisions of what to include or omit, which words to use, and the tone of the narrative. The bas-relief sculptures of the World War II Memorial described in Chapter 6 give an account of the war. Like all accounts they include some things and leave other things out. Textbooks give a different account of the war. And primary sources provide other unique accounts. No account is complete or untainted by its creator's purposes. Each account provides clues about the past, resources historians sift through as they reconstruct past events. Approaching each text with the understanding that it is an account leads the historian/student to consider the source, read critically, and accept or reject each idea it includes.

Significance

The process of historical inquiry requires historians and others to determine when an event, person, era, or even civilization is worth studying. Determining historical significance is one of the main roles of historians and history teachers. For instance, there is little interest in what Ms. Jensen ate for lunch on December 11, 1973. And without interest there is no significance and thus no history. On the other hand, a biographer of Abraham Lincoln might devote a great deal of energy trying to uncover what Abraham Lincoln ate in the evening of April 14, 1865, his final meal. The biographer creates historical significance by his interest in and investigation of this topic. Perhaps the most compelling case for considering historical significance is that of the Indus River society, a civilization that flourished 3,500 years ago in a large region near the Indus River in modern Pakistan. For many years, even after the British occupation of India, there was little interest in Indus ruins, besides scavenging building material for use in the construction of railroad lines. Eventually, after the discovery of their unique writing system, interest began to grow and a new civilization was "discovered" in the early 20th century. A more accurate description of this "discovery" would be that historians began to place significance on a society which had been known of for ages. Significance relates to topics as large as a civilization or as small as a grandson's search for records of his grandmother's life.

Time

It is unthinkable to study history without a grasp of the metaconcept of time. Time is particularly helpful in establishing sequence and duration. And an understanding of duration is critical in distinguishing between a single event and a long-term process (Lee, 2005). However, students sometimes have distorted views of time. For instance, students often fail to comprehend the important distinction between long eras, such as the tens of thousands of years of the Ice Age, and shorter eras, such as the years of the New Deal. Lee contends that "the attempt to transfer common-sense ideas about time from everyday life to history may pose problems" (2005, 42). For instance, although the development of the first agriculture evolved over thousands of years, students may view the change to farming as being an invention of a single generation or even the choice of a single individual. Further, students are often literal and inflexible in their understanding of time, basing it on clocks and calendars. Historians, on the other hand, think of time in terms of processes or patterns. For instance a historian might refer to the "greater 20th century" in order to link events of the late 1800s with similar 20th century trends.

Change and Continuity

Many students have distorted views of the metaconcept of change as well. For instance, young people often confuse the notion of event and change (Lee, 2005). Although events are not, in and of themselves, change, patterns of events can mark changing conditions. Historians recognize that the absence of change is not the absence of events, but acknowledge, instead, the notion of *continuity* (Lee, 2005). Additionally, students tend to view change as perpetual progress, failing to understand that progress is not inevitable and that changes sometimes result in regression.

Cause and Effect

Without an understanding of causation, history becomes "one damn thing after another" (Toynbee, 1957) – simply a parade of events. Causes and effects are what link events into historical narratives. Much of the work of historians involves identifying the causes of observed phenomena. In doing so, they impose a sense of order on the past. Thus chronology is not simply a time sequence, but is a series of causes and effects. Nor should chronology be considered a simple chain of causes and effects, but a complex network of causes, and potential and actual effects with both predictable and unpredictable outcomes (Gaddis, 2002). An understanding of cause and effect, as well as change, time, significance, account, evidence, and other metaconcepts lays the groundwork for students to engage in historical literacies. Ms. Jensen's lesson on the home front during World War I was designed to help students understand the metaconcept of evidence.

Building Historical Literacies with Visual Text

In the remainder of this chapter I consider the building of historical literacies, including the building of metaconceptual understanding, using visual texts. The focus is on teaching with visual texts, understanding the challenges students face in working with visual texts, and methods of building students' historical literacies with visual texts. I provide case studies of four types of visual texts: maps, political cartoons, paintings, and photographs. I conclude the chapter with a consideration of students using and creating visual texts for instruction and assessment.

Teaching with Visual Texts

Today's students live in a visual-oriented world. They are regularly exposed to images through Internet sites, movies, ipods, and television. Interestingly, they typically receive very little formal instruction on how to construct meaning with visual texts, relying instead on their instincts. Their intuition may be sufficient to comprehend, critique, and use some types of visual texts, such as a photograph of a group of friends on a Facebook page. However, many of the texts that are useful in historical inquiry require in-depth analysis using unique strategies – visual literacies. History classrooms provide a suitable context for building students' visual literacies because visual texts serve as valuable evidence for historians.

Visual texts may be primary or secondary sources depending on the historian's questions and the source of the text. Some of the oldest evidence used by archeologists and historians are visual primary sources. Cave paintings at Lascaux, France, for example, are over 17,000 years old. Human forms of art, from prehistoric times to the present, offer a glimpse into values, attitudes, and cultures, and serve as invaluable evidence – particularly when studying illiterate cultures that did not produce written records. Since the invention of the camera, photographs have added a new genre of historical primary sources. Individuals involved in historic events make sketches or draw maps. Political cartoonists capture public opinion in their work. Governments sponsor propaganda posters. Corporations pay for ads in magazines and newspapers. And the list of visual texts that historians use as evidence goes on and on. Imaginative history teachers have a nearly limitless supply of visual primary sources from which to choose.

In addition, secondary and tertiary visual sources are important in learning history. Paintings often reveal how past events were viewed by later generations, and, thus, serve as both secondary sources of the events they depict and as primary sources of the time period during which they were produced. Modern textbooks are filled with colorful images, both primary and secondary sources, that illustrate the events described in the writing. Historians produce maps to help others visualize the geographic setting of events. Illustrators support the narrative in magazines and children's books. As with all other texts, visual texts have an original source, and history students should make a distinction between primary and secondary visual texts.

Historical thinking can be fostered with visual texts. For instance, Ashby, Lee, & Shemilt observed students trying to make sense of paintings as historical sources. Through a teacher's coaching, eventually a student acknowledged, "You would need to know about the painter who actually painted it. You need some background information." Through continued dialogue another student wanted to know, "What period of time it was painted and whereabouts it was painted" (2005, 99). These students demonstrate the strategy of sourcing applied during an analysis of visual texts. Further, their statements reveal that they understand the metaconcepts of evidence and account.

The Challenges of Reading Visual Texts

There are several challenges that students face in working with visual texts. First, there are often subtle symbol systems in visual texts that are difficult to decode. For example, in topographical maps the elevation is shown using lines drawn at certain elevations (i.e., at 5000′, 5500′, 6000′) (see Figure 7.3). A person who understands the symbol system can break the code of lines and construct meaning,

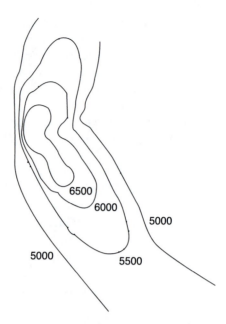

FIGURE 7.3 A topographical map.

visualizing the layout of a landscape. Topographical maps have many applications in teaching history. For example, a topographical map of the Battle of Gettysburg can show how the lay of the land was influential in determining the outcome of the battle. But the usefulness of topographical maps is based on the ability of the reader to construct meaning with them. Such is also the case with other visual resources: their usefulness is based on the reader's ability to decode, comprehend, use, and critique the text in constructing interpretations.

There are some visual texts that use symbol systems even more subtle and difficult to decode than topographical maps. For instance, artists use colors, symmetry, movement, and theme to convey a message more subjectively to the viewer. In negotiating meaning with art, students may lack the background knowledge necessary to decode or comprehend the artist's intended meaning. Because a painting often says as much about the artist as it does about its subject, the historical context for the creation of art is extremely important. Additionally, students often experience an initial reaction to a work of art that may interfere with their ability to effectively negotiate meaning. They might confuse realism with historical accuracy, for instance. Compounding the difficulties, students often feel quite confident in their ability to break the code and construct meaning with many visual texts in a mere glance. This creates the dangerous combination of incompetence and confidence as students engage with art. Thus artwork presents a particular literacy challenge.

Students face a different challenge in working with photography. They often assume that photographs are isomorphic with historical "reality," forgetting that photographs always have a source, were created for a purpose, and sometimes have been manipulated to achieve that purpose. For example, during the Great Depression photographers working for the Farm Securities Administration were commissioned to build public support for government programs that aided poor farmers. Their photographs of dust bowl farms, immigrant farm workers, poor farming families, and wealthy bankers were not simply produced to document events, but were politically motivated. Nor did the photographs always capture naturally occurring situations, but they were often manipulated. Historians, for example, have discovered what they call the "perambulating skull," a prop that was moved from location to location to add emphasis to the desolation of dust bowl farms. Like their work with textbooks, students often view photographs as being sourceless and thus exempt from the criticism that they would use in analyzing other sources. To summarize, students face particular challenges in working with visual texts, namely unfamiliar symbol systems that present challenges in code breaking; overconfidence in their ability to construct understanding at a glance; and overestimation of the reliability and validity of photographs.

Building Students' Visual Literacies

Because different formats of visual text use different symbol systems, learning with unique visual texts requires unique literacies. Depending on the research questions, visual texts that are important in building historical meaning might include propaganda, maps, political cartoons, paintings, photographs, cartograms, flags, billboards, organization or corporation symbols, product packaging, and countless other genres. It is impossible to elaborate on all forms of visual text in this volume. Instead, I consider four types of visual texts in some detail: maps, political cartoons, paintings, and photographs. Effective teaching with all visual texts includes the same standards: students must be able to break the code, which sometimes requires explicit instruction on unfamiliar symbol systems. They must construct meaning with the text, and critically evaluate the image, which involves strategies of sourcing, contextualization, and corroboration. With these skills, students can use visual texts as historical evidence.

Maps

Historians acknowledge that geography has a profound influence on history. So maps serve as important primary and secondary sources in the study of history. Historians can trace, for instance, changing knowledge of and attitudes about the land or bodies of water through historical maps, using them as primary sources. For example, a lesson found on the Stanford History Education Group's website uses early colonial maps to study colonists' evolving attitudes toward Native

Americans (Stanford History Education Group, 2012). Additionally, maps are used as secondary sources, to illustrate this connection between geospatial context and history. A historian might produce a map showing colonial settlements to illustrate the importance of rivers. Students who understand the metaconcept of context want to know, among many other contextual factors, the details of the physical location of an event. So history students must become skilled in constructing meaning with maps.

Teachers can facilitate students' learning with maps by providing explicit instruction on map-reading skills. As with all sources, students should consider the source and purpose of each map and become familiar with their common features. Students should know that there are a wide variety of maps each having a unique function. The features of a map suit its particular purpose. Students should be taught to look at the title, the legend or key, and the scale. They should be aware of an index on some maps, which narrows down a search to one small section, thus improving students' facility with the map. Decoding the map involves traditional decoding, identifying words; symbolic decoding, recognizing the meaning of different symbols (i.e. green lines representing interstate highways and broken parallel lines representing dirt roads); and structural decoding, using the index and coordinates to locate details.

Although the decoding and constructing meaning with maps require unique skills, the critique and use of maps as evidence require more familiar historical literacies. For instance, knowing the source of a map can help a historian infer things about the context of its creation. Further, the purpose of the mapmaker and the attitudes of the time can often be inferred by the decisions made about inclusions on the map, as in the case of the colonial maps mentioned above. Through sourcing, contextualization, and corroboration across several maps that were produced within a few decades, students can make interpretations about changing colonial attitudes toward Native Americans.

Political Cartoons

Political cartoons, depicting both current and historic events, present a particular challenge to students. Unlike their work with other types of visual texts, students often recognize and acknowledge that they "don't get it" after their initial glance at a political cartoon. Further, students are often unwilling to put forth the effort to decode and construct meaning with political cartoons because of their difficulty. However, political cartoons are an important part of America's political culture and a valuable historical resource. They provide evidence of popular opinions associated with politics and events, both currently and in the past.

Breaking the code of political cartoons is sometimes tricky for students. They are often very literal in decoding, failing to understand that each image and interaction in a political cartoon symbolizes a more abstract idea. Students' ability to decode political cartoons is aided when teachers talk explicitly with students about their nature. To aid with decoding, students can be shown that political cartoonists often give hints of what symbols represent, sometimes going so far as to label the symbol. For example, in Dr. Seuss' 1941 cartoon (see Figure 7.4) some symbols are labeled with words, such as the names of countries written on the trees; some symbols are labeled by other symbols, such as the black woodpecker with the Nazi symbol, or the eagle with the starred and striped hat; and some symbols are not labeled at all, such as the eagle's closed eyes, smile, and twiddling thumbs (Seuss, 1941). The process of breaking the code requires students to

FIGURE 7.4 A political cartoon.
Source: Seuss (1941).

identify the symbolic meaning of the various images. Additionally, the process of breaking the code requires students to figure out the meanings implied in the relationships between images. For example, the American eagle's back is turned to the Nazi woodpecker and, as noted, his eyes are closed. So, students' ability to break the code rests in their identification of the symbolic images in the cartoon and clarification of the relationships between the images. In many instances, decoding and comprehending also require students to understand rhetorical devices such as irony, sarcasm, forced connections, and exaggeration. For example, in Dr. Seuss' cartoon the eagle's foolish optimism is exaggerated in the quote. Dr. Seuss did not believe those words he wrote.

As students break the symbolic code they can work to construct meaning with the cartoon. The construction of meaning with political cartoons is facilitated by whole-class or small group discussions as students brainstorm, suggest inter-pretations, and critique each other's ideas. As with the analysis of other types of visual texts, there is a synergy that develops as students work together, play off one another's ideas, and collaboratively construct meaning. Additionally, when teachers require students to make explicit their thinking processes, stu-dents model literacies for each other. For example, when a student puts forward an evidence-based interpretation, the teacher can demand that he she cite the evidence upon which the interpretation is based. Thus, teachers demonstrate the need to rely on evidence as they reveal to struggling students the manner of thinking that constitutes proficiency. Mrs. Jensen's oft-asked prompt: "How did you figure that out?" is intended to make explicit the skilled students' otherwise hidden thought processes.

Early on, teachers can facilitate students' comprehension of political cartoons by creating checklists, worksheets, or posters that prompt students to a) consider the source and context of the cartoon, b) identify and decode word-labeled, symbol-labeled, or unlabeled symbols; c) describe important relationships be-tween symbols; d) activate or build appropriate background knowledge; e) find instances of irony, sarcasm, forced connections, or exaggeration; and f) summarize the message the cartoonist is trying to send. Figure 3.4 (see page 44) serves as an example of such a poster. Over time and with practice, as students gain profi-ciency in decoding and comprehending political cartoons, teachers can provide less support.

Once students understand the meaning of a political cartoon, they can use it as historical evidence by asking questions such as: When was the cartoon produced? What do we know about the cartoonist? Is the tone of the cartoon humorous or serious? How well did the artist do in presenting his/her message? Who would be likely to agree with this message? Who would be likely to disagree? What other evidence would we need to fully comprehend and critique this cartoon as historical evidence?

Eventually students should be required to critique the cartoon. For example, a teacher can ask students what this cartoon reveals about Dr. Seuss. Questions should be raised whether his opinion reflected a majority or minority opinion in the United States at the time. Why might he have advocated this position? What were the flaws in his logic in this cartoon? Research might be conducted to search for political cartoons that show an opposing point of view. As with all literacies, with practice students become more proficient in using political cartoons as evidence in the development of historical interpretations, and, in the process, become more literate with current political cartoons.

Paintings

Students' tendencies in constructing meaning with paintings contrast sharply with the challenges they face in reading political cartoons. Instead of quickly admitting an inability to comprehend, with paintings students often believe that they have achieved complete comprehension at a glance. Frequently the challenge in working with paintings is to get students to slow down and think more deeply about what they see, what it might represent, and what it suggests about the artist and his/her time – in other words, to engage in the strategic reading of paintings and to use them as evidence.

One way I have had success in helping students think deeply about historic paintings is through the use of the Observation/Inference (O/I) chart (Nokes, 2008). The O/I chart is a graphic organizer that breaks down the process of analyzing paintings into the stages of observing and inferring (see Figure 7.5). The O/I chart is a basic t-chart with two columns. In the left column students keep a record of the things they observe in a painting. In the right column students record inferences they make about the painting and the author's intended message. In connection with the use of the graphic organizer, teachers can provide

Observations	Inferences

FIGURE 7.5   The Observation/Inference (OI) chart.
Source: Nokes (2008).

explicit instruction on strategies that make students more observant and more skilled at making inferences. For instance, students can be encouraged to take their time, in essence, to slow their reading speed; to look at the details of the painting quadrant by quadrant; to look at each of the images included in the painting in isolation; and to look at the relationships between images. Additionally, allowing students to work together increases and improves the quality of their observations. One student's discovery often stimulates a flurry of new observations.

The metaconcept of *evidence* comes into play when working with the O/I chart. Students keep a record of observations, evidence upon which to base inferences. For each inference they list on the chart, students should be able to identify the evidence upon which it is based. Arrows linking observations to inferences can be drawn on the O/I chart to explicitly demonstrate the connection between evidence and inference. The O/I chart is effective for a number of reasons. It provides scaffolding by reminding students about the process of making observations and inferences. It gives them a place to record their thoughts, thus freeing up cognitive resources and allowing them to return to their thinking later. It helps them be metacognitive by requiring them to slow down and think about their cognitive processes in making inferences. The O/I chart promotes self-critique because students must justify their inferences. And, the O/I chart allows students to make their thinking processes explicit, allowing others to evaluate their analysis. It creates a record for the teacher to use to assess and provide feedback on their analysis.

As with all other texts, history teachers should choose carefully the paintings that they use with their students. Considerations should include whether a painting contains appropriate material for the students, a message that students can interpret and use when given the proper support (such as peer support and the O/I chart), and a topic that will support the content objectives of the class. In working with paintings, as with all other texts, students should keep the artist in mind and attempt to discern the artist's message, remembering the historical context during which the painting was produced.

Photographs

Since the mid-19th century, photographs have become a useful resource for studying the past. Students should be taught how to use them as historical evidence. As mentioned, students should acknowledge that photographs have a source; do not represent an objective reality; are created with a purpose in mind – sometimes to document, sometimes to persuade – and can be manipulated to exaggerate or distort their subject. In working with photographs, students should seek to find the source and its sponsorship. With the source in mind students can analyze photographs in much the same way recommended in analyzing paintings. I have found that the O/I chart works equally well with paintings and photographs (as well as other types of non-print texts such as artifacts or even movie clips). In helping students work with photographs teachers should ask the follow-ing questions: a) What basic background knowledge do students need in order to effectively read this picture? Without the necessary background knowledge students are not likely to be able to construct appropriate meaning with the photograph. However, teachers should not do the reading for students, which can happen if they provide too much background knowledge. b) How can students' attention be drawn to important details in the photograph? Teachers might sug-gest that students analyze specific sections of the photograph, or particular items, in addition to analyzing the photo as a whole. c) What challenges might students face in dealing with the details in the photograph? For example, are there objects, people, or activities that students are not likely to accurately identify? d) How can students be led to consider the photographer's purposes in taking a particular picture? For instance, why did he/she choose a certain perspective, certain light-ing, etc? And e) how can this picture be used as evidence in the development of historical interpretations? In other words, how does this photograph help us understand the past?

The online "Image Detective" is an interactive Internet site that guides stu-dents through the analysis of historical photographs, considering how the camera was used as a tool for social reform (Education Development Center, 2002). On this site, a historian models his analysis of a photograph of an immigrant family engaged in "piece work" at their kitchen table. Students are given other photo-graphs that they can analyze in a supportive environment. Students are encour-aged to ask historical questions about observations they make in the photos. As they search for clues to answer their questions, their attention is drawn to smaller sections of the photograph. Students can access basic facts if they don't understand something that they see in a photograph. The website provides a place for them to take notes on the various clues that they observe. After analyzing the photograph, students are given access to their notes and are asked to draw conclu-sions – find answers to their questions – based on the evidence they have gath-ered. Finally, they are asked to formulate new questions. Whether or not teachers use the website, they could provide the same type of interactive experience by finding appropriate photographs, building the necessary background knowledge, allowing students to pose questions, drawing students' attention to specific parts of the photograph, answering questions about unfamiliar things shown in the photograph, modeling effective thinking processes, and encouraging students to develop their own interpretations based on evidence in the photograph.

Students Creating Visual Historical Texts

Historians often illustrate and/or provide evidence for their work with carefully selected visual texts. For example, in a PowerPoint presentation, a historian might include photographs, artwork, or maps – both primary and secondary sources – to illustrate important points that he/she is trying to make. Historians' books and articles often include images. Thus, historians create with visual historical texts. Students can be taught to use visual texts to illustrate or persuade the way historians do. As they present their historical interpretations, whether through PowerPoint presentations, posters, or in written format, visual texts can be used to attract or hold audience attention, clarify confusing concepts, help the audience visualize events and locations, or persuade that their interpretations are sound. One of the main challenges students face in creating with visual texts is in text selection – finding the right historical text for the intended purpose. Teachers can help students make wise choices in texts by reminding them to pay attention to the source and context of the image's production. Additionally, teachers should help students consider their purposes for using a visual text, their intended audience, and the proper citation of their sources.

In addition to using visual texts that others have produced, students can create visual texts to display their development of literacy skills, to increase their understanding of visual texts, to encourage their interaction with historical ideas, to make history content personally relevant, or as part of their engagement in historical inquiry. For example, one way a teacher can assess whether students understand the literacies involved in constructing meaning with political cartoons is to have them draw a political cartoon based on a current or a historic topic. Teachers can use student-produced cartoons to assess students' content knowledge, understanding of symbolism, and ability to work with political cartoons. Students could be assigned to produce a propaganda poster, a map of their community, or other visual texts in order to assess their ability to work with various symbol systems. A closely related purpose for assigning students to create visual texts would be to help them increase their understanding of a particular text genre. For example, a teacher might assign class members to document and build sympathy for those suffering from the current "Great Recession" by taking photographs similar to those taken by the Farm Securities Administration in the 1930s. They would be creating a visual account of current conditions, like visual accounts created in the past. Doing so would help students understand the photographer's use of perspective and context to achieve a certain purpose. Such work would deepen students' understanding of the use of photographs as historical evidence and of the meta-concept of *account*.

Alternatively, a teacher might assign students to produce a visual account as a means of having students interact more deeply with historical ideas. For example, a teacher might ask students to create a collage depicting a historical era. Students could develop a list of significant events, trends, and ideas from that era and collect images that represent them. Similarly, a teacher might invite students with unusual talents or interests to produce paintings or drawings depicting events or eras. Although these types of activities do not parallel the type of texts historians produce, they can make historical ideas personally relevant for students. And, in the process of creating, students are required to engage in many of the same reading and thinking processes that historians use: determining historical significance, constructing interpretations, and using evidence to support and persuade. Thus, the process involves historical thinking though the product may be more suited for history students than for historians.

Chapter Summary

Metaconcepts are concepts that cut across all historical study, the understanding of which is vital in historical thinking. Metaconcepts include concepts like *evidence*, *account*, *change*, and *time*. Evidence includes visual texts. History teachers can help students increase their visual literacy by helping them learn the unique symbol systems of various genres of visual texts, such as propaganda, maps, political cartoons, paintings, and historical photographs. Students have different literacy needs when working with different types of visual texts. Teachers can help students critique and use visual texts as evidence in constructing historical interpretations. Additionally, the creation of visual texts, even texts that are not typically created by historians, can help students engage in historical processes and can make historical themes relevant in their lives.

8

DEVELOPING HISTORICAL EMPATHY AND PERSPECTIVE TAKING THROUGH HISTORICAL FICTION

In a few weeks, Miss Anderson will start a unit on the Civil Rights Movement in her 8th grade U.S. history class in her Midwest suburban school. She wishes there was a way to help students experience the conditions across America at the outset of the Civil Rights movement. She's heard of teachers doing simulations that recreate feelings of anger over discrimination but she's afraid that a simulation might trivialize the realities of the period. She wouldn't think of doing a simulation on the Holocaust or the Middle Passage and, for the same reasons, is hesitant to do a simulation related to the Civil Rights Movement. In former years she has started the unit by telling the story of Emmett Till, a fourteen-year-old African American boy from Chicago who was murdered while visiting his cousins in Mississippi. White men tortured and brutally killed Emmett Till because he whistled at a White woman. His killers, who later confessed to the murder, were acquitted by an all-White jury in spite of overwhelming evidence against them. Eighth-grade students can relate to Emmett Till. They are about his age. And most of them have committed a prank, have taken a dare, or said something dumb. It's shocking for them to imagine that such a minor offense could be used to justify murder in the segregated South in 1955. She tells the story because it draws students into a world very different from current conditions, a world that seems remarkably foreign to students in spite of its closeness in both time and space.

As Miss Anderson begins to research Emmett Till's story, she discovers a historical novel that was written about him, *Mississippi Trial, 1955* (Crowe, 2002). She checks it out from the library and reads it over the weekend. She finds a story that she believes would appeal to her predominantly White students, and will immerse them in the culture and conditions of Greenwood Mississippi at the time of the Emmett Till murder. She finds in the novel the story of otherwise good people who are so invested in a culture of segregation that they commit heinous acts to "preserve their Southern way of life." Pooling her annual supply money with some resources from the school's Social Studies department, English Department, and school library, she has the school secretary put in a rush order for a classroom set of novels.

The books arrive a few days before her Civil Rights unit is scheduled to begin. In the mean time, she has spoken with some of the Language Arts teachers at her school about what they do to motivate students to read, to make them accountable for reading, and to assess their learning with the novel. She creates a reading schedule for the students, expecting them to read two or three chapters for homework each evening. To monitor and assess their comprehension and to motivate students to read, she assigns them to create a double-entry journal (see Figure 8.1), a t-chart for recording elements of the story that are particularly relevant to history in the left column, and reactions, questions, or connections in the right column. She intends to give a short reading quiz in class each day, before forming students into discussion groups that will reflect on issues, themes, and questions about the book. She assigns the books to students a few days before the Civil Rights unit starts.

In addition to the quiz and discussion groups, instructional methods designed to help students comprehend the text, Miss Anderson wants to help students critique the novel – to think about it not just as an average reader would, but to read it as a historian might. She wants students to understand the genre of historical fiction and to be able to distinguish between historically accurate elements of the story, both events and conditions, and fictional and literary elements of the story. She understands that historical fiction is not typically used as evidence by historians, nor is it generally produced by professional historians. But nonetheless, it is a genre of historical writing that her students will be exposed to throughout their lives. What better place to learn how to deal with historical fiction than in a history classroom? She gathers primary sources on the Emmett Till case for students to use to assess the accuracy of the book. She builds several document collections on topics addressed in the novel including segregated schools, African American working conditions, White Citizen Councils, Jim Crow Laws, the murder of Emmett Till, and the trial of those accused of his murder.

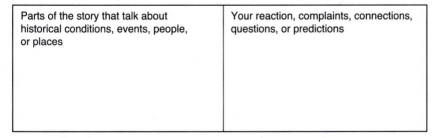

Parts of the story that talk about historical conditions, events, people, or places	Your reaction, complaints, connections, questions, or predictions

FIGURE 8.1 A double-entry journal to support students' work with a historical novel.

Students are surprised when she passes out the books at the end of class one day. Miss Anderson hasn't had them read historical fiction all year. She gives them the reading schedule and, amid groans, explains that they will have a short quiz to start class each day to assess their comprehension of the chapters from the evening before. She also tells them that she will give them a few minutes in class each day to discuss what they have read with their classmates, to ask questions, and to consider some questions she will ask them. "I think that reading and talking about this book will be a good experience for you," she explains.

"Why do we have to read a whole book," Isaac whines. "This isn't an English class is it?"

"I'm glad you asked," responds Miss Anderson. "This book is an example of historical fiction. Do you remember what fiction is, from your English class?"

"It's a story that's made up. It isn't true," Jenna answers.

"So why would I be asking you to read something that isn't true in a history class?" Miss Anderson asks.

"Exactly!" Isaac continues his protest.

"They are based on something that really did happen, but some parts of the story aren't true," Jenna explains, getting the class back on track.

"That's exactly right. This book is the story of Hiram Hillburn, a boy from Arizona who goes to Mississippi to spend a summer with his Grandpa in 1955. Hiram and his grandpa are made up, fictional characters, but some of the people Hiram meets, and some of the events he witnesses really happened. What's most important for you to learn as you read this book are the conditions he finds in the South, in the Mississippi Delta. The main reason that I want you to read this book is so that you can get a sense of the relationships between African Americans and White people in the South during the 1950s. I want you to go with Hiram to a place that might seem foreign to you, to experience what people were feeling and thinking at the time. So as you're reading I want you to focus on race relations – what do people say and do that helps you understand how the races interacted in the South." Using a term students have heard in previous lessons, she continues, "I want you to experience the historical context of one part of the deep South in the early years of the Civil Rights Movement. I think it will help you with *contextualization*."

"You mean we're reading this whole book just for contextualization?" Seth complains. "Why don't you just tell us what it was like?"

"It's not that easy," Miss Anderson responds. "I could tell you about events that might help you understand some aspects of the context, but you know how reading a novel, or watching a well-made movie can help you experience an unfamiliar time or place in a way that I can't just tell you about. It can also help you understand why people made some of the choices that they did that seem crazy to us today. Historical fiction can help you see the world from other people's perspectives – to engage in what is called *historical empathy*." She writes the phrase on the board as she says it.

"Do they have a movie of this book?" Isaac asks, still hopeful of finding some way to get out of reading. "I think a movie would be better at helping me get historical empathy," he says, reading the last two words from the chalkboard.

"No movie yet, but I hear Spielberg has purchased the rights to make one," Miss Anderson teases. "It's a very good book. I read it in a couple of days a few weeks ago. I think that you'll really enjoy it once you get into it." She knows that not all of the students will read it, but believes that that shouldn't prevent her from providing the opportunity for the majority of her students who will read it and who will learn from the experience.

A week or so later the Civil Rights unit is well underway. The students have read through Chapter 11 in their novels and Miss Anderson has planned an activity that will immerse students more fully in the context of the Civil Rights Movement. Students are used to the routine by now. Class starts with a five-question quiz on Chapters 10 and 11 with questions that assess their comprehension of the story. After the quiz is corrected, students form groups where they discuss the chapters they read. Miss Anderson has prepared questions for the discussion groups: "What is your reaction to Grandpa's involvement in the 'White Citizens' Council?'" "Do you agree with the editorial 'A Just Appraisal?' Why or why not?" Some of the questions are intended to promote historical empathy: "Did good people participate in White Citizen Councils? Why or why not?" "Why didn't Mr. Paul do something when he realized the Black students were attending inferior schools?" Students spend a few minutes talking informally about these and other questions they have. Miss Anderson doesn't care whether they get through all of her questions, skip some of them, or if they discuss their own questions about the book. The questions, the time, and the format of the discussion groups are to stimulate authentic conversation about the book – an opportunity for students to think more deeply about the issues surrounding the origins of the Civil Rights Movement.

Miss Anderson wants students to consider the context of the Civil Rights Movement including the segregated school system, African American working conditions, White Citizen Councils, and Jim Crow laws. She has collected sets of primary sources on each of these topics. For one class period, she assigns students to get into groups and critique the novel's depiction of one topic. Students begin by reading an excerpt from the novel related to their study, and then search for evidence in the primary sources that supports or contradicts it. One group, for instance, reads a passage in the novel that shows Hiram Hillburn, the visitor from Arizona to the Mississippi Delta, seeking to understand segregated schools. Hiram asks, "But don't Negroes want their own schools just like we do?" (Crowe, 2002, 73). Mr. Paul, another fictional character in the novel, then paints the picture of the inequities between White and Black schools for Hiram and for the reader. After reading the passage from the novel the group of students turns to the primary sources to answer Miss Anderson's question, "Does the novel accurately portray the segregated schools of the South?" Her lesson plan calls for students to spend about 30 minutes exploring one of the four text sets and then take a few minutes to report to the class, critiquing the book's accuracy in its portrayal of schools, working conditions, social attitudes, or legal discrimination.

For a different day, Miss Anderson has created another document collection that all students will use to analyze the Emmett Till murder, trial, and national response. This collection features an interview with Emmett Till's accused murderers, during which they brazenly describe the night of the murder (Huie, 1956). Other texts include trial transcripts, an autopsy report, photographs, and letters sent from around the country in reaction to the Emmett Till murder and to the killers' published confession. These letters paint a picture of an America deeply divided by the murder. Miss Anderson is hopeful that these texts, which all of the students will review, will help them experience a different America, one in which many people condoned the killing of a teenage boy for crossing the lines of segregation. Together with the novel, Miss Anderson is confident that the texts will help students contextualize the Civil Rights movement and, perhaps, experience historical empathy for both the Whites who stubbornly clung to traditional, oppressive race relations, and the Americans of every background that fought for change. For the remainder of the class period, students will work in small groups with a copy of this text set.

Just before allowing students to get into groups to work through the documents, Miss Anderson asks them to try to feel historical empathy for the characters involved in this struggle. She points out that doing so will be easier when considering the perspective of those who were fighting for change than it will be when trying to understand the perspective of those fighting for tradition and segregation. "To be able to understand their perspective doesn't mean that you support their racist ideas and definitely not their actions," she explains. "It means that you are trying to understand the social context that would produce people who viewed African Americans as inferior, and who saw the world around them changing, threatening their way of life. They viewed the quality of their children's schools being threatened as resources might be diverted toward other schools – or even worse, from their perspective – their children might be sent to a run-down school with African American children. I know it will be difficult to understand their thinking, but consider people like Grandpa in the novel – these aren't people like Walt Disney villains who run around singing about how great it is to be evil. They are people who are fighting for what they think is best – even willing to kill to preserve their way of life."

"I'm sorry, but I just can't do it!" exclaims Amy, who has been reading ahead. "Have you read these letters, Miss Anderson? It makes me sick to my stomach. Listen to this garbage. 'Roy Bryant and J. W. Milam did what had to be done, and their courage in taking the course they did is to be commended. To have followed any other course would have been unrealistic, cowardly and not in the best interest of their family or country' (American Experience, 2009). I'm sorry but my imagination just isn't good enough to imagine a world where anyone could call what those murderers did 'courageous.' You want me to try to feel sorry for Bryant or Milam or the racist who wrote this letter?"

"No. Don't get confused about what historical empathy means," Miss Anderson reminds the class. "It's not the same thing as feeling sorry for someone or even having empathy for someone in the traditional sense. It means to be able to understand why they behaved the way they did. It's based on the idea that people's actions generally make sense to them, given their situation. This letter was not written by a person without values, but it was written by a person whose value system was very different than yours or mine. A historian would not look at this letter and say, 'That guy was crazy.' The historian would look at this letter and might say, 'Wow. The context that produced a person like this must have been very different than my experience growing up. I wonder what I can figure out about that context based on this person's values.' Do you understand? The historian assumes that the person was not inherently evil, stupid, or crazy but that he lived in a culture with values and standards very different from ours. Again, think of Grandpa Hillburn in the novel – he's a pretty loveable guy isn't he, in spite of his racist attitudes? I told you this was not going to be easy, but hopefully it will give you a better understanding of the context during which the Civil Rights Movement emerged. The Civil Rights Movement was not about politically overpowering a handful of extremists or lunatics in the South. That would have been easy. The Civil Rights Movement was about changing an entire nation where many otherwise good people viewed traditional segregated society as a good and natural thing. That was, and is, extremely difficult."

Some of the students are starting to understand what Miss Anderson is talking about as they form groups and explore their text sets. They take notes on a study guide Miss Anderson has prepared with a place for them to list the justifications that some people put forward for the murder and a place for the arguments raised by those who opposed the murder. She again makes it clear to the students that she, personally, could not be in greater disagreement with those who supported the murder. "But in order to understand the time period, we have to understand their ways of thinking," she explains. "We've got to try to see the world from their perspective. We need historical empathy."

Historical Empathy and Historical Fiction

Miss Anderson wanted her students to show historical empathy and she thought that using the novel with the supplemental primary sources would help them do so. In the remainder of this chapter I explore two ideas: the notion of historical empathy, and methods of teaching with historical fiction, children's books, poetry, and song lyrics. I first explore historical empathy and perspective taking as historical literacies. I then consider the advantages, disadvantages, and challenges of using historical fiction. I continue with the exploration of the use of children's books, poetry, and song lyrics as both accounts and artifacts. The chapter concludes with ideas for helping students develop historical empathy by producing historical fiction.

Historical Empathy and Perspective Taking as Historical Literacies

Historical empathy, as Miss Anderson explained to her students, is the ability to comprehend a historical individual's actions as a logical effect of his/her worldview. Historical empathy is closely related to the strategies of contextualization and perspective taking. Contextualization, as described in previous chapters, is the process of conceptualizing the physical, social, and interpersonal context of a historical event. Perspective taking is the ability to imagine and assume the identity of another in an attempt to understand his/her actions. Historical thinking and historical literacies require students to engage in perspective taking, contextualization, and to show historical empathy (Nokes, Crowe, & Bausum, 2012).

Because of the way people learn, no other element of historical literacy presents a greater challenge than developing historical empathy. Most modern learning theories acknowledge and highlight the role of background knowledge and personal connections in the learning process. For instance, schema theory proposes that factual knowledge is stored in nodes and links, and that learning something new requires the learner to link new nodes of information within his/her existing network of knowledge (Alba & Hasher, 1983). Constructivist theories suggest that a learner's new experiences are filtered through his/her prior experiences and so perceptions, conclusions, and learning are dependent upon background knowledge (Anderson, Reynolds, Schallert, & Goetz, 1977). These models of learning present a dilemma for history teachers. If all learning is dependent on the learners' prior knowledge and experiences, and learning history involves trying to understand actions, values, and events from times and places that are foreign to us, then it follows that learning history involves a distortion of the past to fit our experiences. When we understand the actions of historical characters through the lens of our own experiences – and it's difficult to learn in any other way – we don't really understand their actions. In response to this dilemma, Wineburg called learning history an "unnatural act" (2001).

Historians forge ahead through this dilemma using the heuristic of contextualization, explained in Chapter 5, and by developing historical empathy, the ability to understand an individual's actions in light of *their* experiences, context, values, and perspective, rather than ours. Fostering historical empathy and nurturing students' ability to view the world from multiple perspectives are vital elements of building historical literacies. Historical empathy and perspective taking, as Miss Anderson's students found out, are among the most difficult of dispositions to develop, because they require unnatural thinking. For instance, current theories of reading comprehension focus on the readers' interaction with a text. Instead, to fully comprehend historical resources it is more important to focus on the writer's interaction with the text. What was he/she seeing, hearing, feeling, and thinking as the text was produced? In historical inquiry, not only the reader's, but the writer's background knowledge, values, perspective, and reaction assume great importance. In addition to focusing on what *we* feel and think as we investigate the evidence, we have to focus on what the creator of the evidence was feeling and thinking as they produced it.

Further, teaching in a manner that discourages unrestrained personal connections and reactions, cuts against the grain of traditional learning theories and, as a result, often clashes with the instincts of good teachers. Many teachers would perceive Amy's outburst as a good thing – as a signal that she is engaging deeply with the text, that she is active in the learning process, and that she is highly motivated as a reader and thinker. Good teachers want this from their students. However, such a reaction decreases the likelihood that Amy will understand the challenges of the Civil Rights Movement's fight against traditional institutions. Unrestrained connections and reactions, like Amy's, while highly valued in many teaching situations, become problematic in history teaching. What on the surface appears to be good teaching, might actually be ahistorical thinking, interfering with historical literacies.

The experiences of Miss Anderson's students suggest that historical empathy comes easier in some circumstances than others. Her students had an easier time assuming the perspective of Emmett Till, Hiram Hillburn, or the writers of letters that called for reform than they did of Grandpa, or the individuals who praised the murder. It's not surprising that it was easier for them to see the world from the viewpoint of people who were similar to them in age, beliefs, interests, and/or motives than to assume the perspective of those who held dramatically different beliefs. However, a fair appraisal of historical events requires historians to attempt to observe the event from diverse perspectives. Miss Anderson worked hard to help her students feel historical empathy for both those who held beliefs similar to theirs and those who held opposing viewpoints. The historical novel and other resources that she brought into the classroom helped.

Historical Fiction

Some researchers suggest that one of the keys to building historical empathy is providing students with opportunities to immerse themselves in historical contexts through detail-rich historical fiction (Nokes, *et al.*, 2012; Tomlinson, Tunnell, & Richgels, 1993; Tunnell & Ammon, 1996; VanSledright & Franks, 1998). They argue that through fiction, students can vicariously experience conditions and events that occurred in distant times and places, in a manner that is impossible with textbooks (Schwebel, 2011). Contextualization and historical empathy require the ability to immerse oneself into the physical, social, economic, and historic conditions of an event. Doing so is extremely difficult for students, who often lack background knowledge of the details of historical times and places (Nokes, *et al.*,

2007; Reisman, 2012; Wineburg, 1991). The elaborate descriptions and imagery included in well-researched historical novels and movies may hold a key to building the background knowledge students need to engage in historical empathy.

Because historical fiction is a popular genre in young adult publishing, history teachers have an increasingly large selection of novels to choose from, with books available dealing with diverse time periods and themes. However, there are a variety of types of historical novels. Some are set in a historical time and place but do not describe historical events or people. Others have a historical setting with a plot that only tangentially involves noteworthy historical events. Some historical fiction, like *Mississippi Trial, 1955,* weaves significant historical events into the plot line, with fictitious characters interacting with historical characters. Still other historical novels describe actual events, filling in minor details with some creative reconstructions. Each of these types of fiction might serve a purpose for history teachers, depending on their objectives. Further, historical fiction varies significantly in its historical accuracy, depending, to a great degree, on the historical research conducted by the author.

Advantages

Well-written historical fiction has several advantages over other types of text. As mentioned, a novel's detailed dialogues, setting descriptions, character development, and depiction of events can transport students to historical settings, facilitating contextualization and historical empathy. Further, many students enjoy reading novels more than they do textbook passages or even primary source documents. The phrase "I couldn't put it down" is used more often with novels than textbooks. Additionally, historical fiction, as all good literature does, presents truths that run deeper than historical facts. Lee contends that historical fiction "makes us feel ... what otherwise would be dead and lost to us. It transports us into the past. And the very best historical fiction presents to us a truth of the past that is not the truth of the history books, but a bigger truth, a more important truth – a truth of the heart" (Lee, 2000). Historical fiction can introduce students in a powerful manner to significant historical themes and concepts, such as the clash of cultures, the quest for freedom, surviving hardship, or correcting societal ills.

Disadvantages

Historical fiction carries with it several disadvantages. Admittedly, the ease with which Miss Anderson procured her classroom set of novels was exaggerated in the vignette – schools typically devote fewer resources to purchasing novels (for the History Department) than they do textbooks. However, an ambitious history teacher will find English teachers, media specialists, grant adjudicators, and principals who were extremely supportive of efforts to gather historical novels.

Additionally, reading a novel takes a great deal of time, time that otherwise could be devoted to other assignments or classroom activities. As with all curricular decisions, there is an opportunity cost associated with taking time to read historical fiction. Further, students' diverse reading abilities and interests make it impossible to find historical fiction that is universally appropriate or appealing. However, this same argument could be made about any text or topic studied in a history class and has rarely been applied to rule out the use of textbooks, which appeal to few students. Finally, teaching with novels is an unfamiliar process for most history teachers, presenting challenges in motivation, assessment, and instruction. Miss Anderson sought advice from Language Arts teachers. Such advice, combined with experience, can help history teachers develop satisfactory methods for working with novels, a genre that is outside of traditional disciplinary reading and writing.

Challenges

Simply providing students with historical fiction is not guaranteed to help them develop historical empathy or the ability to contextualize historical events. Research on students' work with movies, one genre of historical fiction, is illustrative. Seixas (1993) showed history students two movies related to 19th century Native American/White relations. Students judged the movie that showed characters acting and reacting according to modern values and conditions to be more "realistic." The movie that captured the context with greater accuracy was considered less "realistic" by students because the characters did not respond to conditions the way one would expect given current conditions. Seixas expressed concerns that students were looking for realism rather than accuracy in Hollywood's accounts of historical eras (a tendency also common in students' work with historical artwork). His research suggests that students have a difficult time distinguishing between fictional accounts that accurately present historical settings and fictional accounts that twist the past to attract modern patrons.

One of the biggest challenges students face in learning history with historical fiction is distinguishing fictional from historical elements of the story. "Based on a true story" can mean many different things. However, the challenges students face in sifting the historical from the fictional in historical fiction are similar to the challenges they face in distinguishing evidence from claims in secondary sources, or relevant from irrelevant material in primary sources. In fact, the process of learning to work with historical fiction may facilitate general historical thinking. For instance, historians are hesitant to accept information that is found in only one source, remaining skeptical until they find corroborating evidence. To give students the opportunity to engage in corroboration, Miss Anderson provided them with collections of primary sources that gave eyewitness accounts of conditions. Passages from the novel were compared and contrasted with primary sources. Using these text sets, students could not only make judgments about the research that went into writing the novel, but could further immerse themselves into the context of the Civil Rights Movement, her objective for using the novel in the first place.

Teaching with Historical Fiction

As with any other type of text, history teachers need to consider their objectives to identify when historical fiction would be a wise choice. In Miss Anderson's case, she wanted students to experience the effects of segregation on Southern society in the years leading up to the Civil Rights Movement. She didn't believe that students could understand the significance of the movement or the bravery of Civil Rights leaders without feeling the context. And the novel, *Mississippi Trial, 1955,* which detailed an outsider's attempts to understand Southern society within the context of the Emmett Till murder and trial, seemed to be the right text for the job. One of the first issues Miss Anderson faced was finding a way to motivate her students to read. She established a reasonable reading schedule, replacing the normal homework assignments that she would give with a small amount of reading each night. She developed quizzes and discussion questions that were intended to make students accountable for reading and to support and assess their comprehension of the novel, with a particular focus on those elements that were relevant to the Civil Rights unit. Most significantly, she created collections of documents that would engage students in historical thinking related to the novel. As part of her instruction she allowed students to make their own evidence-based judgment of the accuracy of the novel, using evidence that she supplied. At the conclusion of the unit, students were not only knowledgeable of the Emmet Till case, but of general conditions that led to the Civil Rights Movement. Further, they were more informed about the nature of historical fiction, more skilled in sifting between fictional and historical elements of a story, and more able to engage in historical thinking.

Miss Anderson stumbled on the novel quite by accident. But there are systematic ways that history teachers can search for appropriate historical fiction. For instance, each year, the Scott O'dell Award for Historical Fiction is given to an outstanding historical novel written for children or young adults. Reviewing the list of O'dell Award recipients a teacher would find novels on a great variety of U.S. history topics including colonist/Native American relations, the Revolutionary War, slavery, the Civil War, Reconstruction, the settlement of the Midwest, the Depression and Dust Bowl, World War II home front, and the development of the atomic bomb. Fewer titles relate to world history events. Other young adult book awards, though not dedicated to historical fiction, include additional titles. Further, the National Council for the Social Studies publishes an annual list of notable tradebooks for young people, with a large collection of titles of young adult fiction and children's books going back to 1972. These lists are available online or in an annual publication.

Miss Anderson sought advice from Language Arts teachers as she prepared for instruction with the novel. Other history teachers have formed stronger collaborations with English teachers. In many cases Language Arts teachers will coordinate their instruction so that they teach the literary elements of the novel as a history teacher teaches its historical features. Such cooperation can split the time commitment between two courses, making the use of historical novels more feasible.

Children's Books, Poetry, and Song Lyrics

In addition to historical novels, there are short stories, plays, children's books, and movies that blend fictional and historical elements, paint vivid pictures of historical settings, and present memorable and moving depictions of the past. Each of these genres carry the same advantages, disadvantages, and challenges as historical novels, providing opportunities for teachers to immerse students in historical contexts and to teach historical thinking. Through the creation of multi-genre text sets that include images, fiction, primary sources, picture books, and video or audio clips related to the same topic, teachers can foster historical thinking while differentiating their curriculum.

For instance, a teacher might build text sets relating to any number of incidents that occurred as part of the Civil Rights Movement, in addition to or in place of the activities Miss Anderson planned. A text set on Jackie Robinson, who was the first African American to play in all-white Major League Baseball, might include books such as *A Picture Book of Jackie Robinson* (Adler, 1997), *Testing the Ice: A True Story about Jackie Robinson* (Robinson, 2009), *The Story of Jackie Robinson: Bravest Man in Baseball* (Davidson, 1996); primary sources such as a handwritten note containing a death threat to Robinson, the transcript of an interview of Robinson's wife, a letter that Robinson sent President Eisenhower; photographs; video clips; the lyrics from the song "Did You See Jackie Robinson Hit that Ball?" (Johnson, 1948); etc. Students, in small groups, could be assigned to explore Jackie Robinson's contributions to the Civil Rights Movement. With the teacher's guidance, a student who struggles with reading might explore the children's book and the threatening note, while those who are more proficient at reading would be expected to search other, more challenging texts. The group could collaboratively analyze the photographs, song, and other sources. Similar text sets could be created exploring Rosa Parks and the Montgomery Alabama bus boycott, Freedom Riders, The Little Rock Nine, the Woolworth's lunch counter sit in, Birmingham anti-segregation protests and violence, voter registration in Mississippi, the Black Panthers, and numerous other topics. Thus text sets, particularly those that include children's books, photographs, and music, provide an opportunity for teachers to differentiate the curriculum based both on students' interests and abilities. Diverse text sets allow teachers to engage even struggling readers in historical literacies.

I should point out that resources such as children's books or song lyrics might be used as primary source or secondary source accounts. In the example in the preceding paragraph, the books listed would be considered secondary accounts, recently produced interpretations of historical events. However, the song "Did You See Jackie Robinson Hit that Ball?" serves a different function as an account that was produced by Robinson's contemporaries. As such, it serves a double purpose in corroborating other accounts of Jackie Robinson, but also to provide clues as to how he was perceived by others during his lifetime. Thus, as teachers search for resources they should consider things that were produced recently that might be particularly appealing to students (such as the slide show/video of the song at http://www.youtube.com/watch?v=r-7Ac2LVVYU) and things that were produced historically that provide insight on people's thinking at the time, such as the lyrics and music of the song.

Students Developing Historical Empathy by Producing Historical Fiction

In addition to reading historical fiction, writing historical fiction can help students engage in perspective taking, can promote historical empathy, and can allow teachers to assess students' historical thinking skills. Language Arts teachers often assign students to produce "realistic fiction," to extend students' thinking. Though the term "realistic" might ruffle some historians' feathers, the notion that students can write fictional descriptions of historical settings has applications for teaching history. History teachers could assign students to produce carefully researched, short, fictional stories describing important events. Depending on the instructional objective, teachers could focus students' writing on a dialogue, a perspective, a character, a setting, or an event.

Dialogue

For instance, a teacher might build a writing activity around the Norman Rockwell painting, *Moving In* (1964), which shows the African American children of a family that has moved into a suburban neighborhood meeting the children of their White neighbors. Students could write the dialogue that they believe might have transpired in this hypothetical event. In order to prepare students to write the dialogue, the teacher could spend some time analyzing the painting, considering Norman Rockwell and what he might have been thinking and showing as he painted. Students can further prepare to write the dialogue by discussing historical events that were occurring at the time the painting was created. What were the children thinking and how would their thoughts play out in a dialogue? After writing, students could assess their peers' ability to accurately capture the context as they read their dialogues to each other.

Perspective Taking

Additionally, teachers might have students write fictional reactions to historic events from alternative perspectives. For instance, after teaching about the Louisiana Purchase the teacher might have students write the fictional reaction of Jefferson, Napoleon, a Native American living along the Missouri River, a French plantation owner living outside of New Orleans, an American farmer living along the Ohio River, a justice of the Supreme Court evaluating its constitutionality, a Spanish ambassador to the United States, or other historical or made-up characters. Students could read their peers' fictitious reactions in order to consider multiple contrasting perspectives of the event. Teachers can use writing assignments that require perspective taking to assess students' ability to engage in historical empathy.

Character Development

Students' research on a historical person could be presented in the format of the rich character description typical in novels. For instance, students could write a description of Genghis Khan, Ferdinand Magellan, Sundiata Keita, Sitting Bull, General Patton, or any other historical character. In order to explore classes of people, students could write a vivid description of a Christian crusader, an Irish immigrant, a 12th-century Chinese merchant, a sodbuster, a suffragette, or another class of person. After conducting research, looking at primary source descriptions, students could blend what is known about people with reasonable, research-based conjectures. Further, drawings of the character could supplement written descriptions. Such writing can help students position themselves in historical contexts.

Setting Descriptions

Instead of writing about individuals, students could be assigned to write about the physical or social setting of a historical event. For instance, an in-depth understanding of the physical context of Valley Forge, Jamestown, Gettysburg, the Acropolis, King Tut's tomb, Mecca, or Omaha Beach might help students contextualize historical events. In these and countless other circumstances the physical setting of an event affected history. In other cases the social context was more significant than the physical context. For instance, the social context of Jackie Robinson's entry into Major League Baseball, John Hancock's signing of the Declaration of Independence, Kristallnacht, or the Black Death's arrival in Egypt in 1347, could be explored by creating rich written descriptions of the social context. Miss Anderson was hopeful that reading the novel would immerse her students in the social context of the Emmett Till murder and subsequent trial. Writing a rich research-based description of the social context could have served the same purpose. As with the other examples, students' written descriptions of physical and social contexts would allow a teacher to assess their understanding of historical contexts.

Event Depictions

Instead of focusing on characters or settings, students could be assigned to write rich descriptions of historical events. The process of writing these descriptions could involve students in historical research, historical thinking, and creating research-based conjectures to fill in the details. As with the other examples of fiction writing, described above, teachers can use writing about events to promote and assess contextualization.

Chapter Summary

Well-researched historical fiction may foster students' ability to engage in historical empathy and contextualization. Historical empathy is the ability to understand the actions of historical characters. It is closely associated with perspective taking and contextualization. Historical empathy involves recognizing that individuals' actions, though sometimes hard to understand by modern standards, made sense to them given their conditions and values. Historical fiction includes details that can immerse students in the physical and social context of unfamiliar historical eras and, by doing so, can promote a greater awareness of historical contexts and historical empathy. Children's books, poetry, literature, and many movies hold the same potential to help students develop historical empathy. Writing historical fiction can support the development of historical empathy as well as allow teachers to assess this element of historical literacy.

9

FOSTERING HEALTHY SKEPTICISM USING TEXTBOOKS AND SECONDARY SOURCES

At a parent teacher conference Mr. Johnson is confronted by a father who wants to know why his daughter Sandra is not using a history textbook.

"I haven't seen her bring it home all year," he complains, not certain whether Sandra is being lazy or whether her excuses are legitimate. "She says that you didn't even assign them textbooks, but I find that hard to believe."

Mr. Johnson is not sure how to respond. He has spoken before with parents and colleagues like this who think that if students aren't reading lengthy selections from textbook chapters for homework every night, their history class lacks rigor.

"Sandra is telling the truth about the textbook," Mr. Johnson replies. "We have a classroom set that we use occasionally, but I don't assign students a lot of reading from the textbook. She should bring home from time to time collections of documents or other resources that she has to use to try to build her own interpretations of historical events. And you might see her working online, searching digital archives for historical documents. She should be doing some historical writing at home, putting the finishing touches on the work we've been doing in class. We spend a lot of time doing case studies related to important events, with students figuring out what happened and developing their own opinions."

Sandra's father doesn't get it, "I thought people have already figured out what happened and wrote it in textbooks. These kids don't need to figure it out – they just need to learn it. When I was in school my best history teacher gave me one hour of reading from the textbook every night, and I learned history and loved it. Teachers these days don't push kids hard enough and that's the problem with our education system . . ."

Most parents and students appreciate the way Mr. Johnson teaches history but there are a few, like Sandra's dad, who don't understand why he doesn't rely heavily on the history textbook as the main source of information for the students. Mr. Johnson reflects on his attitude about the textbook. One of the goals of his class is to help students understand the textbook's place as *a* text rather than *the* text. He wants them to acknowledge that the textbook, like all accounts, has a human source. Textbook authors have to make interpretive choices, such as what to include and what to omit, where to begin the historical narrative, how to integrate the histories of majority and minority groups, how to address historical controversies such as slavery and American imperialism, and whether to raise questions about the flaws of heroes and heroines. He would like to help students develop a healthy, historian-like skepticism toward all texts, including textbooks, viewing them as the products of imperfect individuals with limited perspectives and specific purposes for producing them. Luckily, he has an entire school year to do this with his students, much more time than the few minutes he had to try to explain his rationale to Sandra's father.

To help achieve these objectives and to help his 10th grade world history students learn about the Mongols, Mr. Johnson decides to conduct an activity giving students numerous descriptions of the Mongols from Chinese, European, Muslim, Mongol, and contemporary perspectives. In preparation, he creates a packet of primary sources for each student, and decides to assign students to compare and contrast the different documents, consider the source of each text, and write on one of a number of questions that he poses such as, "How do you explain the patterns in the way the Mongols were viewed by people from a wide variety of backgrounds?" "How did the Mongols use psychological warfare to subject their enemies?" "How did religion play a role in the expansion of the Mongol Empire?" The answers to these questions cannot be found in any single text, but in a synthesis of the documents. In addition, Mr. Johnson decides to assign his students to write a textbook-like summary of Mongol warfare based on the documents that he gives them and any other primary sources they find.

On the day of the lesson he moves around the classroom as students, in small groups, work with their document packets.

"Which question are you focusing on?" he asks a group of students as he approaches them.

"We're doing the one on psychological warfare," Dillan answers.

"What have you figured out so far?" Mr. Johnson asks.

"I really like this source, *The Secret History of the Mongols* (Cleaves, 1982). The Mongol enemies are trying to decide whether to go to battle against them or not, and the old chief doesn't want to and the younger men are making fun of him."

"Yeah," Zane adds. "They really knew how to insult somebody."

Mr. Johnson thought they would react strongly to this text, but he also notices they aren't thinking about it very critically. "Who wrote *The Secret History of the Mongols?*"

"The Mongols, I think," Tyler guesses.

"Right," Mr. Johnson says. "And who is doing the talking in the document?"

"The Mongols' enemies," Tyler offers with a little more confidence.

"That's right. And how would the Mongols know about this conversation so that they could record it in their history?" Mr. Johnson continues.

"I don't know," Ryan admits. "Maybe one of the Mongols had been taken captive and he heard the conversation."

"Maybe. Does the text say anything about a Mongol prisoner?"

"No, but it says they captured a horse," Ryan adds.

"I think it would have said something if they had captured a Mongol warrior because they are guessing about the strength of the Mongol army by the condition of the horse," Dillan suggests. "If they had a Mongol soldier they would have said so."

"So if there isn't a Mongol witness to their debate over whether or not to go to war, how would the Mongols know the debate took place?"

"Maybe after the battle they got the story out of one of their prisoners," Zane guesses.

"So you think the conversation took place and someone heard it who was then captured by the Mongols and retold the conversation to them and then the Mongols wrote it down. Does that worry you about its reliability – that it had gone through that many people?" Mr. Johnson continues to probe.

"Yeah. Maybe the Mongols made it up completely without any source – just imagining what went on in their enemy's camp," Tyler suggests.

"That's another possibility," Mr. Johnson responds. "Maybe they made it up as a lesson for their own people: 'united we stand, divided we fall.' So the bottom line is that when the Mongols wrote their history they wanted people to know or think that their enemies were extremely afraid to go to battle against them, that their tactics divided their enemies and gave them that advantage."

"Yeah, so that brings us back to the question – the Mongols were using psychological warfare to terrorize their enemies and cause them to be divided rather than united like Mongol armies were," Zane concludes.

"Or at least that's what they want us to think, because they were the ones to write the account of their enemy's fear and division," Tyler adds.

Mr. Johnson spends time with other groups as they work on different questions. At the end of class he assigns students to use the resources in the text set, and any other primary sources they can find online to write a two-paragraph description of the Mongols' war tactics. He emphasizes that they should write something original but that sounds like what they would read in a textbook – just a summary of the most important characteristics of their war practices.

When class starts the next day, Mr. Johnson projects for the students a textbook account of Mongol warfare. He asks them to create a Venn diagram comparing and contrasting the content of their paragraphs with the textbook account (see Figure 9.1). Additionally, he asks students to write a few sentences explaining why their account differs from the textbook, justifying the choices they made about what to include. After students have a chance to work on their own for a while, he leads the class in a discussion of their experience comparing the texts.

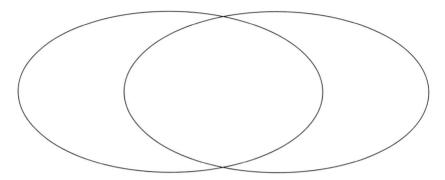

Expository Account 1: The Textbook   Expository Account 2: My Account

Why do the two accounts differ?

FIGURE 9.1 A Venn diagram for comparing a textbook account with a student's account.

"I assume that your account was not identical to the textbook account. Why do you think there were differences?" Mr. Johnson begins the discussion.

"I couldn't believe everything that the textbook left out," Sandra responds.

"Yeah, it didn't say a thing about psychological warfare, which was part of the reason they won so many battles," Zane criticizes.

Other students add their criticism of omissions of the textbook. Mr. Johnson changes the subject a little, "Did the textbook have things that weren't included in your accounts?"

"Yeah, it talked about battle maps, but the stuff we looked at yesterday didn't say anything about maps," Cassie explains.

"So do you think that the textbook is wrong in talking about the Mongols' use of maps?"

"No, probably not."

"So does that mean your account is wrong, because it didn't mention maps?"

"Not wrong, really. I just left that out."

"So the important question that I want you to consider now is why there can be differences in textbook accounts, if all textbook accounts are just trying to give basic factual information?" Mr. Johnson asks.

"Well, different authors might disagree about what is most important to include, like psychological warfare," Zane answers. "I still can't believe they didn't say anything about that."

"I guess it also depends on the sources they look at to get their information. Like the sources we looked at didn't say anything about maps," Cassie adds.

"Do you notice anything about the word choice or tone of your account that is different from the tone and word choice in the chapter?" Mr. Johnson continues.

"Yeah. The textbook seems happy about the Mongols and their expansion.

I thought they were barbaric, violent, and murderous and I was critical of them in my summary," Kathy answers.

"What do you mean?" Zane disagrees. "I thought they were really smart in the way they tried to scare people before going to battle."

The conversation continues for a while, before Mr. Johnson summarizes his class' findings, "I think it is important to understand that textbooks are like other historical accounts. They are written by an author who has purposes in writing. The author has to make tough decisions about what to include and what to leave out. The author also has opinions that are sometimes shown in the choice of words or the tone of the writing. In the future, as you use the textbook in this class and in other history classes you need to remember to read it with the same critical eye that you use when you read other types of historical sources."

Healthy Skepticism, Textbooks, and Secondary Sources

One of the characteristics that distinguish historian readers from history students is that they approach every text with a healthy skepticism. They do not accept the content of a text at face value. Instead, historians understand that each text has a context, which includes its historical and physical setting – the occasion of its creation. Further, every text has a subtext, which includes the author's proximity to the event in time, space, and emotion; the intended audience; the author's perspective; and the author's motives (Lesh, 2011; Wineburg, 1994). Any text represents an extension of an individual, blending the value of unique insights with the flaws that characterize human perception and communication. Historians do not simply collect information from texts, but they use texts as evidence, both rationally and strategically, choosing how to interpret the text's content. Wineburg put it best when he explained that to historians, "what is most important is not what the text says, but what it does" (2001, 65). A healthy skepticism is the filter through which text content is evaluated, allowing a text to serve as evidence rather than as a conveyer of information.

Unfortunately, most students display a remarkable lack of skepticism. Since this is particularly true when they work with textbooks, I discuss skepticism within the context of history textbooks and secondary sources. I explore a) skepticism and historians' thoughts about textbooks, b) skepticism and students' and teachers' thoughts about textbooks, c) supporting students' historical thinking with textbooks and other expository texts, d) introducing students to the role of secondary sources and historiography, and e) helping students develop historical literacies by producing expository texts.

Skepticism and Historians' Thoughts about Textbooks

Textbooks are not a source historians typically use in their original research. However, the few studies of historians' reading of textbooks show that historians approach them with the same healthy skepticism that characterizes their work with other historical accounts. They understand that textbooks, like other forms of historical evidence, have a source, context, and subtext. Wineburg (1991) tested this notion by observing historians' reading of a textbook excerpt as part of his study of historians' and students' reading of historical sources related to the Battle of Lexington. Not only did historians, using evidence found in primary sources, point out factual errors in the textbook account, they engaged in an analysis of the context of the textbook's creation, and its subtext. Fred, for instance, suggested that terms such as "swift riding" and "stood their ground" celebrated American heroism – something completely absent in primary source accounts, even those representing patriot perspectives (Wineburg, 2001). Another historian, after seeing the source information and publication date, and before even reading the textbook passage, began to anticipate what she would find. "[Textbooks] tend to be a little bit patriotic," she predicted, adding that textbooks reduce historical complexity in order to prepare students to answer multiple-choice questions (Wineburg, 1991). Interestingly, the historians, as a whole, rated the textbook excerpt as the least reliable of the sources that they considered, even lower than an excerpt from a historical novel.

Students' and Teachers' Thoughts about Textbooks

One of the great ironies of history teaching is that textbooks, a resource that historians find little use for, are the staple for many teachers and students. And the traditional use of history textbooks is a barrier to students thinking like historians (Nokes, 2011). Students, unlike historians, have a difficult time thinking critically about textbook passages. In fact, in Wineburg's study, the same textbook account that was rated least reliable by the historians was selected as the most reliable text by the students – more trustworthy than eyewitness accounts that painted a remarkably different picture of events on Lexington Green. Derek, one of the students, whom Wineburg praised for his general literacy skills, trusted the textbook because, as he explained, it was "just reporting the facts" (2001, 68). In Derek's mind, the textbook lacked the bias that was present in the minutemen's sworn deposition and a British officer's journal, two accounts that were highly valued by the historians. Research suggests that students' struggles to think critically about their history textbook stem from the way textbooks are written, and the way textbooks are used (Paxton, 1997, 1999).

Paxton's research focused on the way textbooks were written. He suggested that anonymous, authoritative textbook authors present what seem to be objective historical facts through a powerful, third person voice that is above question (Paxton, 1997). To students, like Derek, textbooks appear to be nearly sourceless. Paxton suggests that students who read traditional textbook accounts are unlikely to give independent thought to the information presented, rarely asking questions, making connections, or offering criticism. Instead, he complains textbooks facilitate "mindless memorization" (Paxton, 1999, 319). Most students do not understand, as the students in Mr. Johnson's class were finding out, that as soon as a textbook author begins to write, he or she makes interpretive decisions about where to start, what to include and omit, and how to handle historical controversies. Further, textbooks often portray claims, theories, and even uncertainties as historical facts – facts that students, and much of the general public, accept without question.

Further, the way history teachers typically use textbooks adds to students' uncritical reading. Teachers often like textbooks for a number of reasons. Textbooks help teachers address the constant concern of coverage by providing a seemingly comprehensive narrative that addresses the required curriculum. Textbooks help teachers organize history into manageable chronological and thematic units, often based on textbook chapters. Supplemental material that accompanies teachers' editions of textbooks provides support in lesson planning and the writing of exams. The use of textbooks can ease the burden of history teachers in many ways.

However, the way textbooks have traditionally been used interferes with the building of historical literacies. My dissertation research investigated, among other things, the use of textbooks and other historical sources. As mentioned in Chapter 1, I spent 72 hours observing eight history teachers, paying particular attention to the texts they used and the way that they had students work with texts (Nokes, 2010a). I found that students rarely had opportunities to develop their own interpretations of historical events or to critique the content of textbooks. Instead, when textbooks were used, and they were the most commonly used resource in seven of the eight classrooms, the accompanying assignments were intended to help students summarize, find main ideas, or answer factual questions using information from the book. Unlike Mr. Johnson in the vignette, teachers didn't ask students to question or critically examine the content of textbook passages. Instead, they promoted students' uncritical acceptance of information from their book. Thus, the way textbooks are written and the way they are used makes it unlikely that students will treat textbooks as interpretive historical accounts with contexts and subtexts. What is missing from students' work with textbooks is the healthy skepticism that historians display. As Wineburg concluded, "Before students can see subtexts, they must first believe they exist" (2001, 76). This is particularly true when students use textbooks.

However, students' lack of skepticism is not isolated to textbook reading. As I illustrate in Chapter 3, recent studies of students' online reading show that they experience the same difficulties in reading informational websites (Leu, *et al.*, 2007) that they have in working with a history textbook. They typically accept information uncritically, focusing more on remembering than critiquing what they read. Students are often seduced by detail-rich text, colorful pictures, and formal language, characteristics of textbooks and many websites.

Supporting Students' Historical Thinking with Textbooks and Expository Texts

Teachers can help students think historically about textbooks when they understand the nature of so called "informational texts," when they design activities that promote skepticism, when they value open-mindedness, and when assessments measure more than basic factual knowledge. I consider each of these ideas in this section.

"Informational Texts"

Textbook accounts and other "informational texts" are referred to as expository text. Expository texts such as essays, encyclopedia entries, Wikipedia and other informational websites, and magazine articles are designed primarily to convey information. However, this classification of "informational text," which is common in literacy research and instruction, should be troubling to historians and history educators who know that all texts, in spite of how generic they might seem, include a context and subtext. In the study of history there is no such thing as "informational text." All historical writing is constrained by evidence and involves interpretive decisions about significance. Teachers can help students become more skeptical about expository texts by designing activities that remind them that all texts have authors, and by encouraging them to think critically about the choices authors make. In Mr. Johnson's class, students went through a process of constructing expository text similar to that which a textbook author might go through. They experienced the challenge of deciding what to include in their accounts. Their analysis, contrasting their accounts with that of their textbook, helped them think more deeply about the interpretive choices that authors, themselves included, make.

Promoting Skepticism

Mr. Johnson wanted his students to search for the subtext in history textbooks and the other documents they read. He was determined to help his students understand that all historical sources, including textbooks, should undergo a critical review. He wanted his students to approach texts with a measure of skepticism, considering contexts and subtexts. For instance, in his interaction with students during group work he discovered that one group was making the same mistake with the documents that students often make with textbooks – they were uncritically accepting information without considering the source. In particular, one document reported a conversation that was taking place in an enemy encampment but was recorded in a Mongol text. In looking at the context, a natural question a historian would ask is: how did the Mongols know what was being debated across the plains from their camps? – a detail about which the document was silent. When Mr. Johnson raised the question with the students, they began to wonder. Thinking as historians might, they started to question the source. They hypothesized several plausible explanations, but concluded that the Mongols may have simply invented the conversation in order to project themselves in a certain way. Students began to see that the document did not really tell them what they originally thought it did. But it was still a useful piece of evidence. It revealed more about how the Mongols wanted to be perceived than about how they were actually viewed by their enemies.

The students' study of the Mongols helped them think critically about the textbook as well. Instead of having students find main ideas, summarize, or outline the textbook passage, as teachers often do, Mr. Johnson had students question the textbook content. Students' role was not that of managing information by reading, summarizing, and taking notes, but that of a historian, critiquing and synthesizing historical accounts. Students noticed and wondered why certain things were included or omitted from the textbook account of the Mongols' warfare. They began to see that textbooks do not simply contain "the facts" but that the authors of the textbook put their own personal spin on their description of the Mongols both by selecting the story to tell and by choosing the words with which to tell it.

Valuing Open-Mindedness

One element of critical thinking that is often overlooked is maintaining an open mind. As described in Chapter 2, historians tend to be open-minded, understanding that historical interpretations are works in progress, in need of constant updating based on new evidence or new ways of considering old evidence. Recent trends in education have created a climate where expository websites like Wikipedia are under constant attack. Ironically, some students uncritically reject certain sites, such as Wikipedia, as historical sources, without investigating them. However, students can be shown the usefulness of textbooks, Wikipedia, and other expository texts in providing a basic understanding of an event that can be corroborated by and integrated with the contents of other resources. Expository texts, in spite of their imperfections, can be useful as one of many types of resources employed to solve historical problems. History teachers can model for students how to synthesize material from multiple sources, including expository texts, to build a coherent understanding. When students are skillful at critically evaluating all sources, they need not avoid or fear expository texts like Wikipedia.

Assessing More than Basic Factual Knowledge

Teachers undermine their efforts to help students think critically about textbook passages when they give students traditional assessments that focus solely on remembering the historical facts of textbooks. History tests are notorious for assessing obscure tidbits of information that have little relevance to the lives of students, facts that are quickly forgotten shortly after, or even before, the test is given. When teachers assess students solely on their ability to remember basic facts, they imply that facts, rather than interpretations, the use of evidence, or the processes of historical literacy, are of primary importance. The literal comprehension of the textbook gains preeminence over the ability to think critically about its content. I have found that most students do not have the cognitive resources to memorize details from their textbooks at the same time they are critiquing what the author has chosen to include, analyzing the tone the author uses, or considering how to wisely use textbook information. However, when students use the details in the text to question the author's motives and perspective, they are more likely to remember what they have read (Beck, McKeown, Hamilton, & Kugan, 1997). Teachers must be certain that their assessments are aligned with their instructional objectives. When their instructional focus is on building students' historical literacies, their assessments must not measure the management and memorization of historical information rather than historical thinking.

In summary, history teachers play an important role in helping students learn how to think critically about textbooks and other expository sources. They can do so by designing activities that require a critical analysis of the textbook rather than focusing solely on remembering the information it contains. They should help students approach expository texts with a healthy skepticism but an open mind. Further, teachers can facilitate historical thinking by designing assessments that measure students' ability to use evidence to build and defend interpretations, rather than simply assessing students' ability to remember historical facts.

Exposing Students to Secondary Sources and Historiography

Historians begin their study of any topic by considering what other historians have already said about it. They become familiar with the writing of those historians who have established themselves as authorities, and learn the theories and interpretations that are most accepted in the field. Often the study of a historical topic changes over time, in the specific areas of interest, the types of evidence used, and the lenses through which evidence is evaluated. Historians refer to the study of the way history has been studied as historiography. They immerse themselves in the historiography of their specialty area because, in order to be successful, a historian must produce original scholarship that complements the work of others. To do so, they must become familiar with the history and trajectory of research on their topic – with historiography.

In contrast, students rarely have exposure to the published work of historians (Nokes, 2010a). Should history students be introduced to the notion of historiography as part of a general effort to build historical literacies? Robert Bain (2005), a history teacher and researcher, suggests that they should, and models how it can be done. He includes historiography in a lesson that he teaches on Christopher

Columbus, during which students are exposed to shifting interpretations of Columbus in historical texts. Students start with the standard, widely accepted, story of Columbus pioneering the notion that the world was round and of his attempts to sail west in order to reach the far east. Students read a series of excerpts from textbooks published between 1830 and 1997 that suggest that the conception of a flat earth was the primary obstacle to Columbus' success. With impeccable timing Bain then introduces new texts that claim that "virtually all major medieval scholars affirmed the earth's roundness" and he shows images of a sculpture of Atlas holding the globe on his back – a representation of a round earth produced around 150 AD (Bain, 2005). Students begin to see that the idea of Columbus pioneering the belief that the earth is round represents an evolving public conception rather than the realities of Columbus' time. Students are introduced to a simplified notion of historiography when Bain asks, "Have stories about Columbus changed since 1492?" The purpose of a lecture that follows is not simply to provide information on Columbus, but to describe how interpretations of Columbus have changed over time. Students begin to see that historical understandings evolve as a result of changing interests, purposes, and evidence.

Other researchers have suggested that teachers provide students with conflicting secondary sources, particularly the work of historians, side by side with conflicting primary sources. For instance, at the Stanford History Education Group website (2012) one suggested lesson provides students with two conflicting primary source accounts of Pocahontas' rescue of John Smith, ironically both from John Smith, and two conflicting interpretations written by scholars. Students are asked to assess each of the historians' interpretations and develop their own interpretation based on the conflicting primary and secondary source accounts. Such activities help students understand the interpretive nature of historical thinking and help them become more skeptical of accounts – even those produced by authorities. Simply put, students cannot accept two accounts at face value when they offer antithetical interpretations. Students must critically evaluate both accounts and search for reasons for disagreeing interpretations. In summary, exposure to the writing of historians can be used to help students understand historiography, and, when given opposing historians' interpretations, to develop a healthy skepticism toward secondary sources.

Students Creating Expository Texts

Mr. Johnson assigned students to create a textbook-like account of Mongol warfare. On the surface his assignment was not unlike traditional writing assignments in history classrooms. Teachers often ask students to write summaries or reports on historical people, events, or eras. However, there were two noteworthy distinctions in Mr. Johnson's assignment. First, students were composing their account from multiple primary source documents. Often, when students are assigned to write a history essay or report, they simply recast information found in one expository text into their own expository text. At best, the process consists of general literacies, such as finding the main idea, summarizing, composing with a logical organizing scheme, writing a topic sentence, etc. At worst, the process entails plagiarizing a single, original source. Students engaged in such writing do little historical thinking. In contrast, Mr. Johnson's students were composing from multiple primary sources. To successfully complete the assignment they had to engage in historical literacies, such as sorting through the sources, evaluating the reliability of each source, corroborating patterns found across multiple texts, determining significance, and writing. Composing their paragraphs involved many elements of historical thinking.

Second, Mr. Johnson had students use their expository writing to critique a textbook account. Students' experience writing gave them insight into the process that the textbook author might go through in selecting material for inclusion, and in the word choices that he/she made. Students' experience in writing expository text gave them expertise that allowed them to be more critical of the textbook author, questioning his/her decisions of what to include or omit from the textbook account. Their experience helped them to see that textbook narratives do not simply contain the facts, and that information in textbooks should not be accepted at face value, but like all other historical accounts, textbooks have a context and a subtext and should be subject to the same evaluation that all historical texts undergo. Their use of the textbook was tempered by a healthy skepticism.

Chapter Summary

Historians approach textbooks with the same healthy skepticism with which they approach all historical texts. Students, on the other hand, trust textbooks, primarily because of the way they are written and the way they are used. Teachers can facilitate students' critical analysis of textbooks and other expository texts by understanding the nature of expository texts, by shifting the focus of assignments from remembering information to questioning why authors have included what they have, and by helping students consider the context and subtext of expository texts. Teachers must carefully design assessments to avoid the uncritical acceptance of the historical facts that textbooks contain. Further, the writing of historians can be used to introduce students to historiography and to foster a healthy skepticism. Mr. Johnson serves as a model of a teacher who helps students critique expository texts by drafting alternative expository texts.

10

AVOIDING REDUCTIONIST THINKING WITH AUDIO AND VIDEO TEXTS

Ms. Chavez is planning to teach a lesson on social trends of the 1920s in her U.S. history class. She wants to focus specifically on the clash between traditional rural society and dynamic urban culture. She feels like this clash between tradition and change is an ongoing phenomena in American history – something that her students can relate to today. She wants to help students recognize the problems that can arise from clinging to some traditions or abandoning others. She knows that her high school students have great interest in music so she decides to use jazz music as the medium through which students can explore the clash between tradition and change in the 1920s. She gathers recordings of several jazz songs, intending to play short clips for students. She also gathers recordings of popular songs from the 1920s that would not be considered jazz. As she collects resources she finds other primary sources, written during the 1920s, voicing various opinions about jazz music. She decides to spend some time with the students helping them discover the unique characteristics of jazz music and then have them debate whether the 1920s should be called "the Jazz Age." It dawns on her that this might be an appropriate time to introduce students to the problems of reductionist thinking by talking about the flaws of historical labels, such as "the Jazz Age."

Ms. Chavez establishes the following objectives for her lesson on "the Jazz Age."

1. Students will identify the characteristics of jazz music, including the types of musical instruments commonly used; the role of improvisation and individual interpretation; the combination of a soloist's melody and the rhythm section's countermelody; and the various genres of jazz music, such as Dixieland, blues, and swing.

2. Students will explore the reaction to jazz music in the 1920s and the clash between tradition and change, debating whether the 1920s should be called "the Jazz Age."

3. Students will be exposed to the flaws of historical labels, such as the "Jazz Age," considering forms of popular music of the 1920s that provided an alternative to jazz.

Ms. Chavez finds a number of jazz songs and other popular tunes from the 1920s on "Youtube" and other Internet sites. She will use some songs as examples of jazz music. She will use other popular songs of the 1920s as counter-examples. In addition, she makes copies of magazine articles criticizing jazz music (Faulkner, 1921) and defending the flappers' lifestyle (Page, 1922). She also finds a short animated movie produced in 1936 that captures the conflict between traditional music and jazz music (Schlesinger & Avery, 1936).

Ms. Chavez starts class with a "concept attainment" activity, a way for students to inductively discover some of the defining characteristics of jazz music. She explains to students that she is going to play some examples of a certain type of music, each example followed by a counter-example. She tells them that she is not necessarily looking for a name of the type of music, but for the common characteristics found in all of the examples. The students must try to figure out what all of the examples have in common and how they differ from the counter-examples. She starts by playing one minute of Louis Armstrong's *When the Saints Go Marching In* (1968), while the students listen. She then plays the counter-example of Gene Austin's *Carolina Moon* (Burke & Davis, 1928). After playing the second audio clip she asks students to identify the differences between the first and second recording.

"The first one has a faster beat," James offers.

"The first one has different instruments – a trumpet and a trombone, I think," Andrew guesses.

"Let's play a couple more songs and see if you notice more differences," Ms. Chavez says. She plays one minute of *When You're Smiling* by Louis Armstrong (Shay, Fisher, & Goodwin, 1929) followed by one minute of *I'll Be with You in Apple Blossom Time* by the Andrew Sisters (Tilzer & Fleeson, 1920).

"I think it's the same singer in both of the examples," suggests Jacob, with several other students voicing their agreement.

"Any other theories?" Ms. Chavez probes.

"All of the examples are old," offers Kathy.

"Yeah, but all of the counter-examples are old too," responds Sam.

"Oh yeah, it was just a guess," Kathy admits.

Ms. Chavez steps in, "That's right, Sam. All of the songs – both examples and counter-examples – became popular within about a ten-year span of time. What about James' idea of the faster beat?"

"The last example you gave didn't have a very fast beat," James admits. "But the examples all have a cool rhythm. They're all jazzier."

"Do the rest of you agree with this?" Ms. Chavez allows several students to comment on James' idea about a cool rhythm. "How about Andrew's comment about the different instruments? Listen to a couple of more examples and counter-examples and see if his idea checks out." Ms. Chavez alternates between playing an example and a counter-example, pausing for more discussion after each pair. Eventually students rule out Jacob's idea of a common singer in all of the examples, and become quite certain that the examples are all jazz music. They have identified common instruments in jazz bands and have found that there is a wild and free feel to the jazz music.

"They aren't reading the music but making it up as they go," Amber suggests.

"So you say there is some improvisation going on?" Ms. Chavez helps Amber with more formal vocabulary.

Ms. Chavez fills in a few other gaps in the students' definitions of jazz music, discussing the revolving role of the soloist and the rhythm section. Once the characteristics of jazz have been identified, Ms. Chavez asks the class to see if they can identify each characteristic as she plays a video of the first jazz song students heard, *When the Saints Go Marching In*. She projects the video of the musicians and singers, which makes the characteristics more obvious. "Go ahead and call out what you see as the video is playing."

"There are all of the instruments we talked about," James points out as soon as the video starts. "Piano, trumpet, trombone."

"They're not reading music – they're just making it up as they go," Callie observes. "They're improvising."

"They're taking turns soloing," Amber calls out.

"And listen to the lady singing. She's not even singing words," observes Malia. "She's singing nonsense."

"I don't want to sound rude," starts Peter, "but does race have anything to do with jazz music? This band is mostly Black."

"That's a good observation, Peter. We'll talk more about that tomorrow," responds Ms. Chavez.

The students are highly engaged, so Ms. Chavez plays the entire song. After showing the video, she makes a transition into the larger issue of tradition and change. "How do you think people responded to jazz music like this?"

"I think they loved it. The other stuff was so boring. It sounds like what my grandma listens to," suggests Ben.

"Do you think everyone loved it?" Ms. Chavez questions.

Sandra answers, "I'll bet people had different taste in music then like they do now. I bet some people hated it."

Ms. Chavez explains a new assignment. Students will read two opposing viewpoints written in the 1920s about jazz music. She reminds them to consider the source and context of each article as they read. After reading and discussing in small groups, they'll write a paragraph explaining whether the nickname, "the Jazz Age," is an appropriate label for the era. Ms. Chavez passes out the materials and circulates as students read them.

"So what do you know about the lady that wrote this?" Amber asks, as Ms. Chavez walks by, referring to the woman who wrote the criticism of jazz music (Faulkner, 1921).

"What difference does it make who she was?" Ms. Chavez replies, playing devil's advocate.

"Well she's probably White and just doesn't like it because she's racist," Amber explains.

"Maybe. I wonder whether there were African Americans who didn't like jazz, or whether it was just a handful of White racists that didn't like it, " Ms. Chavez questions.

"Can I get on your computer and see if I can find out about this Faulkner lady?" Amber asks.

Amber goes to Ms. Chavez's computer and the other students continue to read, discuss, and write. After a few minutes, Ms. Chavez takes a straw pole of the class to see whether the name "Jazz Age" fits the era, finding that the students are fairly evenly divided. She calls on one student from each side to argue his/her point. After a few minutes of discussion, she asks, "What is the problem with calling this time period the Jazz Age?"

"I don't think there was a problem at all," answers Amber. "Jazz was a new type of music and it was popular with a lot of people so I think it fits."

"Yeah, but it makes it sound like jazz was the only kind of music from this time period," argues Ben. "And we heard a lot of songs that weren't jazz that were just as popular in the 1920s. Calling it the 'Jazz Age' ignores all of the other music."

"Where did the name 'Jazz Age' start?" asks Chelsey. "Who thought it up?"

Ms. Chavez gets a puzzled look. "I don't know where that name came from. Now that you ask, I wonder whether people called it the 'Jazz Age' during the 1920s or whether that's a name that historians or other people just came up with later on. I'll look into it and see what I can find out."

As the discussion continues, the main argument students come up with against the title "Jazz Age" is that jazz music wasn't the only form of popular music of the period. Ms. Chavez agrees, suggesting that historical labels are a form of "reductionist thinking" that people often engage in. She writes the words *reductionist thinking* on the board.

"Reductionist thinking is oversimplifying the past. Sometimes we forget about how diverse people's taste in music was during the 1920s because we use the label 'Jazz Age.' Historical labels like 'Jazz Age' are useful for helping us make sense of a time period, but they are also flawed because they oversimplify things. Calling the 1920s 'the Jazz Age' might give the impression that jazz was the only form of music in America during the time – which we've learned isn't true."

Continuing the lesson on reductionist thinking, she explains, "Historical labels create an oversimplified sense of history, sometimes forgetting the point of view of minorities, or, in the case of jazz, ignoring less interesting trends. Historians create labels for time periods, like the Jazz Age or the Stone Age; for groups of people, like the Robber Barons or the Mound Builders; or places, like the Dust Bowl or Bible Belt. The key thing to remember about labels like these is that there are almost always exceptions to general trends. Do you remember the Mound Builders we studied at the start of the year? They didn't wander around all day making piles of dirt. The most noticeable features of their civilization for us today are the large mounds of dirt they built. So we sometimes refer to them as the Mound Builders, but that was certainly only a small part of their culture. So again, you should remember that historical labels help us make sense of a time period, but they can cause us to forget or ignore things that don't fit in with the label. Historical labels are one type of reductionist thinking and we'll talk about more later in the year."

At the end of class she shows the animated movie, *I love to singa*, which captures the clash between traditional music and jazz (Schlesinger & Avery, 1936). Before showing it she asks students to consider the source and whether the producers of the cartoon were more inclined to listen to jazz music or to traditional music. After showing the video, she previews the next day's lesson. "Tomorrow we're going to continue to consider the idea of tradition versus change and we'll get back to Peter's observation about race and jazz music."

Patterns in Reductionist Thinking

In this chapter I explore two elements that were addressed in Ms. Chavez's lesson. First, I consider reductionist thinking, warning about specific examples that are common in history classrooms. Second, I discuss the use of video and audio resources, like the music and the video clips that Ms. Chavez used. I explore potential audio and video resources, three different purposes for showing videos, challenges students face in working with audio and video texts, and ways that teachers can promote historical thinking by having students create audio and video texts.

Reductionist Thinking

Reductionism is an effort to explain complex processes in terms of the inter-action between simpler, fundamental parts. There is something appealing about explaining history in simple terms. For instance, in his extremely popular book, *Guns, Germs, and Steel*, amateur historian Jared Diamond explains the economic inequalities between modern societies as a result of relatively simple geographic factors such as the north-south or east-west alignment of continents (1999). Many historians have been critical of his work, however; true historical literacy requires the ability to understand and appreciate a complexity that is absent from his analysis. For purposes of this chapter, and, ironically, in simplifying this element of historical literacy for working with students, reductionism is defined as any effort to simplify historical content and/or causation in order to avoid historical complexity. Reductionism is the tendency to reduce history to the single narrative contained in textbooks by eliminating the disorder that is inherent when alternative viewpoints, exceptions to rules, and multiple interpretations are allowed. One of the challenges of building students' historical literacies is helping them understand the complex nature of historical causation, changes, trends, and events (Gaddis, 2002), without overwhelming them.

Reductionist traps must be avoided in building students' historical literacies for many of the same reasons that teachers must address students' epistemic stance. If history is viewed as a single narrative to be remembered, then explaining it in simple chains of cause and effect, and dividing it up into clean categories with clear labels makes the task more manageable. However, since history is constructed through the skillful use of multiple pieces of evidence, with diverse perspectives being recognized, then multiple narratives must be considered. Categories and labels must be open to critique. Minority perspectives must be included. And, exceptions to general trends should be acknowledged. Building students' historical literacies requires teachers, like Ms. Chavez, to introduce increasing complexity into their history classrooms. For her, the "Jazz Age" continues to serve as a framework around which to build an understanding of the 1920s. However, the students' analysis of 1920s music (both popular and jazz) gives them a more complete picture of the clash of culture that developed during the decade.

In traditional history classrooms teachers oversimplify historical complexity quite often. This statement is not meant to be critical of teachers – in fact, in light of the emphasis on learning historical facts in many educational settings, wise teachers have found ways to simplify, categorize, and label in order to help students manage the volume of historical facts they are expected to remember. However, as teachers shift the emphasis of history teaching away from the exclusive learning of historical facts toward the skilled use of historical texts, they must also expose students to the greater complexities of thinking historically. If building historical literacy is an objective of a history class, then minority perspectives must be included in evidence sets, exceptions to general trends must be acknowledged, and historical assumptions must be critiqued.

Common Examples of Reductionist Thinking

In the vignette, Ms. Chavez pointed out to her students one example of reductionist thinking – historical labeling. Other examples of reductionist thinking that often occur, and are sometimes promoted, in history classrooms include categorization, stereotyping, stagnation, viewing outcomes as inevitable, dualism, single or simplified causation, looking for *the* answer (Lesh, 2011), group personi-fication (Barton, 2010), the expectation of linear narrative progression toward the present (Barton, 1996), and ignoring minority viewpoints. Each of these will be considered.

Historical Labeling

Historians are adept at giving labels to historical eras, i.e. "Jazz Age" or "Stone Age:" locations, i.e. "Fertile Crescent" or "Balkan Powder Keg;" and groups of people, i.e. "Robber Barons" or "Mound Builders." While doing so, historians understand the dangers of such labels: reducing complex trends, places, and people to a single prominent attribute. Historians remain open-minded about the char-acteristics of eras, places, and people who carry such labels. For example, the Stone Age is so named because most of the artifacts that remain from that time period are made of stone. However, historians understand that this is a trick of evidence rather than the realities of the era. They recognize that societies' technologies changed over the tens of thousands of years and the thousands of miles of their migrations. Stone Age humans used cords, textiles, baskets, ceramics, animal skins, bone, and stone tools in different locations at different times. Few non-stone artifacts remain, but the stone artifacts give clues as to the other technologies that people possessed (Angier, 1999). Aware of the risk of historical labels, Ms. Chavez's lesson plan explores the label the "Jazz Age" to help students appreciate the diverse forms of popular music at the time. Ms. Chavez helps students see that traditional music continued to be popular even as a new type of music gained fans. In doing so she is preparing students to discuss the clash between tradition and cultural change during the 1920s.

Categorization

Categorization is another way teachers help students manage historical infor-mation. Just as combining bits of information into "chunks" can serve as a mem-ory aid, creating categories as an organizational framework can help students understand and remember historical content. For instance, when I taught about Franklin D. Roosevelt's New Deal, I discussed its purposes in terms of the three Rs: relief, recovery, and reform. Following an introduction to this framework, I would have students consider several of the alphabet agencies and categorize each based on its purpose: to provide relief, to help the economy recover, or to make needed reforms to avoid future economic calamities. However, I acknowledged that most alphabet agencies served more than a single purpose. Thus, while categorization was a helpful way of thinking about the New Deal, I tried to help students see that the categories do not capture the complexity of the agencies. Like most categorization systems, it oversimplifies the historical complexity.

Stereotyping

One particularly dangerous way of categorizing is through stereotyping, assuming that all individuals within a group possess the same characteristics. Often history teachers address stereotyping by attempting to replace negative stereotypes with positive stereotypes rather than addressing the real issue – stereotyping reduces the complexity of trying to comprehend a spectrum of individual personalities into a more manageable but less accurate understanding of group dynamics. In the vignette in Chapter 5, for example, Mr. Richins helped students see that not all Native Americans – even within the same tribe – reacted the same way to the arrival of colonists. Additionally, often stereotypes include racist or sexist notions that reflect the traits of a small sample of individuals within and across groups. Stereotyping can lead to ahistorical thinking. For example, Wineburg (2001) found that students misidentified an image of a peace-protester during the Vietnam War because he did not fit the stereotypical "hippie" image. Pop culture creates simplistic images of racial groups, women, soldiers, pioneers, Pilgrims, hippies, and countless others, which misrepresent and oversimplify the complexities of understanding the past.

Stagnation

One specific type of stereotyping is viewing a group of people as unchanging over time. History teachers often present an oversimplified account of history by failing to consider the changes that occurred within societies, presenting instead the story of stagnant, unchanging peoples. They do this by focusing on groups at a particularly interesting time and failing to acknowledge the lifestyles of peoples at different times. Egyptians were always building pyramids and mummifying their pharaohs. Native Americans rode horses and hunted buffalo. The Europeans built castles, wore armor, and erected cathedrals. The Romans watched gladiator fights and sent their legions to battle barbarians and rebellious subjects. When teachers fail to acknowledge how cultures changed over time, students get a distorted view of history. Instead, when studying Native Americans, for example, a teacher must not only address issues of diversity by considering *where* they lived, but also by considering *when* they lived. Native American cultures changed significantly over time due to technological development, the spread of agriculture, climate change, the rise and fall of Native American empires, the spread of European diseases, access to horses and other European livestock, and numerous other factors. Without exception, people's culture changes over time and history teachers must avoid presenting snapshots of stagnant, unchanging people.

Viewing Outcomes as Inevitable

Approaching historical events with hindsight creates the illusion that the outcomes of historical events were inevitable. Part of the process of contextualization, showing historical empathy, and taking a historical perspective is understanding that historical characters faced uncertain outcomes. Patriots did not know whether the United States would win its struggle for independence. Many pioneers in the fight for women's rights did not see women vote. Muhammad could have had no idea when he led a handful of followers to Medina that his teachings would change the world. Part of the valor of historic heroes is that they persevered in the face of uncertainty. Students sometimes forget that things did not have to turn out the way that they did. Further, students can find fault with historical actors, forgetting that they did not have the advantage of hindsight that those who study history have.

Dualism

Students, particularly young students, tend to see the world in dualistic terms of black or white, good or evil, and helpful or harmful (Nokes, 2011). They have a difficult time acknowledging that men like Thomas Jefferson, who Americans revere, owned slaves, or that Hitler's policies improved Germany's depressed economy. In an effort to categorize policies as good or bad, students fail to see that many policies that favor one group hurt other groups. It is difficult to find policies that face no opposition. I found that the Reconstruction period following the Civil War is an ideal time to help students face the problems of dualistic labeling – their tendency to label something as good or bad. For instance, during the early years of Reconstruction, Lincoln's policy of leniency toward former Confederates was often praised by my students as "good." As a nation, America celebrates the words from Lincoln's second inaugural address, "with malice toward none, with charity for all" (Lincoln, 1865). However, it was impossible to show mercy to the former slave owners without disadvantaging the former slaves. When students realize that Lincoln's proposed policies left most former slaves in a dire position without food, jobs, homes, or education, they begin to understand the complexity of Reconstruction. The issues the government faced were not about whether or not to have mercy, but were about to whom they would show mercy. Decisions during Reconstruction are one of many opportunities to confront dualistic thinking by showing students that things are rarely absolutely right or wrong or exclusively good or bad.

Single or Simplified Causation

Often students, with the aid of their history teacher, identify a causal chain, i.e. a single cause leading to a single event, which then causes a new event, and so forth. Most teachers know that causal chains create a logical system for remembering the relationship between historical events, much superior to memorizing a random list of facts (Bransford, Brown, & Cocking, 2000). However, causal chains oversimplify the complexity of relationships between historical events. Instead of a chain, historians would be more likely to use the metaphor of a causal network to represent the multiple interlinked causes that lead to multiple interlinked effects. The notion of a network creates more room for individual interpretation and debate about the relative strength of diverse causal strands and the relationship between effects. Further, the image of a network leaves room for students to consider potential effects that were unrealized (Gaddis, 2002). Avoiding the reduction of a complex network of related events into a single causal chain sets the stage for students to use historical literacies in debate and argumentative writing.

Looking for the Answer

Bruce Lesh (2011) suggests that another way teachers reduce historical complexity is by laying out a curriculum that directs students to a single correct answer. Instead, he suggests that teachers allow students to interact with evidence in a way that promotes questioning and diverse interpretations. He acknowledges that initially students feel frustrated when placed in a situation that requires them to develop original interpretations. But he describes how teachers can ease students into a position where they ask questions themselves and contemplate multiple possible answers. For instance, he describes an activity during which he gives students a series of straightforward questions about the Nat Turner slave rebellion then gives different students each a different text with which to answer the questions. As students come together in groups they find that their peers have different answers, at first perceived to be "wrong." He then provides groups of students the source information for the texts that they originally read, a process that helps them understand why conflicting answers exist. Lesh shows that it is questions rather than answers that should drive the history curriculum. He concludes that this and other similar activities, which give students a degree of agency in choosing how to interpret the past, "changed the atmosphere in [his] classroom" (50), energizing both his students and him, increasing students' content knowledge, and building students' historical literacies. Students need to be weaned away from the expectation of a single, textbook-driven historical narrative.

Group Personification

Keith Barton (2010) discovered that students often adopt simplistic notions of historical agency, projecting the traits of individuals onto groups, in particular to nations. For instance, during a unit on World War II he found that students in New Zealand commonly made statements, such as "New Zealand feared Japan." When questioned, they began to realize that they didn't know what this meant. Certainly not all of the people of New Zealand feared all of the people of Japan. Did they mean that individuals within the government of New Zealand feared Japanese military aggression? Or did they mean that the majority of the people of New Zealand were afraid? Can a nation feel fear or other human emotions?

Barton found that students' language repeatedly demonstrated a distorted view of agency by describing individuals' actions as a nation's. Barton suggests that students should be questioned when they make comments such as "Europeans were becoming curious …" or "America was upset over the tax on tea …", which reduce the range of opinions that typically exist on any issue into a single continent- or nation-wide response.

Expecting Linear Progression toward the Present

Students often understand history as a linear progression from less civilized times through increasingly enlightened societies, culminating in the present. For Americans, the United States is viewed as the crowning achievement of this constant and consistent progress. The manner that Western Civilization courses have been taught through the years perpetuates this reductionist view of progress: civilization was born in Mesopotamia, nurtured in Egypt, flowered in Greece and Rome, and, after a short Medieval Period, during which barbarians attempted to destroy it, was reborn during the European Renaissance, eventually being transplanted to America where it reached its full potential. During each era, earlier technologies were improved upon and more enlightened ideas were developed. Achievements in non-Western societies were, more or less, failed attempts at being Western and are relegated to the fringes of historical interest. In contrast, historians understand that history includes many more rises and falls, false starts, wrong turns, and enlightened ideas being replaced by less enlightened ideas. Although there are certainly patterns, and even global patterns at times, the trajectory of different societies often lies in different directions, some of which would be considered progress and some of which, including some modern changes, would be considered regression. Students with the distorted view of history-as-progress are less likely to be able to engage in historical empathy, an important element of historical literacy described in Chapter 8.

Ignoring Minority Viewpoints

"Balboa was the first person to see the Pacific Ocean." Although students might say this, they will quickly admit their error when reminded that people lived throughout the Pacific Islands millennia before Balboa was born. However, there are much more subtle ways through which minority perspectives are eliminated from students' study. For example, most U.S. history teachers include a unit on "western expansion," failing to acknowledge that such a title ignores the perspective of Native Americans or the Spanish living in the West – for them the unit would be called "eastern encroachment." Ms. Chavez, in the vignette, attempted to expose students to the perspective of Americans who embraced Jazz music as well as those who opposed it. Her purpose was to help students explore alternative perspectives that might be ignored in a typical unit on the 1920s.

Using Audio and Video Texts as Evidence

Potential Audio and Video Resources

Some have argued that today's young people are growing up in a visual world (Lesh, 2011). They are also growing up in an aural world. Never before in world history has sound, particularly music, been more accessible on demand to a wider range of people. The Internet makes available diverse audio texts that can be used as evidence in constructing and defending historical interpretations. Ms. Chavez felt that jazz music and other popular music of the 1920s – not the lyrics, but the music itself – was useful evidence in analyzing the clash between tradition and change during the Jazz Age.

There is something exciting and engaging in working with audio texts. For example, although the words used in Martin Luther King's "I Have a Dream" speech demonstrate his genius, his masterful delivery, which can be shown through audio or, even better, video recordings, reveals a force that students might miss in simply analyzing his words. Twentieth-century historical evidence includes a wealth of recorded speeches, radio broadcasts, music, debates, and historical sounds. Video recordings, further, make available similar evidence with the added resources of clothing styles, body movements, facial expressions, etc. Audio and video texts, as well as other visual texts, can supplement traditional written texts in ways that make primary source collections come to life. For instance, in studying the popularity of Ronald Reagan, students might conduct a case study of the assassination attempt during which he sustained life-threatening injuries (Fiso, unpublished). They could listen to and watch a video recording of the attempt itself, analyze still photographs of the event, read newspaper articles from the time, analyze official documents summarizing the government investigation, and watch a video recording of Reagan's subsequent State of the Union address. They might also critique secondary sources dealing with the assassination attempt.

Additionally, students who struggle with traditional reading can often decode and comprehend audio and video texts. Incorporating audio and video sources can invite poor readers into historical thinking activities.

Three Different Purposes for Showing Videos

It should be pointed out that although videos can be an outstanding source of evidence they are not typically viewed as historical evidence by teachers or students. There are three content-related purposes for showing videos in a history classroom that correspond roughly with the traditional purposes of using of textbooks, historical fiction, and historical evidence.

Videos as Expository Teaching

First, documentary videos, which history teachers are notorious for showing, are typically used for expository teaching. Documentary videos are typically used to convey to students information similar to other traditional methods of expository teaching: lecture and textbook reading. Teachers sometimes give students a worksheet or other assignment to help them manage the information presented in the video – similar to what they would do to help students manage the information presented in a lecture or during a textbook reading assignment. Commonly, students' role in working with documentary videos is to receive and remember information and to prepare to regurgitate it during assessments. In most classrooms this is the most common use of videos and the least helpful in nurturing students' historical literacies. Instead, teachers might foster critical thinking about the content of documentary videos in a similar manner to the methods recommended for critiquing textbooks in Chapter 9.

Videos as Historical Fiction

Teachers sometimes show Hollywood-produced, entertainment movies. These types of movies, like historical fiction, can be a good way to help students engage in contextualization by immersing them in a historical time period. However, the utility of entertainment movies depends on the quality of research that went into the production of the movie as well as the preparation that teachers give students to learn with them. Similar issues arise in the use of entertainment movies as develop when students are exposed to historical fiction (see Chapter 8). For example, can they distinguish accurate from fictitious elements of the story? Additionally, research has shown that students have a difficult time critically analyzing historical movies. As described earlier, Seixas (1993) found that students mistakenly judged a movie "more realistic" when the characters in the movie reacted to situations in a manner similar to the way the students would react, rather than in a way that reflected the values and standards of people within the historical context being portrayed. In other words, students are drawn to characters who are more like them than to characters who reflect the traits of historical people. Teachers can help students learn with entertainment videos using many of the same techniques described in Chapter 8 for working with historical fiction.

Videos as Historical Evidence

In contrast to using videos to convey information or to immerse students in a historical context, Ms. Chavez used the recording of Louis Armstrong's band playing *When the Saints Go Marching In* as historical evidence, part of a collection of resources on jazz music. Such use of video texts requires students to use many of the same strategies they use in working with other artifacts (see Chapter 6) and primary sources (see Chapter 5). Using video texts as evidence presents a challenge to students because they might be inclined to believe that a video, like a photograph, simply captures a moment of reality. However, video texts, like all other texts, have a source, an intended audience, a purpose, and a context, all of which are useful in interpreting their content. It is possible to corroborate across texts, and use the other heuristics and habits of mind associated with historical thinking when working with video texts.

For example, when I taught about the psychological effects of the Cold War on the American people, I showed excerpts from the movie *Rocky IV* (Brubaker & Stalone, 1985) as an artifact from 1985 America. Students could make observations as they watch clips from the movie, and then make inferences about American attitudes about the Soviet Union using the movie as evidence. What was the message that the producers of the movie were trying to send? What can historians infer about an American (and a global) audience that was drawn to the movie? As with the use of more traditional texts, there were things that I did to help students with their analysis. At times I would stop the movie and show still photographs to allow students to engage in something akin to "close reading." By doing so, students could pay attention to details, decoding such things as the color in the background or the facial expressions of secondary characters, that they might otherwise miss when the movie was being played at normal speed. I allowed students to discuss their ideas in groups and provided students with a graphic organizer, the O/I chart described in Chapter 7, with a place to record observations and inferences. I provided other documents for students to use to corroborate their movie-based interpretations.

The use of videos for this third purpose, as historical evidence, is rare in history classrooms. Providing students with multiple opportunities to work with video artifacts in connection with other genres of evidence, coupled with explicit reminders about strategy use, can foster historical thinking and make the history content more memorable. Using videos as evidence is a much nobler purpose than simply conveying historical information to students, as they are normally used. They can be used to build students' historical literacies.

Overcoming Challenges in Using Audio Texts

Students face unique challenges in learning with audio texts. In some instances they might have trouble decoding or comprehending the literal meaning of texts. Old recordings might be poor in quality or the recordings might capture people talking quickly or with distracting background noise or, as with any text, using unfamiliar vocabulary or subtle, unnoticed symbols. As with all texts, if students cannot decode or comprehend the literal meaning of an oral or video text, they cannot engage in a critical analysis of it. Non-native English speakers experience particular difficulty in listening to muffled recordings of spoken English, or, as with any text, cultural references of which they have no background knowledge.

For instance, I would sometimes play for students an audio recording of Abbott and Costello's "Who's on First" routine as part of an analysis of the changing nature of humor during the 20th century. However, some students could not comprehend the quick, whiney voice of Costello. Others did not have knowledge of baseball positions. I supported students' code breaking and meaning making by building background knowledge, providing vocabulary instruction, and giving students a transcript of the dialogue to read as they listened.

There are several other things that a teacher can do to help students get more out of their use of oral and video texts. Ms. Chavez, for example, provided multiple opportunities to learn with the texts. Much of her lesson was designed to help students "decode" jazz music, identifying its defining features. If students could not distinguish the elements of jazz after the first recording, they might do so after the second, third, fourth, or fifth example. She exposed students to one song twice – once early in the activity and once at the end, to reinforce key points. Like Ms. Chavez, teachers can play a song or a recorded speech multiple times, with students focused on different elements – perhaps the words the first time and the delivery the second time. Unlike some other types of texts, there is often a need for students to hear oral texts multiple times in order to fully decode and comprehend. Additionally, teachers can provide students with written transcripts of speeches or song lyrics. Both non-native English speakers and English speakers benefit from being able to follow along with the words. Depending on instructional objectives, a teacher might play a recording once to try to recreate the context, with students listening as individuals would have at the time that the speech was delivered, then play it a second time after giving students a written transcript, with students listening as a historian.

With oral texts or video texts it is wise for teachers to pause the text from time to time to allow students to summarize, discuss particular details, or offer critique, much as a teacher might have students pause in reading a traditional text. In the vignette, Ms. Chavez interspersed exposure to the audio recordings with opportunities for students to discuss what they were hearing. She knew that as with analysis of most historical resources, students need time to think deeply and to make interpretations with audio texts.

Promoting Historical Thinking with Student-Produced Audio and Video Texts

The increasing availability of digital technologies, combined with students' increasing experience producing digital and audio recordings, creates a setting where history teachers can assign students to produce oral and video texts. Almost any assignment that students can record, revise, and edit in traditional, written format can be produced in a video format that might be more appealing to create and easier to publish with peers. For instance, currently, the National History Day competition includes a category for documentary video. Students' interpretive videos are judged based on many of the same criteria with which historical writing is evaluated, such as students' use of primary source evidence, critique of sources, and historical analysis. With the expanded notion of texts that is used throughout this book, it follows that the literate act of writing should also be expanded to include the creation of the genres of texts valued by 21st century teens, including audio and video texts.

Chapter Summary

Ms. Chavez has found outstanding texts for teaching about the clash between tradition and change in the 1920s: samples of music from the period. As part of the lesson she attacks the reductionist trap of historical labeling by teaching students that the label of "Jazz Age" can create a distorted understanding of the 1920s. She will find other times during the school year when students can be warned about other reductionist traps, such as dualism, simplified causal chains, and ignoring minority perspectives. She has pulled together primarily oral and video resources to use as historical evidence and has built into her lesson multiple opportunities to listen, knowing that students might struggle to fully decode and comprehend an oral text in a single exposure. She uses a video as historical evidence, rather than in the more traditional use of video as expository text or as historical fiction. Thus her lesson pulls together several elements that nurture code breaking, meaning making, text use and text critique in her ongoing quest to build students' historical literacies.

11

BUILDING AN ARGUMENT WITH QUANTITATIVE HISTORICAL EVIDENCE

Mr. Erikson is planning a unit on industrialization, immigration, and urbanization for his 11th grade U.S. history course. He realizes that statistical records allow historians to explore the past using unique tools and methods. He wants to introduce students to some of these techniques. As he discusses his ideas with one of the other history teachers, his colleague recommends that he look at a census from the early 1900s. She is quite certain that he'll be able to find census figures that have to do with immigration. As Mr. Erikson explores, he finds a table from the 1910 census showing the number of foreign-born people living in the United States (Durand & Harris, 1913). The table breaks down the number of immigrants by their native country and region or state of residence. Students can find, for example, how many German immigrants lived in New York in 1910 and whether that number had increased or decreased since 1900 or 1890. Browsing the table, he realizes that there are a nearly limitless number of possible comparisons that his students could make to explore immigration trends (see Figure 11.1).

Mr. Erikson has found a great text for discovering immigration trends. Next he considers the support his students will need to decode, comprehend, use, and critique it. He realizes that the layout of the table might not be easy for some students to read. It even takes him a few minutes of reflection to realize that the numbers do not indicate the number of new immigrants during a ten-year period, but instead show a cumulative figure. The same people were counted in subsequent decades if they continued to live in the same location. As he struggles to decode and comprehend the meanings of the numbers, Mr. Erikson realizes how difficult it's going to be to help students decode the census, let alone use it as historical evidence. He determines that during the first part of his lesson he will need to provide strategy instruction on how to decode it.

834   POPULATION.

FOREIGN-BORN POPULATION BY COU[NTRY]

| Table 33 | | | PERSONS BORN IN— | | | | | | | | | | | |
| | | | Northwestern Europe. | | | | | | | | | | | |
DIVISION OR STATE AND CENSUS YEAR.	Total foreign born.		Eng-land.	Scot-land.	Wales.	Ireland.	Ger-many.[1]	Nor-way.	Swe-den.	Den-mark.	Neth-er-lands.	Bel-gium.	Lux-em-burg.	Fran[ce]
UNITED STATES														
1 1910	13,515,886		877,719	261,076	82,488	1,352,251	2,501,333	403,877	665,207	181,649	120,063	49,400	3,071	117,
2 1900	10,341,276		840,513	233,524	93,586	1,615,459	2,813,628	336,388	582,014	153,690	94,931	29,757	3,031	104,
3 1890	9,249,560		909,092	242,231	100,079	1,871,509	2,784,894	322,665	478,041	132,543	81,828	22,639	2,982	113,
4 1880	6,679,943		664,160	170,136	83,302	1,854,571	1,966,742	181,729	194,337	64,196	58,090	15,535	12,836	106,
5 1870	5,567,229		555,046	140,835	74,533	1,855,827	1,690,533	114,246	97,332	30,107	46,802	12,553	5,802	116,
GEOGRAPHIC DIVISIONS														
NEW ENGLAND:														
6 1910	1,825,110		155,932	48,421	3,702	334,486	70,267	8,448	70,777	7,689	2,144	3,264	13	10,
7 1900	1,445,237		139,087	42,157	3,909	387,570	73,814	5,244	59,415	6,058	1,278	1,168	7	7,
8 1890	1,142,432		133,569	38,896	3,603	412,846	63,022	3,927	35,821	3,958	817	647	8	6,
9 1880	793,612		84,822	23,208	2,265	370,749	36,338	1,051	8,805	1,397	796	343	42	3,
10 1870	648,001		65,044	17,319	1,791	360,299	28,030	543	2,031	541	675	158	5	2,
MIDDLE ATLANTIC:														
11 1910	4,351,173		306,360	88,995	37,921	615,756	754,993	32,684	87,719	20,637	26,581	10,601	162	39,
12 1900	3,317,559		295,944	78,459	43,952	720,306	848,030	16,290	74,175	15,176	20,312	7,116	146	34,
13 1890	2,745,746		318,352	80,576	47,478	828,270	835,299	12,157	51,935	11,239	16,942	5,136	92	34,
14 1880	2,020,903		228,110	56,434	37,533	829,029	589,274	2,795	20,361	5,354	13,748	2,095	672	32,
15 1870	1,872,605		207,074	49,838	36,294	851,388	531,049	1,180	8,342	2,772	10,189	1,574	365	34,
EAST NORTH CENTRAL:														
16 1910	3,073,766		170,189	48,718	18,259	179,266	921,443	99,192	178,140	42,875	59,661	22,925	1,092	19,
17 1900	2,625,226		181,843	47,065	22,122	238,613	1,073,976	100,159	170,923	40,498	52,215	14,629	1,101	20,
18 1890	2,510,924		211,758	51,250	22,997	287,815	1,054,278	104,626	141,291	33,938	47,095	11,003	711	26,
19 1880	1,916,630		177,554	43,823	24,566	307,331	782,552	70,199	64,272	19,564	31,710	8,967	4,906	28,
20 1870	1,661,674		164,475	41,205	23,749	322,026	691,172	53,629	37,616	10,876	25,620	7,808	2,773	35,
WEST NORTH CENTRAL:														
21 1910	1,616,695		69,052	21,817	7,840	78,614	426,539	198,786	213,531	63,910	21,010	6,146	1,472	9,
22 1900	1,533,248		78,526	25,058	9,615	111,192	496,096	185,413	207,946	59,347	16,560	3,849	1,523	10,

FIGURE 11.1 A portion of a table from the 1910 census.
Source: Durand & Harris (1913).

Next, Mr. Erikson considers how he is going to have students use the census to construct and defend historical interpretations. What background information will he need to give? Do 11th grade students know what a census is, or how census data is gathered? He also starts to think about what he wants students to discover as they work with the table. He wants them to understand the major trends in immigration, particularly the patterns that historians have labeled "old immigration" and "new immigration." In reviewing the census, he can find powerful evidence of these immigration trends. He wonders how he can lead students to make those same discoveries. With so many numbers on the page he anticipates that students' attention might be scattered or misdirected. The challenge, he decides, lies in helping students attend to those numbers that represent the important trends he wants them to "discover." But, he also wants to let students explore freely, raise their own questions about statistics they see, and, perhaps, make new discoveries about immigration trends. He creates a study guide (see Figure 11.2) that will give students practice decoding and comprehending; draw their attention to numbers that reveal patterns of old and new immigration; allow students to record their own observations and inferences, raise questions, and make claims about immigration trends; and defend their claims using data from the census.

Mr. Erikson prints the study guides and makes copies of the table for his class. On the day of the activity he passes out the table and study guide, and reads through the background information. He explains to students what the census is, and how they are going to use it. "On your study guide the first question asks you 'How many people who had been born in a foreign country were living in the USA in 1910?' Look over the census for a minute and raise your hand when you know how many." Mr. Erikson waits until most of the hands are up and then he calls on Thomas to give the answer.

"Thirteen million, five hundred and fifteen thousand, and eight hundred and eighty six," Thomas proclaims.

"How many of you think that is the correct number?" Mr. Erikson follows up. Most of the students raise their hands but there are a few who seem unsure.

"How did you figure that out, Thomas?" Mr. Erikson asks.

"I just looked at the first number on the chart."

"How did you know that was the number for the whole United States?"

"It says right above it."

"Where?"

"In the right column above the year 1910."

"So you knew I was looking for the year 1910 for the whole U.S. so you went across the row from that date. How did you know which column to look in?" Mr. Erikson waves his hand back and forth across an overhead transparency of the census page that he projects for the class.

"The first column says total foreign born and that's what you asked," Thomas explained.

"OK. Thanks for explaining how you did that. The questions are going to get tougher. Look at the second question on your study guide. 'Is this number higher or lower than the number of immigrants in 1900?' When you know the answer, turn to a partner and explain how you figured it out." Mr. Erikson knows that this first part of the lesson will be a little tedious, especially for those who are confident in their use of the table, but he wants to be certain that everyone in the class will be able to read it. It's worth the few minutes at this slow pace at the start of the lesson.

Mr. Erikson continues through part one of the study guide, working with the class, making students explain their answers, having them discuss their use of the columns and rows with their classmates. Mr. Erikson explains that the numbers do not represent the number of immigrants arriving in that decade but the total that are still there from previous decades added to those who arrived in the most recent decade. When Mr. Erikson has gone through the few questions on the first part of the study guide he feels like some students are still struggling with decoding. He decides to do a formative assessment and to give students an opportunity to practice more. "Please number from 1 to 5 in the left margin of

Exploring Immigration Trends

Background: The Constitution requires the federal government to conduct a census every 10 years. During a census, surveys are mailed or interviewers are sent to each home in an effort to count the number of Americans. Through the years censuses have collected information about farming, industry, poverty, education, and immigration. You are going to use a table from the 12th census, conducted in 1910, to explore immigration trends at the turn of the century.

I.   Practice reading the census
   a.   How many people were living in the USA in 1910 who had been born in another country?
   b.   Is this number higher or lower than the number in 1900?
   c.   How many people born in Wales lived in the USA in 1870?
   d.   How many people born in Italy lived in New Hampshire in 1900?
   e.   Which geographic division had the most Irish immigrants living in it in 1890?

II. Discovering trends with the census
   a.   In 1870, which five foreign countries were represented by the greatest number of immigrants? (Rank in order from first to fifth.)
      i.
      ii.
      iii.
      iv.
      v.
   b.   Where are all of these countries located geographically?

   c.   In 1910, which five foreign countries were represented by the greatest number of immigrants? (Rank in order from first to fifth.)
      i.
      ii.
      iii.
      iv.
      v.
   d.   Which new countries have joined this list?

   e.   Which other countries experienced the most dramatic increase in numbers between 1890 and 1910?

   f.   Where are all of these countries located geographically?

   g.   What general statement could you make about changing trends in immigration at the turn of the century based on your observations?

FIGURE 11.2 A worksheet to support students' work with the 1910 census table.

III. Exploring the census data
   a. Identify a trend, surprising statistics, or some other characteristic of immigration, and complete the following:
      i. Write a brief description of the trend, surprise, or characteristics that you notice giving specific numbers:

      ii. Write a question or possible hypothesis for your observation:

      iii. Research your question or hypothesis and report here any information that you can find:

      iv. Make a claim explaining the trend, surprise, or characteristic that you observed:

IV. On a piece of graph paper construct a bar graph that demonstrates the trend or characteristics that you based your claim on. Below the graph give a written explanation telling how the data on the graph supports your claim.

FIGURE 11.2 *(continued)*

your worksheet. We are going to have a quiz to make certain that everyone knows how to use this census. Question 1: How many people who were born in China lived in Maine in 1900? Question 2: Which geographic division had the largest population of immigrants from Denmark?" He continues with three more questions, grades the quizzes with the class, answers a few questions, and finally is satisfied that each member of the class will be able to read the census, comprehending what each number means, and knowing where to look to find the information they are curious about.

Mr. Erikson moves into the second part of the worksheet, which helps students distinguish between "old" and "new immigration." He assigns students to work in small groups. As they work, he circulates. One group calls him over to them. "What can I help you with?" he asks.

"We don't get this question: 'Where are all of these countries located geographically?'" Ben explains.

Mr. Erikson looks at Ben's paper and sees that they have correctly listed the top five immigrant nationalities in 1870: Ireland, Germany, England, Canada, and Scotland. "Where on a globe are these countries located? They are all fairly close together, with the exception of Canada." Mr. Erikson rephrases the question.

"They're all in Europe," Taylor answers.

"That's right," Mr. Erikson responds. "But can you be even more specific? What part of Europe?" When the students hesitate to answer, Mr. Erikson gives a hint. "Look at the top of the census. All of those countries are listed under which heading?"

"Northwestern Europe," several in the group say simultaneously.

"You got it."

Mr. Erikson continues to circulate helping students answer the questions on their study guides. When each of the groups has completed the second section, he calls for the class' attention and leads them in a discussion of immigration trends.

"What numbers on the census jumped out at you when it comes to big trends in immigration?" he asks.

"Well, if you look at Ireland, its numbers drop from 1.8 million in 1870 to 1.3 million in 1910 and in that same time the number from Russia increase from 4 thousand to 1.6 million," Kristin answers.

Mr. Erikson allows a few others to share numbers from the census that support their interpretation of immigration trends. Eventually he explains that historians have discovered the same trend that students have found and that they make a distinction between "old" and "new" immigration. "How do you think they would define old immigration – immigration through most of the 1800s?" he asks.

"Immigrants were mostly coming from northwestern Europe," Bailey answers.

"And how would they define new immigration?"

"A lot more immigrants were coming from southeastern Europe," John responds.

"And when did this transition take place?"

"It looks like it started in the 1880s and really sped up between 1900 and 1910." Maddie explains.

"Did you notice any exceptions to this trend?" he continues to ask.

"The worksheet didn't ask us to look for those," Taylor suggests.

"Yeah, but see if you can see any exceptions to the general rule now," he perseveres. Students look down at their censuses, running their fingers across columns and rows.

"Well the numbers continued to go up for some of northwestern Europe too, just not from Ireland where a lot of the immigrants had been coming from," Bailey explains.

After a short discussion of old and new immigration, Mr. Erikson explains the third part of their assignment, which students will do as homework. It requires them to look for some other trend, something surprising, or some other characteristic of the census numbers; develop research questions or a hypothesis for the trend they observe; conduct research on their observation; and make a claim to explain the trend. The last part of the assignment will be to create a bar graph that uses data from the census to support their claim. During the next few minutes of the class, Mr. Erikson models this process. He explains to students that his ancestors immigrated to Minnesota from Sweden in the late 1800s, so he's curious about that area. He flips through the census with the students, showing them a pattern. "Look at all of the Swedes in Minnesota," he reacts. "So the question I have is why did so many Swedes immigrate to Minnesota rather than to any other state – why not Florida?" He turns a page and notes that there were only 729 Swedish immigrants living in Florida in 1910 compared to over 122,000 in Minnesota. "So this is my research question – why did so many Swedes, including my ancestors, immigrate to Minnesota?"

With the class observing, Mr. Erikson does an Internet search on the subject of Swedish immigration and explores a couple of websites. After consulting these sites he concludes that Swedes immigrated and settled in Minnesota because Minnesota's climate and geography are quite similar to Sweden's. Curious, he checks the weather in Minneapolis, Stockholm, and Tallahassee, finding that the forecast calls for similar high and low temperatures for the day in Minnesota and Sweden, but drastically different temperatures in Florida. He further theorizes that a first wave of Swedish immigrants drew later immigrants to the same regions through "chain migration." He admits that there might be other reasons for the immigration patterns, but after consulting with the class, he hypothesizes that the pattern was primarily a matter of geography, climate, and chain migration.

"Historians need evidence to support any hypothesis that they make. So what evidence do I have that Swedes immigrated to Minnesota because of the climate?" Mr. Erikson asks.

"The fact that many of them went there says there must have been something special about that place for Swedes," Taylor answers.

"And several Internet sites say that they went there because of the climate, and we saw that the climate really is the same – at least the temperature is today," Carrie adds.

"So do you think that is enough evidence to support the claim? What other evidence might help?"

"I wonder whether you might find a journal or letter written by a Swedish immigrant to someone in Sweden," John offers. "They might talk about why they chose to settle in Minnesota or why they like it there."

Other students chime in with suggestions for where he could search for evidence. Eventually Mr. Erikson is confident that students understand the process of looking for trends in the census and searching for explanations and evidence to support claims. He is ready to allow the students to explore the censuses on their own. "Take about 15 minutes and search for patterns that make you curious, that you think are interesting, or that are somehow related to you. You might focus on a single country and look for patterns in the immigration from that country, like we did with Sweden. You might look at a single state and look at the type of immigrants that came there. Or you might look at regions and see if you can find trends. Or you might compare two countries. Look at Japan and China, for instance. Or you might look for exceptions to the general rule of "old" and "new" immigration. Once you find something interesting, be sure to work on the third part of your study guide. You're welcome to use my computer to look for other sources if you get that far."

Mr. Erikson allows students to explore, circulating and asking them about their discoveries.

"I think it's interesting that Chinese immigration dropped off so much after 1880," Maddie says, pointing at the census. "Look, the numbers went way up from 1870 to 1880, leveled off in 1890 and then dropped in 1900 and again in 1910. Something must have been going on with Chinese immigrants."

"I wonder about the Greeks," responds Helen, when Mr. Erikson approaches. "Their numbers were different than any other country because they went from just a few in 1870 and 1880 and 1890 to hundreds of thousands in a single decade from 1900 to 1910. And look at their numbers in the Mountain region. Utah went from three Greeks in 1900 to over 4,000 in 1910."

"Do you have a hypothesis about why their immigration didn't increase gradually, like it did in most other places?" Mr. Erikson asks.

"There must have been something really bad going on in Greece to drive this many people out in this short of a time."

"Good thinking, Helen. You'll have to research that to try to find out what was going on in Greece. Now why would they have been attracted to the mountain region? Do you have any theories?"

"I'm still working on that one."

Mr. Erikson kneels by Andrew's desk. "What are you finding?" he asks.

"I was looking at Mexico but I really didn't see much except that their numbers really went up from 1900 to 1910."

"Where were the Mexican immigrants settling?"

Andrew runs his finger down the column that shows Mexico. "There were a lot in California, a lot in New Mexico, some in Arizona." His finger stops at Texas. "Look at this, Mr. Erikson. There were over 125,000 Mexican immigrants in Texas. That's more than half of all of them that were in the United States. OK, so I get it now. They were mostly settling in states on the border with Mexico."

With about ten minutes left in class, Mr. Erikson calls for the students' attention and models using the census to create a bar graph. On his model graph he contrasts Swedish immigration to five states with climates similar to Sweden (Minnesota, Illinois, Michigan, Wisconsin, and Nebraska), with Swedish immigration to five states with climates dissimilar to Sweden (Florida, Georgia, South Carolina, Kentucky, and Tennessee). On the board he demonstrates how to lay out the horizontal axis with five similar and five dissimilar states, each with a column for 1890, 1900, and 1910. On the vertical axis he helps students see how he determines the scale to create. If he uses numbers in the millions, then the difference between the states does not appear remarkable. If he uses numbers in the hundreds, the graph becomes too large to manage. By choosing a scale with numbers in the tens of thousands he produces a graph that will highlight the differences between the states in a way that is manageable. He points out to students that the states he chooses and the scale he chooses are primarily for purposes of argumentation. He wants to present evidence that will convince the viewer that his climate/weather thesis is not only plausible, but is the best explanation for immigration patterns. His selection, use, and portrayal of the census numbers serve a purpose of supporting his claim.

As class ends, students are sent home with a copy of the census table, a piece of graph paper, and with the assignment to research an interesting trend or feature that they have observed, make a claim that explains the trend and construct a bar graph that provides evidence to support the claim.

Argumentation and Quantitative Historical Evidence

Historians' writing blends narration, description, and argumentation. Publishing cutting edge historical research requires historians to interpret evidence in new ways and to defend interpretations through the skillful use of evidence. Much of their writing, then, consists of a justification of their use of resources and an explanation of how their interpretations flow from the evidence. Visual aids such as tables, graphs, and maps serve not only to clarify historical concepts, but to persuade readers that claims are supported by evidence. In this chapter I focus on the historical literacy of argumentation, with an emphasis on the use of numerical data, such as the census records Mr. Erikson gave students. The connection between argumentation and numerical data is not meant to imply that quantitative data is the only evidence which historians use in argumentation. On the contrary, numerical data is only one type of the vast array of evidence historians use. Every possible genre of evidence can and should be used in argumentation. In this chapter I explore a) argumentation and historical thinking, b) teaching argumentation, c) finding numerical data, d) helping students interpret numerical historical data, and e) helping students use numerical data in constructing historical arguments.

Argumentation and Historical Thinking

As described throughout this book, historical thinking requires healthy skepticism, a critical assessment of every source, a questioning of every interpretation, and an evaluation of every claim. Historians do not only interrogate primary sources, but they question secondary sources as well. They require from their colleagues a careful accounting for each piece of evidence, including that which supports their thesis and that which seemingly contradicts it. Historical thinking and historical writing involve a great deal of argumentation. As historians write they must visualize a mildly resistant audience. In addition to telling a story, they have to convince their audience that their story is not only plausible, but that it makes the most sense given the available evidence. The most graceful of historical writing, then, seamlessly blends a story of the past with the story of how the evidence has been used to reconstruct it.

Argumentative writing, and by extension argumentative speaking, have several characteristics. They require the writer/speaker to take a strong stance on a debatable claim. The writer/speaker must "go out on a limb" taking one of multiple possible positions on a controversy. Statements of fact are not good topics in argumentative writing because they do not invite a critical response. For instance, "the number of Greek immigrants to America dramatically increased between 1900 and 1910" is not a good thesis because there is no reason anyone who is familiar with immigration trends would contest such a statement. Additionally, claims must be specific enough to be contestable. Vague statements are easy to defend because they can be modified to fit any evidence. Argumentation includes logical reasons for claims. Perhaps the most important element of argumentative writing/speaking, particularly in historical writing, is that it must be evidence based. Further, historical argumentation must use evidence in a manner that is generally accepted by historians (i.e. sources have been carefully evaluated, multiple perspectives must be represented, an exhaustive search of the evidence has to be completed). In argumentation, writers anticipate opposition – there is often evidence that contradicts a thesis that must be accounted for. Skillful writers foresee criticisms of their thesis and, through logic, strike down counter-arguments before they surface. Much historical writing is argumentative to one degree or another.

As students construct arguments, they must make the distinction between questions, claims, reasons, and evidence. Argumentation typically begins with an authentic research *question*. As phenomena are observed, historians ask why? In Mr. Erikson's case he wondered why so many Swedes immigrated to Minnesota.

Within the discipline of history, *claims* are most often explanations for historical phenomena. They emerge from the evidence-based interpretations of causation. Mr. Erikson claimed that geography, climate, and chain migration all played a part in Swedish immigration trends. *Reasons* include logical support for a claim. For instance, Mr. Erikson argued that the climates were similar, and that the patterns in immigration were remarkable, and that it made sense that new immigrants would be drawn to a region that friends and family had already settled. *Evidence* includes the primary sources, artifacts, and, in this case, numbers that support a claim. Mr. Erikson's evidence included the specific weather patterns, the numbers of Swedes in Minnesota and neighboring states, and, potentially, letters sent from immigrants to their friends at home.

Argumentation involves numerous other historical literacies. For instance, a writer cannot make a strong claim with weak evidence. And the strategies of sourcing and corroboration are essential in evaluating evidence. Further, corroboration and sourcing are often useful in discounting contrary evidence. When one source contains information that contradicts other sources that are deemed more reliable, corroboration and sourcing can explain the discrepancies. Further, a resistant audience appreciates signs that a writer approaches evidence with a healthy skepticism. Doing so allows the writer to anticipate and confront potential skeptics. In addition, the ability to make logical, evidence-based inferences allows the writer to make interpretative, defensible claims. Contextualization and historical empathy embolden the writer in his/her analysis of the evidence. In summary, argumentative writing requires the orchestrated use of numerous historical literacies such as sourcing, corroboration, healthy skepticism, inference making, contextualization, and historical empathy. Making evidence-based claims is a substantial element of historical thinking. And the skillful use of evidence in making an argument is a vital historical literacy.

Teaching Argumentation

The recently published Common Core State Standards for writing in social studies, history, and science suggest that students should be able to engage in and evaluate argumentation (2010). For instance, the standards for 12th grade include the ability to

> a. Introduce precise, knowledgeable claim(s), establish the significance of the claim(s), distinguish the claim(s) from alternate or opposing claims, and create an organization that logically sequences the claim(s), counterclaims, reasons, and evidence. b. Develop claim(s) and counterclaims fairly and thoroughly, supplying the most relevant data and evidence for each while pointing out the strengths and limitations of both claim(s) and counterclaims in a discipline-appropriate form that anticipates the audience's knowledge level, concerns, values, and possible biases. c. Use words, phrases,

and clauses as well as varied syntax to link the major sections of the text, create cohesion, and clarify the relationships between claim(s) and reasons, between reasons and evidence, and between claim(s) and counterclaims.
d. Establish and maintain a formal style and objective tone while attending to the norms and conventions of the discipline in which they are writing.
e. Provide a concluding statement or section that follows from or supports the argument presented.

(Common Core State Standards, 2010, 64)

As a result of these common core standards there is growing interest among history teachers in teaching argumentative writing and speaking that reflects disciplinary norms. In other words, the standards are asking history teachers to teach their students to argue like a historian.

Historians do not start with a claim and then search for evidence to support it. Instead, they start with historical or modern observations that spark curiosity, develop questions, and then hypothesize possible historical reasons for things being the way they are. Gaddis explains that historians notice a current or historical condition and then seek a historical explanation for the condition (2002). Mr. Erikson's approach to teaching argumentation is authentic to the discipline of history. Questions spring out of observations, and claims flow from evidence. It is through the exploration of the census figures that students begin to notice patterns, raise questions, develop hypotheses, and conduct research. After a period of exploration, the censuses, along with other evidence that students have collected, support their claims about immigration trends. The bar graph, that Mr. Erikson prepares with students, is a key element of argumentative writing and speaking. It is not just a matter of presenting facts, but the decisions that Mr. Erikson makes on which data to include on the graph were made purposefully. Mr. Erikson wants to present evidence for his claim in a persuasive manner. The bar graph, as Mr. Erikson has constructed it, supports the claim that Swedish immigrants were attracted to Minnesota and other states with Scandinavian-like climates. Other evidence that he gathers further explains and justifies his claim. Modeling a historian's thinking and writing (graphing) process is an important part of Mr. Erikson's teaching.

Finding Numerical Data

One of the challenges of helping students work with historical numerical data is finding the sources. An experienced co-worker directed Mr. Erikson to the census records that he found so useful in exploring immigration. U.S. census records could be used to study a great many topics and to explore trends at various locations across decades. For instance, census records include statistics on the number of enslaved people; trends in farming, industrial, and mining production; trends in ages, family size, and other social issues; and immigration trends. The United

States Census Bureau's web page at http://www.census.gov/ includes links to a wide range of resources for teachers including lesson ideas (though these ideas primarily focus on current rather than historical data). Other government agencies provide statistics on a wide range of historical trends. For example, the Bureau of Labor Statistics' website at http://www.bls.gov/home.htm provides data on unemployment rates; the consumer price index; earnings by occupation, race, and sex; and numerous other statistics over the past decade. At these types of websites teachers can find data that students could use to explore historical topics related to a great variety of course objectives.

Additionally, websites sponsored by historical organizations often provide links to numerical data. For instance, The Friends of Valley Forge Park have made available the muster rolls from Valley Forge through the winter of 1777 to 1778 (The Friends of Valley Forge Park, 2011). These rolls include statistics on the monthly strength of divisions, brigades, and regiments including the number of soldiers who were fit for duty, who were assigned, who died, who deserted, who were discharged, and who enlisted. A student could use these statistics to assess a claim made on an introductory page of that website that "the encampment experience [at Valley Forge] could be characterized as 'suffering as usual' for privation was the continental soldier's constant companion." The website goes on to suggest that misery ascribed to Valley Forge is romanticized in order to create a "parable to teach us about American perseverance." The number of deaths compared to the number of enlistments could be used, along with other primary sources such as diary entries or letters, to evaluate the website's claims of a "romanticized" notion of Valley Forge.

Teachers who spend time searching the Internet will be able to find a wealth of historical numerical data – compelling texts around which to build lessons on topics as diverse as the spread of AIDS in Africa, World War I or American Civil War battle casualties, global population trends, urbanization trends in America and the world, global literacy rates, and countless other topics. Teachers can also use graphs and tables to explore historical statistics, such as in the vignette when Mr. Erikson helped students read a census table and assigned students to construct a bar graph. Graphs are persuasive texts that show historical trends, such as income inequality and U.S. tax policy (Crocco, Marri, & Wylie, 2011), global urbanization trends, disease rates, population trends, or historical gas prices. The World Wide Web has made available a wide range of historical sources including historical numerical data, tables, and graphs.

Helping Students Interpret Numerical Historical Data

Whether using census records, charts or graphs, or other numerical data, working with quantitative evidence presents some unique challenges for students. As explained in Chapter 3, a history teacher must help students in each of their four roles as readers: code breaker, meaning maker, text critic, and text user. Mr. Erikson's lesson was designed to help students in each of these four areas, but primarily in the first three. First, Mr. Erikson formatted his study guide and his lesson to support students' development as code breakers and meaning makers. As with all tables and graphs, the census figures were organized within a structure that was difficult for some students to comprehend. Mr. Erikson taught students explicitly about the structure of the table, particularly the meanings of columns and rows. He supported students' code breaking by asking them to help each other, showing each other how to use the structure of the table to find the data they wanted. He understood his responsibility to help students decode and comprehend the meaning of the data on the census table. Further, he modeled the process involved in constructing a bar graph, explaining to the students the meaning of the horizontal and vertical axes and suggesting ways to determine an appropriate scale for the data they wanted to present. Mr. Erikson's work with the students involved a great deal of instruction on decoding and comprehending tables and graphs.

Further, Mr. Erikson modeled for students how to use quantitative data to discover historical trends and as evidence to support a historical argument. Mr. Erikson's study guide drew students' attention to features of the census that would allow them to "discover" the distinction between old and new immigration. The census numbers served as a springboard into research, inspiring a research question, sometimes suggesting a hypothesis, and providing evidence. Through the process of the lesson, students could see how a historian might use quantitative data in historical argumentation.

Mr. Erikson did not do much to support students' role of text critic. He did little to critique the census as a source, nor did he suggest to students the need to be skeptical about the census data. The numbers on the census were accepted as being accurate without question. Students did not consider the methods used to conduct the thirteenth census, whether it might under- or over-represent certain groups, or why some nations were not listed in the table. For Mr. Erikson, it was a conscious decision not to question the reliability of census data during this lesson. He thought that the thinking that he required was sufficiently challenging without introducing more complexity. However, his lesson was not completely void of the notion of the reader's role as text critic. He raised questions with the students about other sources that should be used as evidence to support his claim. His search for additional evidence showed students that a single source, the census, was not enough to build a solid argument. Additional evidence in the form of journals or letters was required. In a subsequent lesson, he might devote more time to issues of reliability in census data collection.

In most cases the students' role as text critic should not be ignored. As described earlier in this book, students tend to accept information at face value. This is particularly true with statistics, which appear to simply present objective facts. However, students must become aware that statistics are often manipulated to achieve a particular purpose. Mr. Erikson modeled this to some extent with the bar graph that he created, purposefully selecting data that suited his purpose and ignoring other data. Students need to understand that private entities commission surveys with loaded questions, that organizations design websites containing statistics that support their purposes, that politicians spin data to promote their platforms, and that authors purposefully use statistical data as evidence to support their claims. As with all evidence, students must consider the origins, the author, the audience, and the context of numerical historical data.

Helping Students Use Numerical Data in Constructing Arguments

The culmination of students' interaction with the census in Mr. Erikson's class was their use of numerical data to independently develop a research question, search for evidence, make a claim, and support that claim with numerical data displayed in a bar graph. His census work is meant as a mini-lesson on not only immigration, but on historical argumentation, with much of the class period spent with him modeling argumentative processes. As the school year continues, Mr. Erikson will require more argumentative writing and speaking from his students, including more substantial research projects. And as students engage in independent research projects, Mr. Erikson will encourage them to find numerical data that support their claims. The census project has demonstrated for students both the advantages and disadvantages of numerical historical information. Numerical data are compelling evidence – often erroneously viewed by an audience as objective and unbiased. Numerical data, in contrast to primary sources like letters or journal entries, often provide a view of broad trends. Further, historical statistics provide a springboard for authentic questions, as historians seek explanations for phenomena. In spite of these strengths, numerical data present some disadvantages. Statistics do not stand alone as evidence but need documentation from other sources. Further, statistics, like textbooks in students' eyes, may seem to be above criticism. Mistakenly, the student might pay little attention to the origin, author, context, and audience of statistical reports. Further, the selective use of certain statistics and the omission of others can distort data. Like all other types of historical evidence, it takes great skill in effectively using numerical data to develop historical arguments.

Chapter Summary

Argumentation, including question formulation, claims, reasons, and evidence, requires historical literacies. Strategies discussed throughout the chapters in this book, such as sourcing, corroboration, contextualization, historical empathy, and skepticism are vital in working with evidence to build solid arguments. Numerical historical data, such as the census table that Mr. Erikson used, are evidence that can bolster a historian's argument. The Internet increases the availability of numerical data such as census records, government statistics, and assorted charts and graphs. Students need support in decoding, comprehending, critiquing, and using numerical historical data to support an argument.

PART III

Putting It All Together

In the previous section, the literacies and texts are considered in isolation. In my experience, focusing on a single literacy, such as sourcing or showing historical empathy, or a single genre of text, such as political cartoons or propaganda posters, is an effective way to introduce students to different aspects of historical thinking. Trying to introduce several aspects of historical literacy or multiple genres of text too quickly can overwhelm students. However, limiting instruction on historical literacy to a single strategy or text format does not reflect the authentic practices of historical reading and reasoning. For historians, the heuristics, habits of mind, and literacies described in the preceding section occur simultaneously and harmoniously. Historical research often involves multiple genres of text and always requires multiple literacies.

The chapters in this section integrate the strategies, literacies, texts, and instruction described in the previous chapters. The reader will be introduced to Mrs. Powell who takes her class to the school's computer lab where they explore mosques from around the world. Her students jump from images to written text to audio and video texts as they consider the things architecture can teach them about Islam. Their work involves a critical intertextual analysis of the evidence, a process that requires a range of historical literacies. The concluding chapter shifts the focus from the student to the teacher, providing practical advice for teachers who want to build students' historical literacies. A pattern of planning and teaching, implicit in the vignettes, is made explicit for the reader, with some final words of practical advice.

12

ENGAGING IN CRITICAL INTERTEXTUAL ANALYSIS WITH MULTIMODAL TEXTS

Mrs. Powell is planning a lesson on the spread of Islam for her 10th grade world history course. She wants students to consider the ability of Islam to adapt to diverse global cultures as it spreads, a feature that has contributed to both its status as a world religion and its profound influence on world history. In addition to her content objective, Mrs. Powell has several literacy objectives. Knowing that there is an aesthetic element of literacy, she wants to help students gain a deeper appreciation for the beautiful art and architecture of Islam. Further, she wants students to be able to use architecture, particularly architectural *function* and *form*, as historical evidence. Finally, she wants to help students become more skilled in Internet research, with the ability to synthesize across hyperlinked multimodal online texts.

She believes that a good way to reach these objectives would be to have students work online to explore mosques from around the world. She schedules a time at the school's computer lab for her class, planning to spend about 45 minutes (of the 90-minute period) there with students investigating mosque architecture. In order to illustrate Islam's adaptability, she decides to have students explore the features of mosques that are common across cultures and those characteristics that show cultural distinctions. She thinks that students can learn about Islam by considering the functionality of the common features of mosques, such as minarets, courtyards, and arcades. She also thinks that the activity will dispel some stereotypes of Islam – such as that it is unyielding or backward. She creates a list of mosques that she will require students to study, but she also intends to give students some freedom to explore mosques of their own choosing.

Mrs. Powell's lesson will focus on the essential question: "In what ways did Islam remain true to its origins and in what ways did it evolve as it spread?" She creates a study guide that students will complete while in the computer lab (see Figure 12.1). The study guide includes four columns. In the first, students will draw a sketch of the mosque. In the second, they will write a brief physical and historical description of it. In the third column, students will create a list of unique features of the mosque, with a special consideration of cultural influences on its *form*. In the fourth column, students will keep track of common features that they find across mosques from around the world, with a special consideration of the *function* of the common architectural elements. To model the thinking involved in "reading" mosques, Mrs. Powell decides to complete the first row of the study guide for the students before making copies.

In preparation for class, Mrs. Powell browses the Internet, finding images and descriptions of mosques that blend cultural and traditional elements of Islam. She decides to start the lesson by modeling an analysis of the Mosque of Sultan Ahmed in Istanbul, Turkey. She likes this mosque because it shows the influence of the Byzantine Empire, which her students have recently studied. She thinks that they will be able to make a connection between this mosque, built in the former Byzantine capital, and the Hagia Sophia, a Christian cathedral built during Byzantine times. She fills in the cells, describing it and testing its unique and common features. Continuing her online search she finds a number of other mosques that she would like students to explore. As she browses, she discovers that Wikipedia provides information on many of the mosques. She spends some time considering how she can model the effective use of sites like Wikipedia. Mrs. Powell also contemplates the sequence that she wants students to view the mosques, determining to have students view more traditional mosques first and to later view mosques that reflect a local culture in their architectural forms.

On the day of the activity Mrs. Powell explains the assignment before going to the computer lab. She passes out the study guide, reads the instructions to students, and models how to conduct the online research. She points out that she has completed the first row for them, and says, "I want to show you how I did the first row. How did I know where to look for information online?"

"Why can't we just google it?" Spencer asks.

"Google might be a good place to start, but how will you know where to go next?" Mrs. Powell questions.

"I just go to the first thing on the list and if that doesn't work I go to the second thing," Spencer explains.

"Well, let me model a way of searching that might be more efficient." Mrs. Powell turns on the projector connected to her classroom computer and continues to talk as it warms up. "The mosque that is on the study guide first is the Mosque of Sultan Ahmed. Like Spencer suggested, I'll do a search using google or another search engine." With the projector displaying her computer screen, she continues, "When I google it, the first thing on the list is Wikipedia. Before automatically going there I want to think about whether it would be the best place to start. What do you think?"

Exploring Mosques from around the World

Your assignment is to consider the questions: "What do mosques suggest about the ability of Islam to adapt to different cultures? What impact would this have on the spread of Islam?" Before you can answer these questions you will need to explore some mosques from around the world. This study guide will help. On the study guide below, quickly draw a sketch of the mosque in the first column, give its name and write a brief physical and historical description in the second column, make a list of unique features of the mosque in the third column (trying to pay attention to how it captures the local culture), and make a list of common features of mosques from around the world in the fourth column. You will have to complete the third and fourth columns after looking at several of the mosques. When you run out of room on this side of the paper, make the same columns and continue on the back.

Sketch	Name/Description	Unique Features (function and form)	Common Features (function and form)
	Mosque of Sultan Ahmed: Istanbul Turkey, 1609–1616, built during the Ottoman Empire, called "Blue Mosque" because of tiled interior	Byzantine style flat domes and half domes – create spacious interior for large gathering	6 minarets for calling to prayer, rectangular courtyard with arcade for prayer and fountain to cool
	Great Mosque of Cordoba:		
	Ibn Tulum Mosque:		
	Great Mosque of Jenne:		
	Mashkhur Jusup Central Mosque:		
	Cheng Hoo Mosque, Indonesia:		

FIGURE 12.1 A graphic organizer to support students' Internet work with mosques.

"Our English teacher says that we can't use Wikipedia. She says that people can just go on it and change things so that we can't trust anything there," Carla explains.

"Well, Carla, your English teacher is right in telling you that people can change Wikipedia, but my experience has been that Wikipedia is usually pretty reliable for getting basic information. One thing is for sure, though. We aren't going to rely solely on Wikipedia or any other site for that matter. I'm always going to look for sources to corroborate what I find at one website. In fact, for this assignment I want you to use a minimum of three sites for each mosque you explore."

With students watching and listening to her think aloud, Mrs. Powell goes to Wikipedia and several other sites, explaining how she decides what to write on the study guide as she goes. She talks through her thought process in choosing which sites to explore and which links to hit, as well as how she identifies the source of a website. She demonstrates that it is appropriate to jump from pictures to written descriptions or video clips showing the mosque. She points out that since they will be drawing a sketch they need to look at pictures. Mrs. Powell recommends that they look at more than one picture before drawing the sketch because each photograph shows a different perspective. "See. This mosque looks like a completely different building from different perspectives. Don't get in such a big hurry that you miss really looking at the pictures of the mosques and enjoying them. Some of the world's most beautiful buildings are mosques."

Mrs. Powell expects that the last two columns of the graphic organizer will be the most difficult for the students to complete because they involve a synthesis of evidence across multiple mosques. "You might have to leave the last columns blank at first until you have looked at a few mosques." Giving a hint, she adds, "Be sure to attend to the function and form of the mosques in those last two columns." She explains that the function is the practical purpose of the building and form has to do with the style.

Mrs. Powell continues, "Do you want me to analyze the Great Mosque of Cordoba with you before we go to the lab?"

The class enjoys having Mrs. Powell do their work for them so most of the students are willing to watch her model the process again. With the class observing her, she explores a few websites, looks at some of the pictures, and, leaving a particularly striking image on the screen, gives students a few minutes to sketch the mosque. Further browsing reveals that after the Muslims were driven from Cordoba, a cathedral was built in the courtyard of this mosque. As Mrs. Powell reads one of the written descriptions, she finds a few words that are unfamiliar to students. She models the use of an online dictionary to quickly learn that a mihrab is a niche in a mosque that shows the direction of Mecca, the direction Muslims face when they pray.

After a few minutes of exploring she finds some contradictory information across two sites. "Wait a minute," she says. "We just read that the cathedral built in the middle of the mosque adds to its beauty and uniqueness. Now we read that it destroys the original purpose and beauty of the mosque. How are we going to deal with these disagreements? Why would two texts that are simply describing the mosque give different information?"

"Go back to that last site," Nina requests.

Mrs. Powell clicks a few times on the mouse and the projector shows a site they had previously visited.

"See," Nina points out. "This site is made by a travel agency trying to get people to come see the mosque and cathedral. Of course they're not going to criticize it – they want to attract Christians and Muslims and people who aren't religious and anybody who will spend money there. Now go back to the site we were just looking at."

Mrs. Powell likes where Nina is going and silently follows Nina's directions.

"Well, I don't know who made this site, but it sounds like it was made by Muslims."

"How can you tell?" Mrs. Powell asks, so that Nina will explain her thinking to the other students.

"It speaks happily about the time when Spain was controlled by Muslims and criticizes the Christian takeover. So from the tone of the writing I would guess that it was produced by a Muslim source," Nina explains. "If that's true, it isn't a big surprise that it criticizes the cathedral."

"Yeah, and look at the pictures of the cathedral," Jens adds. "The photographer picked angles to take the pictures that make it look ugly. It doesn't look like the same building as the pictures on the travel agency website."

"I'm glad you noticed the disagreements and I like the way you used the source to explain them. Jens is even thinking about the source of the photographs. Corroboration and sourcing are two of the strategies we've been working on all year, and it's especially important to remember sourcing and corroboration when using Internet sources," Mrs. Powell reminds. "Remember that when you get to the computer lab."

"Now go ahead and fill in the description in the second column of your worksheet, and then I'll call on a couple of you to share what you wrote."

After a few minutes Mrs. Powell calls on Tia, knowing that Tia has a knack for summarizing. "What did you write for the physical/historical description?"

"I did kind of like you did on the first one," Tia explains. She reads from her paper, "Cordoba, Spain, started in 784 by banished Arabic prince. Cathedral added by Christians. Open prayer hall created by columns."

Mrs. Powell notices that several students in the class are adding to their descriptions as Tia talks. "How did you know what to write?" she asks, giving Tia a chance to model her thinking.

"Well I thought it was good to start with some basic information like where it is and when it was built and who built it, kind of like you did on the first one."

"How did you know to write about the cathedral and the columns?"

"Well the cathedral really jumps out at you in the pictures. It's strange to see a mosque with a cathedral built in the middle of it. I didn't even know what it was until we read the physical descriptions. And all of the websites we looked at made a big deal about the columns, so I thought it was one of the most important features to include in the description."

"So let me see if I understand your thinking on this. You identified what was most important about this mosque based on what was repeated across all of the websites – the columns – and what was really unique about it – the cathedral. Is that right?"

"Yeah, pretty much."

"Did you copy information that you found on any website word for word?"

"No I just thought about what I was seeing and reading and then decided what to write."

"Well done, Tia. Her process is a good rule of thumb for this assignment. If something is repeated across several websites, or if a feature is shown over and over again in pictures, you should pay attention to it. You don't have enough room on the study guide to copy word for word from websites. You're going to have to think for yourselves and decide what to write, like Tia did. Does anyone have anything that they thought was important that they want to add to Tia's description?"

Jason raises his hand, "I had that the columns were thin at the bottom and thicker at the top. I thought this was really strange."

"Good idea, Jason. I thought this was important too. Why would they have columns shaped like this? Does this tell us something about the *function* of the building?"

"It makes it feel more open and roomy at the bottom. Lots of people would be able to fit in it and see what was going on around them," Jason responds.

"Yeah. I really hadn't thought about that, but you're right. If Muslims are engaged in prayer, this hall would create a more communal experience because you would feel connected with the other people who were praying because of the column shape. If the columns were bigger at the bottom you wouldn't be able to see as much of what was going on around you. Great thinking, Jason."

Mrs. Powell moves across the rest of the row of the study guide calling on students to tell what they wrote.

By now students are getting antsy to go to the computer lab. Mrs. Powell gives a few more instructions, "You'll need to study the four remaining mosques on the front of this paper and then find three other mosques of your choice that you can analyze on the back. Explore and see if you can find an amazing mosque that other students in the class miss. We'll come back to the classroom for the last 15 minutes of class and I'll let you nominate a 'most breathtaking mosque.' I'll have the class vote to determine the winner. I have a prize for the student who finds the class' choice for the most amazing mosque." With that preparation, Mrs. Powell walks with her students to the computer lab.

In the computer lab, Mrs. Powell circulates and gives help. She watches as students jump from search engine to website and from picture to written description. A few of them even bring up videos related to mosques. She sees students looking at the same pictures of the assigned mosques: the Ibn Tulum Mosque, the Great Mosque of Jenne, the Mashkhur Jusup Central Mosque, and the Cheng Hoo Mosque. Eventually she sees students looking at pictures of mosques that she has not seen before. Students alternate between browsing on the Internet and then working on their study guides. Occasionally, a student raises his/her hand and Mrs. Powell gives help. Some problems stem from inefficient search strategies, or the inability to create a brief summary that synthesizes, in their own words, across multiple pictures and textual descriptions. After about 40 minutes some students finish the study guide. She gives the class a five-minute warning, reminding them that if they want to nominate a mosque for the "most breathtaking mosque" competition, they should turn in a slip of paper with their name, the name of the mosque, and a website that shows a good picture of it. This keeps students who have finished their study guide engaged in exploring until it is time to return to class.

The students arrive back at the classroom with about 15 minutes left for debriefing. Mrs. Powell knows that this is where much of the teaching and learning from this activity will occur.

"What did you find were the common features of all of the mosques?" Mrs. Powell begins the discussion. "Call them out while I write them on the board."

As students talk she lists "minarets, rectangular courtyards, arcades, mihrabs, prayer halls, and domes."

When students run out of ideas Mrs. Powell asks, "What do most of these things have in common? I'll give you a hint: they have to do with the *function* of mosques."

Students think for a few seconds and hands start to come up. Mrs. Powell calls on Andrea.

"They all have to do with prayer except for the domes."

Mrs. Powell agrees, "Yes. So what general statement could be made about Islam and mosques no matter where they are located?"

"Mosques from all around the world are built as a place for Muslims to pray," Andrea continues.

"And how do they pray?" Mrs. Powell extends the questioning.

"I don't know what you mean. I saw pictures of them kneeling facing the mihrab," Andrea guesses.

"That's true. The mihrab serves a practical function, then, pointing worshippers toward their holy city. Someone else add to what Andrea has said about prayer."

Jesse raises his hand and Mrs. Powell calls on him. "They pray together with other Muslims. That's why they need the courtyards and big, open prayer halls. Even the domes are important because they make a big open area so lots of Muslims can fit in there."

"So look on your study guide and what could you say about the common forms and functions of the mosques you looked at?" Mrs. Powell asks.

"All of the things they had in common like the big courtyards had a function that was related to Islam – mostly something to do with prayer," Telise summarizes.

"That's a great summary of similarities. Now let's talk about differences between the mosques," Mrs. Powell transitions. Students observe that the local cultures often influence the architectural forms.

"I was surprised that the mosques looked like the culture where they were built. The Chinese mosques looked Chinese," explains Jordan.

"How is that possible?" Mrs. Powell asks. "Don't mosques serve a religious purpose? If you change the mosque aren't you changing the religion?"

"No," Jordan clarifies. "The mosques still had the same features that were important to Islam. It's just that the architectural styles were different."

"So are you saying that the *functions* remained the same across mosques, but the *forms* changed?" Mrs. Powell follows up.

"Exactly," Jordan concludes.

Mrs. Powell returns to the original question that started their study: "In what ways did Islam remain true to its origins and in what ways did it evolve as it spread?" Mrs. Powell guides the students as they consider how the central tenets of Islam, such as prayer, remained constant as Islam spread to regions of the world as different as Mali, China, and Indonesia. However, peripheral elements of Islam were adapted by local converts to meet local needs. "What influence would this have on the spread of Islam?" Mrs. Powell asks.

"It would make more people convert," Jason suggests.

"Why?" Mrs. Powell continues.

"Because people are less likely to join a religion that feels completely foreign to their culture. They are more likely to convert if it seems familiar to them," answers Tia.

Mrs. Powell continues, "As world religions spread they pick up features of the local religions and culture, a process called syncretism. Syncretism is not only about architecture but it is about religious ideas. Sometimes a spreading religion will change practices or even doctrines to adapt to local cultures."

"Are we going to vote on the most breathtaking mosque?" Spencer interrupts Mrs. Powell. "Because I think mine is going to win."

"Oh yeah. I almost forgot," she answers. "I have 11 nominations. Let's take a look at each of them . . ."

Critical Intertextual Analysis with Multimodal Texts

The dispositions and skills of historical literacy taught by Mrs. Powell and demonstrated by her students, bring together many of the literacies described throughout this book. Students work with a wide variety of types of online texts using a range of strategies. This type of strategic work with texts has been labeled *critical intertextual analysis* by Bruce VanSledright (2002). Critical intertextual analysis is a synthesis of many of the concepts, strategies, and texts discussed throughout this book, and represents an application of historical literacies to explore questions about the past. In this chapter I a) define critical intertextual analysis in terms of online and historical reading, b) review the distinction between general and historical literacies, c) contrast intratextual with intertextual reading, and d) reflect on the challenges of reading multimodal texts such as the Internet sites that blend and link writing, images, video, and sounds.

Defining Critical Intertextual Analysis

Twenty-first century reading is unlike the reading of previous generations. The availability of the Internet has created literacy experiences that are increasingly responsive to the reader and are richly intertextual. Readers have nearly immediate access to a vast array of resources. Online, one can move from written text to photograph to music to virtual fieldtrip to video by scrolling down a page or clicking on a link. As Mrs. Powell demonstrated, unfamiliar terms, like mihrab, can be conveniently looked up in seconds, without distracting from the flow of study. Evidence found in one text can quickly be cross-checked against other sources. Biographies of "experts" can be verified by a few clicks of the mouse, streamlining sourcing. The nature of the Internet creates a setting where reading is not linear (i. e. the reader starting at the first word and proceeding to the last), but involves numerous jumps, side trips, backtracking, neglected opportunities, false leads, and distractions. In short, the Internet makes it simple to move from text to text, which requires readers to make quick judgments about the relevance and utility of diverse sources.

Then, in some ways online reading is a completely new experience. However, in other ways the movement from text to text that occurs online is not very different from the way historians investigate the past – the Internet just makes it occur more quickly and conveniently. Historians have always had to make judgments about the relevance and utility of different sources, with the accompanying jumps, side trips, backtracking, neglected opportunities, false leads, and distractions. Any historian would agree that none of these frustrations originated with the Internet. Further, historians have been observed to pause from reading one document, set it down, and pick up another, when confronted by discrepancies between texts (Wineburg, 1991). Thus, in the absence of hyperlinks, historians have always made their own hypolinks, forging less convenient connections across available resources. Checking and cross-checking evidence across multiple sources, referred to as corroboration in the research and throughout this book, is a basic strategy employed by historians. So in some ways, the Internet is a setting where all readers can and should read more like historians, creating an even greater need for the building of historical literacies.

In his study of 5th grade students, VanSledright (2002) identified characteristics of mature historical reading – or at least as mature as 5th graders could muster. He labeled students' sophisticated historical reading and reasoning processes, which were rare, *critical intertextual analysis*. Internet reading makes the ability to engage in a critical intertextual analysis essential for all readers. It can be helpful to consider each of its components somewhat independently.

Critical Analysis

An analysis is *critical* when the reader approaches the task with an appropriate, criterialist epistemic stance, understanding the nature of historical study and his/her role as a historian. Critical students understand why contradictory accounts of an event exist and they have cognitive tools to sift through contradictions. Critical analysis requires students to use historians' heuristics of sourcing, corroboration, and contextualization to determine the reliability of various sources. Critical analysis requires a healthy skepticism. Students do not blindly accept information in the text as it is presented, but view texts as evidence to be used according to their discretion and purposes. Similarly, as Mrs. Powell pointed out, students do not blindly reject a source, like Wikipedia or their textbook. When they approach any source with skepticism and the proper strategies for analyzing it, students can find utility in all kinds of texts, even Wikipedia. Critical thinking requires a sophisticated worldview, avoiding the reductionism that is typical of textbooks and traditional history instruction. Critical analysis involves the strategies, dispositions, and habits of mind celebrated throughout this book.

Intertextual Analysis

Further, critical intertextual analysis is *intertextual* because the reader makes frequent connections across different texts, as Mrs. Powell's students did in their online reading. In intertextual analysis the reader moves from text to text looking for agreement and disagreement that allows him/her to gain a more mature understanding. Intertextuality requires exposure to multiple texts and strategies, or heuristics for making connections between them. However, research suggests that students have a difficult time making connections and synthesizing across multiple texts. For instance, Spivey and King found a common pattern for students who were assigned to write research papers using multiple texts (1989). Instead of creating a synthesis, they used a single source for the bulk of their writing. They drew from their main source with little independent thinking, at best simply summarizing, and at worst cutting and pasting directly from the source. When pushed to include other sources, students threw in a token quote or two from other texts, but there was rarely a real synthesis of ideas across texts. Stahl and his colleagues made other discoveries about students' intertextuality in their observations of secondary students working with historical texts. They found that students noticed similarities across texts, and used the similarities to create strong summaries. However, discrepancies between the texts went unnoticed or were ignored. The researchers concluded that students have a difficult time creating sophisticated syntheses from the types of texts that historians use. Making connections across texts is not a natural or easy process for most secondary students (Stahl, *et al.*, 1996).

Again, the reading of historians presents a model for history teachers to consider in supporting students' critical intertextual analysis. Historians don't simply search for a handful of sources. They conduct exhaustive searches for evidence, leaving no relevant archive unexplored. They review every text that might inform their research. Although this type of exhaustive intertextual research is impractical in history classrooms, teachers can facilitate intertextuality by providing multiple texts, or requiring the use of multiple sources for students' research. However, simply providing or requiring multiple sources does not guarantee intertextual reading – history teachers must support intertextuality.

Mrs. Powell included several measures that were intended to help students engage in critical intertextual analysis. First, students both compared and contrasted mosques, which served as the texts for this lesson. Students could not complete the assignment without considering mosques' common and unique characteristics, engaging in the thinking associated with intertextuality. She created a graphic organizer that required students to record the similarities and differences they noticed. Along with making students accountable for their work, the graphic organizer served as a reminder of the need to both compare and contrast. Additionally, it provided a place to record the physical description of mosques, allowing students to move forward and backward between the mosques, searching for similarities and differences.

Second, Mrs. Powell's selection of mosques was done purposefully, to illustrate the concepts she was trying to teach and to facilitate intertextual analysis. Knowing that students have a harder time dealing with discrepancies than with similarities, she required students to study mosques with obvious differences. The mosques in Mali and Indonesia contrasted sharply with those in Spain and Turkey, making it easier for students to contrast. Third, Mrs. Powell modeled the kind of thinking that she wanted students to do. She modeled effective ways of verifying information found on Wikipedia with other sources. She revealed her thought processes in making judgments about which sites to enter and which links to select. She demonstrated the need to use multiple sites and how to identify the source of a site. Additionally, she had students model their thought processes for their peers. When a student made an insightful comment her normal response was the question: "How did you figure that out?" Her purpose in doing so was to have those students who were skilled in their use of texts reveal for their peers the strategies that they used.

Fourth, Mrs. Powell gradually removed the scaffolding students received as the activity continued. She completed the first row of the study guide for students, so that their attention could be focused entirely on her as she modeled her reading and reasoning processes. She made the students complete the second row of the study guide as she and other students modeled their reading and reasoning processes. Students then moved into the computer lab where they analyzed four other mosques that Mrs. Powell had purposefully selected. The graphic organizer continued to support their thinking. Finally, students ventured out on their own, finding and choosing mosques to explore, and creating their own graphic organizer on the back of their paper. Thus, as the assignment continued Mrs. Powell withdrew the support that she provided until students were comparing and contrasting mosques with relatively little support.

Analysis

In addition to being critical and intertextual, a critical intertextual analysis involves analysis. Historical analysis integrates several of the literacies described in the chapters of this book. For example, historical analysis includes the use of evidence to make and defend claims. For instance, Jason claimed that Muslims desire a communal experience when they pray. The narrow base of the columns in the Great Mosque of Cordoba served a purpose: to create a more open room that would facilitate the communal experience. Historical analysis revolves around the use of evidence to create logical, defensible interpretations, and texts serve as that evidence. Additionally, historical analysis calls for the making of inferences. Nina inferred that one of the websites was produced by a Muslim source based on the generous description of the mosque and the history of Muslim rule. Using texts as evidence and making inferences are key elements in historical analysis. Critical intertextual analysis is an application of each of the historical literacies described in this book.

General and Historical Literacies

In developing the notion of critical intertextual analysis, VanSledright tracked the progress of his 5th grade students. One of the differences between less mature and more mature readers was their use of strategies. The poorest readers were not strategic in their reading or thinking. Better readers used what he considered general literacies. The most skilled readers, on the other hand, employed historical literacies. The students in the vignette that opens this chapter illustrate this range of abilities. Carla, for instance, is not particularly strategic in following the hard and fast rule given by her English teacher, "don't use Wikipedia." There is little strategy use in Carla's recommendation not to go to that site. Tia, on the other hand, uses a general summarizing strategy to write a good description of the Great Mosque of Cordoba: if something is repeated across multiple sources it is an indication that it is important enough to be included in a summary. Tia is able to produce a good summary though her thinking involves little critical analysis.

She synthesizes across sources without questioning the information in any source. Nina and Jens, on the other hand, use the historical literacies of sourcing and corroboration in an analysis that is more critical. Nina identifies a website as coming from a pro-Muslim source, based on the tone of the writing. Jens considers the source of photographs, suggesting that the photographer chose perspectives that were less glorifying for the cathedral than they were for the mosque. Thus, in order to engage in critical intertextual analysis a student must employ strategies that are specific to the study of history such as sourcing and corroboration; general literacies, such as summarizing, are insufficient.

Intratextual and Intertextual Reading

Several researchers have investigated the way readers make connections both within and across texts. One of the most interesting studies was conducted by Doug Hartman (1995), who observed eight proficient readers think aloud as they read five texts. He paid particular attention to the links that they made as they read. Hartman found that readers approached a text, or series of texts, with certain attitudes about their role as a reader. Some buried themselves within each text, making numerous connections within the text in order to comprehend the author's meaning, removing themselves, their experiences, and other texts from the comprehension process. The connections a reader makes between two or more elements of the same text can be referred to as intratextual. And some readers, those whose primary focus is on comprehending the author's message, have a tendency to focus on intratextual connections.

Hartman found that other readers were less focused on comprehending the author's literal message, but instead were open to multiple interpretations, based not only on what one text said, but on a synthesis of ideas from multiple texts. These readers remained open to numerous interpretations of a text. He labeled these readers, whose reading most closely mirrors historical thinking, as intertextual. A third type of reader resisted the author's meaning, instead imposing his/her own interpretation based on his/her experiences, which were sometimes only tangentially related to the reading at hand. These readers were not open to multiple interpretations, instead imposing on the source what they viewed as the correct interpretation. These readers approached texts with their opinion firmly in place, discounting evidence that might suggest a different interpretation, and latching on to evidence that confirmed preconceived ideas. In conclusion, Hartman suggested that the way a reader views his/her role influences his/her tendencies to make connections within, across, or without texts. And it is the across-text, intertextual connections that are valued in historical thinking.

In VanSledright's tracking of 5th grade students' historical thinking, he used this distinction between intratextual and intertextual reading as well. He suggested that some individuals progress through phases of intratextual reading, which involves general literacies, into increasingly sophisticated intertextual reading, which involves historical literacies. Like Hartman, he suggests that intratextual analysis is a less sophisticated way of analyzing and evaluating text. In intratextual analysis, a reader focuses on a single text, comprehending, summarizing, and, to a lesser extent, evaluating its content. Judgments of the text are made based on its characteristics such as whether or not it makes sense, is interesting, or is rich in details. Readers skilled in historical analysis, on the other hand, proceed into an intertextual analysis. When engaging in intertextual analysis, they use outside sources to analyze and evaluate a text. Exposure to a first text enriches the students' experience with subsequent texts. For instance, as they encounter more evidence they gain a richer understanding of the context, and they use this contextual understanding to consider the sources of the subsequent texts they read. At the highest levels of intertextual analysis, readers evaluate a text's validity based on its source and how it compares to other texts. VanSledright concludes that as students engage in critical intertextual analysis they systematically refine their interpretation of the event they study based on evidence in multiple texts.

Mrs. Powell understood the importance of moving from an intratextual to an intertextual analysis and of progressing from general literacies to historical litera-cies. Before moving to the computer lab, she helped students create descriptions of mosques that involved little critical analysis, though relying on multiple texts. With increasing exposure to pictures and written descriptions of mosques, stu-dents were able to make connections across texts, noticing disagreements, which resulted in critical thinking about the sources they used. Further, as students pro-gressed through the activity, their study guide required them to compare and contrast across mosques, an intertextual activity.

Challenges of Multimodal Texts

Many literacy tasks, from reading the newspaper to exploring the Internet to skimming a textbook passage, involve learning with multiple genres of text. One of the themes that has been repeated across this book is that each genre of text brings with it unique challenges for students in their roles as code breakers, mean-ing makers, text critics, and text users. Websites can represent particularly difficult reading because they often combine on a single page multiple genres such as writ-ten text, photographs, artwork, video, and audio texts. In addition, websites often bring together material from different sources that vary in reliability. Authors of web pages can produce attractive and entertaining sites that misrepresent, confuse, or distort historical events. Thus, the use of multimodal Internet sites to answer historical questions requires students to use a variety of historical literacies.

At times a teacher might choose to provide explicit instruction on the decoding of a challenging genre of text. However, such instruction can be tedious and time consuming. It would be a mistake to take a significant amount of class time in a single class period to provide explicit instruction on the decoding of multiple modes of texts, such as photographs, architecture, and blueprints. Mrs. Powell sensed this, and chose to focus her instruction on the reading of the function and form of buildings. She purposefully chose not to focus much energy on students' struggles in reading photographs, blueprints, or videos found on web pages. Certainly she took opportunities to model critical analysis of all texts when opportunities arose. And, she celebrated students' critical analysis of photographs and the text on a web page, asking them to make their thinking processes explicit for the class. However, her focus during this lesson was on teaching students to use buildings as historical evidence, and her explicit instruction focused on teaching those literacies. Mrs. Powell understands that the teaching of strategies for reading multiple modes of texts is a year-long process and cannot be the object of a single lesson.

Chapter Summary

Internet literacies, like historical literacies, involve searching for sources, making judgments about their relevance and validity, seeking corroborating evidence, synthesizing across multiple genres of text, pursuing false leads, overlooking potential sources of evidence, and, in the end, constructing a defensible under-standing of the topic of study. Both effective Internet study and historical inquiry require a critical intertextual analysis of evidence. Critical intertextual analysis in history involves sifting through multiple pieces of evidence, synthesizing across different sources, and using history-specific literacies in order to develop and de-fend an interpretation of a historical event. Critical intertextual analysis involves the literacies discussed and celebrated across the chapters of this book.

13

FINDING A PATTERN IN BUILDING HISTORICAL LITERACIES

I opened this book with the story of Ms. Cordova walking through the social studies department at McArthur Middle School observing a variety of teaching methods including lecture, textbook reading, recitation, and the showing of documentary videos. She saw something different, however, in Mr. Rich's classroom, where students sifted through a variety of forms of evidence trying to determine whether child labor in factories was worse than child labor on family farms. A quick review of the vignettes across the chapters of this book shows other teachers, like Mr. Rich, helping students use evidence to answer interpretive historical questions. For instance, the 10th grade students in Mrs. Hansen's class used primary and secondary source accounts of the Crusades to decide whether the crusaders were motivated primarily by religious factors. Miss Anderson's 8th grade students used a historical novel and primary sources to gain a deeper appreciation for the historical context of the Civil Rights Movement – to understand how White people and Black people interacted as the Civil Rights Movement gained momentum. Mr. Erikson's 11th-grade students used census records to identify and explore patterns of immigration to the United States at the turn of the 20th century. And Mrs. Francis' students used tree rings, ruins of dwellings, and other artifacts to consider the changing culture of the Ancestral Pueblo people. In this chapter I highlight a pattern followed by the innovative teachers described in the vignettes throughout this book in the planning and execution of lessons. The pattern involves four stages: a) the selection of objectives, b) the selection of texts, c) a determination of the support and instruction that students need to use the texts, and d) the execution of the lessons. I conclude the chapter with a few other practical suggestions for getting started in building students' historical literacies.

Stage One: Selecting Objectives

Content Objectives

The work of history teachers, like the work of historians, involves interpretive decisions about significance. Historians must decide which historical issues are worthy of investigation, which elements should be included in their narratives, and which can be left out. Similarly, history teachers make decisions about how to use their limited class time. Should they teach about specific battles of the Revolutionary War, or just talk about the war in general? Should they require students to memorize the Gettysburg Address, or should they skip it completely, as Lincoln suggested would be the case? Should they set a pace that allows students to learn about the Vietnam War? Or will the end of the school year arrive while they're still studying the Baby Boom and Civil Rights Movement? From the vast domain of historical understanding, history teachers must make decisions about the content that would be significant, interesting, relevant, and important for their students to understand. State curriculum guides often outline the content to be covered during the year. However, these guidelines typically leave much room for interpretation as history teachers determine the depth of coverage. For instance, the state curriculum guidelines might require teachers to teach about the causes, events, and effects of the Crusades, but the world history teacher decides whether the students spend 20 minutes or six days working toward that standard.

The teachers in this book integrate content and literacy objectives in their planning. Mr. Rich, for example, has high standards for students' mastery of content. He wants them to understand child labor in ways that extend beyond the iconic images of boys and girls standing in front of textile machinery staring emotionlessly at a photographer. He wants them to understand that children have always been involved in labor, and that the Industrial Revolution simply changed the venue for their work. He is quite confident, and the research supports this notion (Nokes *et al.*, 2007; Reisman, 2012), that the analysis of primary sources that his students conduct will help them thoroughly understand and remember issues surrounding child labor, though they may come up with different interpretations about the impact of the Industrial Age on children.

Literacy Objectives

Most state curriculum guidelines say little about the skills that students should develop in their history classrooms. And, pressured to "cover the historical content," many history teachers fail to integrate skill and literacy objectives into their instruction. However, there is enough research on young people's historical thinking that it is possible to identify developmentally appropriate skills that history instruction should include. Further, the Common Core State Standards (2010) and national organizations, such as the National Council for the Social

Studies, have established standards for reading, reasoning, and writing skills for history students (Nash & Crabtree, 1996). This book highlights skills and habits of mind associated specifically with historical literacy that emerge from research on students' historical thinking and that are found in national standards documents.

Mr. Rich establishes literacy objectives, in addition to content objectives, to be achieved during his lesson. In particular, he wants students to focus on the source of texts and to understand how acknowledging the source influences the analysis of evidence. He wants students to think about the photographer behind the images. He wants students to think about the creator's purpose, whether the text is a historical novel or a political cartoon. He wants them to consider the distance between the author and the event being described. He wants students to develop ways of thinking about text that allow them to view all sources as evidence rather than as conveyors of information. And students, with his support, are taught and practice these skills throughout the lesson.

Chapters 4 through 11 of this book suggest eight historical literacy strategies that could become the focus of a teacher over a school year: developing an appropriate epistemic stance, using historians' heuristics, making inferences, comprehending metaconcepts, showing historical empathy, remaining skeptical, avoiding reductionist thinking, and constructing evidence-supported arguments. Mr. Rich's lessons across the school year cycle through these few historical literacy strategies. For example, he taught students about sourcing, one of the historians' heuristics, on one of the first days of the school year, and reminds them about it repeatedly during subsequent lessons, adding to the complexity of their understanding. For instance, as students study events that occurred after the invention of the camera, Mr. Rich talks explicitly about sourcing again, raising awareness that photographs do not simply capture a moment of reality, but that the person behind the camera, with his/her purposes in taking the picture, makes a difference. Mr. Rich provides explicit instruction on analyzing the source of photographs. Mr. Rich will revisit sourcing as other new genres of evidence, such as audio recordings and video recordings are introduced. As strategies, like sourcing, are repeatedly reviewed, students transfer previously developed historical literacies to new genres of text. For instance, they learn the value of considering the source whether the text is a diary entry, a history textbook, a Depression-era photograph, an Internet site, or a current news report.

At the start of each new unit, as Mr. Rich considers his objectives, he reflects on the students' current skill levels and the literacies that can be fostered within the content to be taught. And, from unit to unit, when Mr. Rich considers his literacy objectives, his expectations steadily increase. He starts the year with a vision of what his students will be able to do by the end of the year and provides repeated opportunities for students to learn and practice historical literacies with new genres of evidence, increasingly sophisticated questions, increasingly challenging texts, and decreasing teacher support.

Assessing Students' Mastery of Objectives

The development of assessments goes hand in hand with the selection of instructional objectives (Wiggins & McTighe, 1998). If a teacher's objectives include literacies, then their assessments should measure students' historical literacies. In other words, history tests and other instruments of assessment should evaluate students' ability to engage with diverse genres of historical evidence using target strategies. In Mr. Rich's case he should assess not only students' comprehension of the impact of the Industrial Revolution on children, but he should also evaluate students' ability to use source information to determine the trustworthiness and usefulness of historical evidence. Such assessments of literacies and skills run against the grain of traditional, content-focused, multiple choice history tests. However, historical literacies can be assessed fairly easily. For instance, Wineburg and his colleagues suggested that developing, using, and scoring assessments of historical literacies is not as difficult as it might appear. They contend that the simple task of giving students a painting of a historical event, created during a subsequent era and asking them to write about its usefulness can help a teacher determine whether students view evidence in the same way that a historian would (i.e. looking at the source rather than the content, valuing primary sources over secondary sources, remaining skeptical about text content, etc.) (Wineburg, Smith, & Breakstone, in press). Assessments such as these help history teachers set an appropriate pace for increasing the difficulty level of historical questions and texts.

Stage Two: Selecting Texts

The work of the historian and the history teacher are also comparable in their search for evidence. Historians scour archives searching for the letter, diary entry, or newspaper clipping that will serve as evidence in answering a pressing historical question. History teachers too should search for evidence but for a different reason. The evidence they seek must be accessible to students, allowing them to engage in deep thinking about historical questions. Just as a historian feels euphoric after discovering an important piece of evidence, history teachers get excited when they find something suitable for their students and their learning objectives.

There is no end to the number of possible texts that a history teacher might use to reach his or her content and literacy objectives. Collingwood suggests that anything perceptible to a historian might serve as evidence, given the right question (1993). The chapters of this book describe history teachers using texts as varied as letters, paintings, speech transcripts, music, political cartoons, picture books, pottery shards, Hollywood-produced movies, maps, historical novels, census numbers, tree rings, line graphs, newspaper articles, monuments, and even textbooks. With such a rich array of potential resources, and with access to texts via the Internet, teachers should be very selective about the texts they use. In choosing texts a history teacher might ask questions such as: Will students learn the desired content by working with this text? Will students develop the target strategies by working with this text? Will this text be viewed as evidence by students or will they be seduced by objective sounding language into accepting it as "informational" text? Will this text demand historical thinking on the part of the students? Do students have the literacies necessary to work with this text or can I help them build the needed literacies? Will this text open the students' eyes to a unique perspective of an event? Will this text be interesting and engaging for students? Is this a type of text that historians might use as evidence? Is this a genre of text that students will encounter in their adult world? History teachers must be purposeful in selecting the texts that students explore in their classrooms.

The most instructive historical literacy lessons include multiple texts. Corroboration is impossible without multiple pieces of evidence across which to make comparisons. And sourcing is facilitated when students read conflicting accounts from multiple perspectives – acknowledging the source often helps explain the disagreement. Further, differences between genres can be highlighted when learning activities juxtapose different formats of text. For example, reading a detail-rich account in a historical novel followed by a relatively dry eyewitness account can improve students' understanding of the authors' purposes in producing each. Further, giving students reliable and unreliable accounts, side by side, can foster a healthy skepticism and can help them gain expertise in judging the credibility of the things they read. And introducing diverse perspectives can help students develop a more mature epistemic stance as well as a better understanding of the nature of history. They see that textbooks only present one of many possible interpretations of an event. Historical empathy and perspective taking are improved when students read accounts showing multiple perspectives.

Teachers in the vignettes in this book found texts in a variety of ways. Some received useful tips from colleagues. Some, like Mrs. Dahl who had recently visited the World War II memorial, found texts through their experiences. Journal articles, such as that on dendrochronology, inspired other teachers. Some teachers found texts exploring the Internet. Others remembered powerful texts that they experienced as students. What all teachers had in common, though, was that their planning included a search for engaging texts around which to build historical literacy lessons.

Stage Three: Determining the Support and Instruction Students Need

After gathering texts for a lesson, a teacher should reflect on the support students will need to effectively work with the texts. Freebody and Luke's (1990) model of literacy, described in Chapter 3, provides a checklist for teachers. First, will students need help in their role as a code breaker? Reading old documents, written in cursive script, might present a challenge for students that a typed transcript would resolve. Unfamiliar genres of text, such as propaganda posters, political cartoons, or music, may use symbol systems that are foreign to students. Teachers should to be sensitive to students' needs in breaking the code of each text they use. For instance, in Chapter 11, Ms. Chavez helped students identify the unique features of jazz music, by having them listen to examples of jazz followed by non-examples. Over time, students began to recognize what made jazz jazz, identifying, in particular, improvisation and the unorthodox use of voice and instruments. Their breaking of the code of jazz music, in this manner, allowed them to understand its revolutionary nature and to consider attitudes about tradition and change during the Jazz Age.

Second, will students need help in their role as a meaning maker? There are several steps that a teacher can take to help students comprehend texts. Texts might be modified to suit students' reading levels. Vocabulary help, instruction on text structure, or peer support might aid students' comprehension of a text. In Chapter 11, Mr. Erikson dedicated a significant amount of class time to helping students comprehend the data presented in a relatively complex census table. Students could look at the table and see numbers, thus breaking the code, but many were not able to comprehend what those numbers meant without instruction and practice reading the table. He had students model for their peers how to use the headings and labels to comprehend what the numbers represented. Students must be able to comprehend a text in order to use it effectively as historical evidence.

Third, are students prepared for their role as a text critic? Do they have the disposition to approach a text with the appropriate epistemic stance and a healthy skepticism? Do they know how to use historians' heuristics for working with the text? Teachers can foster students' ability to engage as text critics by providing conflicting accounts, creating a cognitive disequilibrium. In order to achieve a resolution, students must make judgments about the reliability and validity of conflicting sources. Teachers can create a classroom where all ideas and sources are subject to a critical review. For example, in Chapter 9, Mr. Johnson had students use primary sources describing the Mongols to critique their textbook. In the process he modeled for students that all texts, including the textbook, should be considered accounts and that all accounts should be open to criticism. His conversations with students during the document analysis activity helped them think deeply about the source of the documents they analyzed. As a result, they became better judges of the evidence they were exposed to.

Fourth, are students prepared for their role as a text user? In classrooms that build historical literacies, students use texts in ways that are authentic to the discipline of history, and not simply to answer questions on a worksheet. History teachers design activities that require students to use texts as historians do, to solve historical problems, answer historical questions, or settle historical controversies. Good historical thinking lessons begin with an authentic, engaging, and appropriately challenging question to answer or problem to solve. In the vignettes, teachers established a purpose for working with texts. In some instances, there was a closed-ended question for students to consider: Were the Crusades primarily motivated by religious factors? In other cases, teachers presented more open-ended questions: What does the evidence suggest about changes within the Ancestral Pueblo culture? Additionally, throughout this book teachers produced graphic organizers, posters, and activities that facilitate sourcing and corroboration, and otherwise supported students as they worked as text critics and text users. T-charts and matrices were used to help students keep a record of their analysis of texts in order to help them answer the questions and solve the problems around which lessons were built.

Stage Four: Executing the Lesson

In most chapters of this book, I have given a rich description of a teacher who plans and executes a lesson. Several patterns can be seen across the vignettes illustrating successful teaching. In each vignette, the teacher gave students space to develop their own interpretations of the evidence. Mrs. Francis' 8th grade students, for instance, used the evidence to discover that many Ancestral Pueblo moved into homes built in the cliffs, though they disagreed about the reasons for doing so, Christie suggesting that it was because of a changing climate and Curtis contending that it was because of enemies. Mr. Erikson gave his 11th grade students even more room to explore the evidence, allowing them to identify a pattern in the census numbers and then search for an explanation for the pattern. The nature of history as a discipline allows historians to disagree over important historical questions. History classrooms that focus on historical literacies allow students the same room for independent thinking.

Another pattern across all of the vignettes was that the teachers fostered critical and creative thinking through their interactions with students. The modeling of historical thinking took place in whole-class discussions, during small group work, and as teachers interacted with students one-on-one. Repeated throughout the lessons was the question, "How did you figure that out?" This question required students to make explicit their thought processes in working with texts. Students who struggle benefit by this type of modeling and thinking aloud. Interactions with students focused on processes more than products. Thinking properly and strategically about the texts was more important than coming up with a predetermined correct answer. The assumption is that if students work appropriately with texts they will reach interpretations that they can defend using historical evidence. A correct answer, on the other hand, can represent a lucky guess, copying from a classmate, looking something up on Wikipedia, or countless other desirable or undesirable processes.

Additionally, the execution of lessons in this book shows teachers working flexibly in multiple roles with their students. At times they assume the position of the "sage on the stage." They are the classroom authority on historical content and on historical literacies and they share their expertise with students when appropriate. They lecture at times, in order to build the background knowledge students need to approach historical questions. They provide explicit and implicit instruction on strategies and habits of mind, such as sourcing or showing historical empathy.

At other times teachers assume the role of "guide on the side," sometimes even withholding information that they know so that students can work through the process of discovering things for themselves. Rarely do classroom activities revolve around them. Instead activities are centered on students' interaction with texts. The teachers are facilitators, gathering texts, imagining activities, designing support, and providing instruction that will allow students to work effectively with the texts. At times, teachers join the students as learners of history. They admit, without embarrassment, that they don't know everything about history – not even the most seasoned historians do. They show an interest in, and a critical respect for, the ideas presented by students. Like historians, these history teachers remain open to new interpretations that are supported by evidence. Above all else these teachers model a curiosity about the past, with questions answered through the skillful use of evidence, a process that requires historical literacy.

Practical Suggestions for Getting Started

I conclude this book with four practical suggestions for getting started with building students' historical literacies, based on my experience and the experiences of others who have taught history or studied history teaching.

Start Small

First, start with small steps. In the preface I explain the long process I went through in integrating historical literacy into my curriculum. It is remarkably similar to the process described by Bruce Lesh, another high school history teacher with a drive to build historical literacies (2011). During my first years of teaching, I used one or two historical thinking lessons each year. Eventually, I had developed at least one in-depth historical investigation for each unit. I eventually started to reduce the length of my lectures to make room for more regular mini-lessons involving students' work with texts. I was primarily driven by the success of the literacy lessons to try them with increasing frequency. A new teacher, or an experienced teacher attempting a new approach, should not feel pressured to have a literacy lesson each day, but should be satisfied in making the transition to building historical literacies at a pace that will not cause undue stress or burn out. Further, as with many aspects of teaching, it is difficult to have complete success in a first attempt. Unanticipated problems, such as using texts that are too difficult or unappealing to students, can cause literacy lessons to be disappointing. Teachers must be patient with themselves as they try, correct, and retry historical literacy lessons.

Use What's "Out There"

As a new teacher, studying history, planning lessons, grading students' papers, learning school policies, and fulfilling extra-curricular responsibilities left me little time to explore innovative teaching methods. My first attempts at historical literacy lessons were based on materials collected by colleagues and shared with me. Today, with the Internet, teachers have unprecedented access to materials prepared by other teachers. For instance, the Stanford History Education Group has posted over 80 document-based lessons on their website (2012). Other websites, described throughout this book, provide materials for lessons on a variety of historical topics using a wide range of texts. Further, innovative colleagues, those who strive to build historical literacies, serve as valuable partners in developing and refining historical literacy lessons. Teachers can save a significant amount of preparation time, perhaps preserving their sanity, by borrowing published resources and adapting them to meet the needs of their students.

Build Structure and Accountability into Literacy Lessons

With few exceptions, my historical literacy lessons have proceeded more smoothly when I build structure and student accountability into the lesson, often accomplished through graphic organizers. The graphic organizers that were used by the teachers in the vignettes in this book were designed for four purposes. First, as described in this book, they are a source of scaffolding, supporting students' strategic engagement with texts. For instance, the graphic organizers remind students of the need to use sourcing and corroboration. They prompt students to search for similarities and differences across texts. They help students weigh textbook passages against alternative accounts. They help students weigh evidence from opposing perspectives. Well-designed worksheets serve an important role as scaffolding for students as they work with unfamiliar historical literacies.

Second, the graphic organizers provide a record of the students' work that can be used to assess students' historical thinking. By looking at the students' notes in a "sourcing" column, the teacher can get a feel for the students' ability to appreciate the influence of perspective and audience on a source. Well-designed graphic organizers help make students' thought processes more evident to teachers, so that they can adjust instruction according to the students' needs. Thus, graphic organizers serve as an ongoing formative assessment, helping teachers plan future learning activities.

Third, graphic organizers provide a record of the students' work that can be used by the students to review historical concepts and to monitor their own growth. Students can review historical processes as well as historical content using the record of their historical thinking preserved on a graphic organizer. One particularly effective graphic organizer I designed was the "Evolving Concept Worksheet" (Nokes, 2010b). Students would be exposed to a primary source related to a controversial issue (such as the guilt or innocence of Captain Thomas Preston in the deaths of American civilians during the Boston Massacre). After analyzing the first document, students would state their opinion and rank their certainty on a scale of 1 to 5. After reading a second document they could switch their opinion or keep it the same, ranking their certainty on a scale of 1 to 5. This process would be repeated through five or six documents. After completing the activity, students could trace their evolving opinion. Typically, their level of certainty started high, as they accepted without question the evidence presented in the first document. After reading two or three alternative accounts, their certainty would usually decrease and their opinion would sometimes shift. In the end, students would become more certain of their opinion once again, but this time because of their familiarity with the evidence. The Evolving Concept Worksheet provided a record of their thinking throughout the activity and served as a resource in the metacognitive debriefing that followed the activity.

Fourth, graphic organizers build structure and accountability into a literacy lesson. Admittedly, managing a class can be more difficult during small group work than during a lecture, particularly when students are moving at their own pace, searching online, and engaging in lively debates with their peers. Graphic organizers provide structure that helps students focus on the task at hand. Further, knowing that a teacher will collect and evaluate their work can motivate students to stay on task throughout an activity. Other management-related problems may be avoided by establishing clear rules for small group work, appropriately pacing activities, and by purposefully forming groups. Giving students the freedom to develop independent interpretations of historical events does not need to result in a loss of control of the classroom. But it can if teachers do not address potential management issues.

Worry Less about Coverage

Most states have curriculum guidelines for history classes. Teachers should meet these standards. However, the guidelines typically leave considerable room for teachers to make curricular decisions. Unfortunately many teachers choose to supplement the state standards with their own coverage standards. They feel like they are somehow short-changing their students if they don't talk about every presidential election, battle of the Civil War, or New Deal agency. History teachers are notorious for putting pressure on themselves to cover everything (Tovani, 2004). Instead, history teachers must acknowledge that they cannot cover everything – they can't even cover everything that's important. They must get over their concern for coverage, and use literacy lessons to meet their state or local curriculum guidelines. In the debate over depth or breadth, research on learning is firmly on the side of depth (Bransford, *et al.*, 2000). And a focus on depth rather than breadth leaves room for historical literacy instruction.

Chapter Summary

The teachers in the vignettes in this book went through four stages in the development and execution of historical literacy lessons. They chose content and literacy objectives, found appropriate texts for reaching the objectives, designed support for students' use with the texts, and flexibly carried out the lessons. I suggest that teachers who want to build historical literacies do not try to revolutionize their instruction overnight but start small, borrow from colleagues and from online sources, use graphic organizers to build structure and accountability into their literacy lessons, and worry less about content coverage.

REFERENCES

Adler, D. A. (1997). *A picture book of Jackie Robinson*. New York: Holiday House.

Afflerbach, P., & Cho, B. Y. (2009). Identifying and describing constructively responsive reading strategies in new and traditional forms of reading. In S. E. Israel & G. G. Duffy (Eds.), *Handbook of research on reading comprehension* (pp. 69–90). New York: Routledge.

Alba, J. W. & Hasher, L. (1983). Is memory schematic? *Psychological Bulletin, 93*, 203–231.

American Experience. (2009). The murder of Emmett Till. Downloaded April 13, 2012 at http://www.pbs.org/wgbh/amex/till/sfeature/sf_look_letters.html

Anderson, R. C., Reynolds, R., Schallert, D. L., & Goetz, E. T. (1977). Frameworks for comprehending discourse. *American Educational Research Journal, 14*, 367–382.

Angier, N. (1999). Furs for evening, but cloth was a Stone Age standby. *New York Times,* December 15, 1999.

Armesto, F. F. (2010). *The world: A history* (2nd ed.). Upper Saddle River, NJ: Prentice Hall.

Armstrong, L. (1968). When the saints go marching in. On *When the saints go marching in* [Record album]. USA: Delta Entertainment.

Ashby, R. A., Lee, P. J., & Shemilt, D. (2005). Putting principles into practice: Teaching and planning. In M. S. Donovan & J. D. Bransford (Eds.), *How students learn: History, mathematics, and science in the classroom* (pp. 79–178). Washington, DC: National Academies Press.

Bain, R. B. (2005). "They thought the world was flat?" Applying the principles of *How people learn* in teaching high school history. In M. S. Donovan & J. D. Bransford (Eds.), *How students learn: History, mathematics, and science in the classroom* (pp. 179–213). Washington, DC: National Academies Press.

Baker, L. (1984). Spontaneous versus instructed use of multiple standards for evaluating comprehension: Effects of age, reading proficiency, and type of standard. *Journal of Experimental Child Psychology, 38*, 289–311.

Baker, L. (1994). Fostering metacognitive development. In H. Reese (Ed.), *Advances in child development and behavior* (Vol. 25, pp. 201–239). San Diego, CA: Academic Press.

Baker, L. (2002). Metacognition in comprehension instruction. In C. C. Block & M. Pressley (Eds.), *Comprehension instruction: Research-based best practices* (pp. 77–95). New York: Guilford.

Barton, K. C. (1996). Narrative simplifications in elementary students' historical thinking. In J. Brophy (Ed.), *Advances in research on teaching vol. 6: Teaching and learning in history.* Greenwich, CT: JAI Press.

Barton, K. C. (2010). "There'd be a coup if people knew they were scammed: New Zealand students and historical agency." Paper presentation, annual meeting of the American Educational Research Association, Denver, CO, May 1, 2010.

Baumann, J. F. (2009). Vocabulary and reading comprehension: The nexus of meaning. In S. E. Israel & G. G. Duffy (Eds.), *Handbook of research on reading comprehension* (pp. 323–346). New York: Routledge.

Beck, I.L., McKeown, M.G., Hamilton, R.L., & Kugan, L. (1997). *Questioning the author: An approach for enhancing student engagement with text.* Newark, DE: International Reading Association.

Bell, J. C., & McCollum, D. F. (1917). A study of the attainments of pupils in United States History. *Journal of Educational Psychology, 8,* 5, 257–274.

Bransford, J. D., Brown, A. L., & Cocking, R. R. (2000). *How people learn: Brain, mind, experience, and school.* Washington, DC: National Academy Press.

Britt, M. A., & Aglinskas, C. (2002). Improving students' ability to identify and use source information. *Cognition and Instruction, 20,* 485–522.

Brubaker, J. D., & Stalone, S. (1985). *Rocky IV* [motion picture]. U.S.A.: 20th Century Fox Home Entertainment.

Burke, J. & Davis, B. (1928). Carolina moon. [Recorded by G. Austin]. On *Gene Austin: Voice of the Southland* [Record album]. USA: Victor.

Chinich, M. (Producer), & Hughs, J. (Director). (1986). *Ferris Bueller's day off.* [Motion picture]. U.S.A.: Paramount Pictures.

Cleaves, F. W. (Ed.). (1982). *The secret history of the Mongols: For the first time done into English out of the original tongue and provided with an exegetical commentary.* Cambridge, MA: Harvard University Press.

Collingwood, R. G. (1993). *The idea of history.* New York: Oxford University Press.

Common Core State Standards. (2010). Common core state standards. Retrieved February 19, 2011, from http://www.corestandards.org/

Cope, B., & Kalantzis, M. (Eds.). (2000). *Multiliteracies: Literacy learning and the design of social futures.* New York: Routledge.

Crocco, M. S., Marri, A. R., & Wylie, S. (2011). Income inequality and U.S. tax policy. *Social Education, 75*(5), 256–262.

Crowe, C. (2002). *Mississippi trial, 1955.* New York: Penguin.

Davidson, M. (1996). *The story of Jackie Robinson: Bravest man in baseball.* Milwaukee, WI: Gareth Stevens.

De La Paz, S. (2005). Effects of historical reasoning instruction and writing strategy mastery in culturally and academically diverse middle school classrooms. *Journal of Educational Psychology, 97,* 139–156.

Diamond, J. (1999). *Guns, germs, and steel: The fates of human societies.* New York: W.W. Norton & Co.

Dole, J. A. (2000). Explicit and implicit instruction in comprehension. In B. M. Taylor, M. F. Graves, & P. vanden Broek (Eds.), *Reading for meaning: Fostering comprehension in the middle grades* (pp. 52–69). New York: Teachers College Press.

Draper, R. J., Broomhead, P., Jensen, A. P., Nokes, J. D., & Siebert, D. (Eds.). (2010). *(Re) imagining content-area literacy instruction.* New York: Teachers College Press.

Durand, E. D. & Harris, W. J. (Directors). (1913). *Thirteenth census of the United States taken in the year 1910, volume 1, population 1910, general report and analysis.* Washington, DC: Government Printing Office.

Education Development Center. (2002). "Image detective." *Picturing modern America 1880–1920: Historical thinking exercises for middle and high school students.* Downloaded April 12, 2012 at http://cct2.edc.org/PMA/image_detective/index.html

Eisenhower, D. D. (1944). Untitled memo. Downloaded August 19, 2010 at http://www.archives.gov/education/lessons/d-day-message/

Faulkner, A. F. (1921). Does jazz put the sin in syncopation? *Ladies' Home Journal, 38,* 16–34.

Ferretti, R. P., MacArthur, C. D., & Okolo, C. M. (2001). Teaching for historical understanding in inclusive classrooms. *Learning Disabilities Quarterly, 24,* 59–71.

Finucane, R. C. (2002). *Soldiers of the faith: Crusaders and Moslems at war.* Cited in J. R. Mitchell & H. B. Mitchell, *Taking sides: Clashing views on controversial issues in world history, volume 1.* Guilford, CT: McGraw-Hill/Dushkin.

Fiso, J. (unpublished). Teaching activities on the Reagan assassination attempt.

Foster, S. J. (2001). Historical empathy in theory and practice: Some final thoughts. In O. L. Davis, E. A. Yeager, & S. J. Foster (Eds.), *Historical empathy and perspective taking in the social studies* (pp. 167–181). New York: Rowman & Littlefield.

Freebody, P., & Luke, A. (1990). Literacies programs. Debates and demands in cultural context. *Prospect: Australian Journal of TESOL, 5*(3), 7–16.

Gaddis, J. L. (2002). *The landscape of history: How historians map the past.* London: Oxford University Press.

Griffith, D. W., & Aitken, H. (Co-producers), & Griffith, D. W. (Director). (1915). *The birth of a nation* [Motion picture]. USA: Epoch Producing Corporation.

Gurney, G. (2004). Sculpting the World War II Memorial: A conversation with Raymond Kaskey. *American Art, 18,* 2, 96–105.

Halsall, P. (2011). Internet medieval sourcebook. *Fordham University Internet History Sourcebooks Project.* Retrieved April 5, 2012 from http://www.fordham.edu/halsall/source/urban2–5vers.html

Hartman, D. K. (1995). Eight readers reading: The intertextual links of proficient readers reading multiple passages. *Reading Research Quarterly, 30,* 520–561.

Hopps, H. R. (1917). Destroy this mad brute [Poster]. USA: A. Carlisle & Co. Found in H. D. Laswell. (1971). *Propaganda technique in World War I.* Cambridge, MA: MIT Press.

Huie, W. B. (1956). The shocking story of approved killing in Mississippi. *Look, 20,* 46–50.

Hynd, C., Holschuh, J., & Hubbard, B. (2004). Thinking like a historian: College students' reading of multiple historical documents. *Journal of Literacy Research, 36,* 2, 141–176.

Johnson, W. B. (1948). Did you see Jackie Robinson hit that ball? [Recorded by the Count Basie Orchestra]. New York: Victor. (July 13, 1949). Downloaded April 13, 2012 at http://www.youtube.com/watch?v=r-7Ac2LVVYU

Kaskey, R. (2004). The Lend Lease Act [sculpture].

Keppler, U. J. (1904). Next. *Puck, 56,* 1436. Found at http://www.loc.gov/pictures/item/2001695241/

Kuhn, D., Weinstock, M., & Flaton, R. (1994). Historical reasoning as theory-evidence coordination. In M. Carretero & J. F. Voss (Eds.), *Cognitive and instructional processes in history and the social sciences* (pp. 377–401). Hillsdale, NJ: Lawrence Erlbaum Associates.

Langer, J. (1984). Examining background knowledge and text comprehension. *Reading Research Quarterly, 19,* 468–481.

Lee, P. J. (2005). Putting principles into practice: Understanding history. In M. S. Donovan & J. D. Bransford (Eds.), *How students learn: History, mathematics, and science in the classroom* (pp. 31–77). Washington, DC: National Academies Press.

Lee, P. J., & Ashby, R. A. (2000). Progression in historical understanding among students age 7–14. In P. N. Stearns, P. Seixas, & S. Wineburg (Eds.), *Knowing, teaching, and learning history. National and international perspectives* (pp. 199–222). New York: New York University Press.

Lee, P. J., & Weiss, A. (2007). *The nation's report card: U.S. History 2006* (NCES 2007–474). Retrieved from U.S. Department of Education, National Center for Education Statistics website: http://nces.ed.gov/nationsreportcard/pubs/main2006/2007474.asp#pdflist

Lee, R. (2000). History is but a fable agreed upon: The problem of truth in history and fiction. Paper presented at the annual meeting of Romantic Novelists' Association. Downloaded March 15, 2012 at http://www.historicalnovelsociety.org/historyis.htm

Lesh, B. A. (2011). *Why won't you just tell us the answer? Teaching historical thinking in grades 7–12.* Portland, ME: Stenhouse.

Leu, D. J., Zawilinski, L., Castek, J., Banerjee, M., Housand, B. C., Liu, Y., & O'Neil, M. (2007). What is new about the new literacies of online reading comprehension? In L. S. Rush, A. J. Beagle, & A. Berger (Eds.), *Secondary school literacy: What research reveals for classroom practice* (pp. 37–68). Urbana, IL: National Council of Teachers of English.

Levesque, S. (2008). *Thinking historically: Educating students for the twenty-first century.* Toronto: University of Toronto Press.

Levstik, L. S., & Barton, K. C. (2005). *Doing history: Investigating with children in elementary and middle schools.* (3rd ed.). Mahwah, NJ: Lawrence Erlbaum.

Limón, M. (2002). Conceptual change in history. In M. Limón, & L. Mason (Eds.) *Reconsidering conceptual change: Issues in theory and practice* (pp. 259–289). Dordrecht, The Netherlands: Kluwer.

Lincoln, A. (1865). Second inaugural address, endorsed by Lincoln April 10, 1865. March 4, 1865. Found in Series 3, General Correspondence, 1837–1897; The Abraham Lincoln papers at the Library of Congress, Manuscript Division. Found at http://memory.loc.gov/ammem/alhtml/alhome.html

Markham, E. M. (1979). Realizing that you don't understand: Elementary school children's awareness of inconsistencies. *Child Development, 50*, 643–655.

Mayer, H. E. (2002). *The Crusades.* Cited in J. R. Mitchell & H. B. Mitchell, *Taking sides: Clashing views on controversial issues in world history, volume 1.* Guilford, CT: McGraw-Hill/Dushkin.

McKeown, M. G., Beck, I. L., & Worthy, M. J. (1993). Grappling with text ideas: Questioning the author. *The Reading Teacher, 4*, 560–566.

Mitchell, J. R., & Mitchell, H. B. (2002). *Taking sides: Clashing views on controversial issues in world history, volume 1.* Guilford, CT: McGraw-Hill/Dushkin.

Moje, E. B. (2008). Foregrounding the disciplines in secondary literacy teaching and learning: A call for change. *Journal of Adolescent and Adult Literacy, 52*, 96–107.

Nash, G. B., & Crabtree, C. A. (1996). *National standards for history.* Los Angeles, CA: National Center for History in the Schools.

National Center for Education Statistics (2011). The Nation's Report Card: U.S. History 2010 (NCES 2011–468). Institute of Education Sciences, U.S. Department of Education, Washington, D.C.

National Park Service. (2012). Dendrochronology. Downloaded April 2, 2012 at http://www.webrangers.us/activities/dendrochronology

Nokes, J. D. (2008). The observation/inference chart: Improving students' ability to make inferences while reading non-traditional texts. *Journal of Adolescent and Adult Literacy, 51*, 538–546.

Nokes, J. D. (2010a). Observing literacy practices in history classrooms. *Theory and Research in Social Education, 38*(4), 298–316.

Nokes, J. D. (2010b). The evolving concept instructional strategy: Students reflecting on their processing of multiple, conflicting, historical sources. *National Social Science Journal, 35*(1), 104–117.

Nokes, J. D. (2011). Recognizing and addressing barriers to adolescents' "reading like historians." *The History Teacher, 44*(3), 379–404.

Nokes, J. D., Crowe, C., & Bausum, A. (2012). *Finding the story in history: Teaching with stories of diversity.* Presented at the National Council for History Education annual conference, Kansas City, MO.

Nokes, J. D., & Dole, J. A. (2005). Helping adolescent readers through explicit strategy instruction. In T. L. Jetton & J. A. Dole (Eds.), *Adolescent literacy research and practice*, (pp. 162–182). New York: Guilford.

Nokes, J. D., Dole, J. A., & Hacker, D. J. (2007). Teaching high school students to use heuristics while reading historical texts. *Journal of Educational Psychology, 99*, 492–504.

Ogle, D. M. (1986). K-W-L: A teaching model that develops active reading of expository text. *Reading Teacher, 39*, 564–570.

Page, E. W. (1922). A flapper's appeal to parents. *Outlook*, Dec. 6, 1922, p. 607. Downloaded May, 9, 2012 at http://faculty.pittstate.edu/~knichols/flapperappeal.html

Paris, S. G., & Hamilton, E. E. (2009). The development of children's reading comprehension. In S. E. Israel & G. G. Duffy (Eds.), *Handbook of research on reading comprehension* (pp. 32–53). New York: Routledge.

Paris, S. G., Wasik, B. A., & Turner, J. C. (1991). The development of strategic readers. In R. Barr, M. L. Kamil, P. Mosenthal, & P. D. Pearson (Eds.), *Handbook of reading research, Vol. 2* (pp. 609–640). White Plains NY: Longman.

Paterson, K. (1991). *Lyddie*. New York: Lodestar Books.

Paxton, R. J. (1997). "Someone with like a life wrote it:" The effects of a visible author on high school history students. *Journal of Educational Psychology, 89*, 235–250.

Paxton, R. J. (1999). A deafening silence: History textbooks and the students who read them. *Review of Educational Research, 69*, 315–337.

Pearson, D. (2009). The roots of reading comprehension instruction. In S. E. Israel & G. G. Duffy (Eds.), *Handbook of research on reading comprehension* (pp. 3–31). New York: Routledge.

Pearson, P. D., & Dole, J. A. (1987). Explicit comprehension instruction: A review of research and a new conceptualization of instruction. *Elementary School Journal, 88*(2), 151–165.

Perfetti, C. A., Britt, M. A., & Georgi, M. C. (1995). *Text-based learning and reasoning: Studies in history.* Hillsdale, NJ: Lawrence Erlbaum Associates.

Perfetti, C. A., Rouet, J.-F., & Britt, M. A. (1999). Toward a theory of documents representation. In H. van Oostendorp & S. R. Goldman (Eds.), *The construction of mental representations during reading* (pp. 99–122). Mahwah, NJ: Erlbaum.

Perry, J. & Xue, L. (2001). Stephen, Count of Blois and Chartres letter to his wife, Adele. Hanover Historical Texts Project. Retrieved April 5, 2012 from http://history.hanover.edu/texts/1stcrusade2.html

Pulsipher, J. (2003). "Subjects unto the same king:" New England Indians and the use of royal political power. *Massachusetts Historical Review, 5*, 29–58.

Ravitch, D., & Finn, C. E. (1987). *What do our 17 year olds know: A report on the first national assessment of history and literature.* New York: Harper & Row.

Reddy, K., & VanSledright, B. (2010). Epistemic change in history education. Paper presented at the annual conference of the College and University Faculty Assembly, Denver, CO.

Reilly, K. (2007). *Worlds of history: A comparative reader* (3rd ed.). Boston, MA: Bedford/St. Martins.

Reisman, A. (2012). Reading like a historian: A document-based history curriculum intervention in urban high schools. *Cognition and Instruction, 30,* 1, 86–112.

Richard the Lionheart massacres the Saracens, 1191. (2001). EyeWitness to History. Retrieved April 5, 2012 from www.eyewitnesstohistory.com

Robinson, S. (2009). *Testing the ice: A true story about Jackie Robinson.* New York: Scholastic.

Rockwell, N. (1964). *Moving in* [Painting].

Romano, A. (2011). How dumb are we? *Newsweek, 157,* 13/14, 56–60.

Schlesinger, L. (Producer), & Avery, T. (Director). (1936). *I love to singa* [motion picture]. USA: Warner Brothers and Vitaphone. Downloaded May 9, 2012 at http://www.youtube.com/watch?v=akAEIW3rmvQ.

Schwebel, S. (2011). *Child-sized history: Fictions of the past in U. S. classrooms.* Nashville: Vanderbilt University Press.

Seixas, P. (1993). Popular film and young people's understanding of the history of Native American-White relations. *The History Teacher, 26,* 351–370.

Seuss, Dr. (1941). Ho hum! When he's finished pecking down that last tree he'll quite likely be tired. *PM Magazine,* May 22, 1941. Found at Dr. Seuss Collection, MSS 230. Mandeville Special Collections Library, UC San Diego.

Shay, L., Fisher, M., & Goodwin, J. (1929). When you're smiling. [Recorded by L. Armstrong]. On *Louis Armstrong's greatest hits* [Record album]. USA: MCA Music Media Studios.

Spivey, N. N., & King, J. (1989). Readers as writers composing from sources. *Reading Research Quarterly, 24,* 1–14.

Stahl, S. A., Hynd, C. R., Britton, B. K., McNish, M. M., & Bosquet, D. (1996). What happens when students read multiple source documents in history? *Reading Research Quarterly, 31,* 430–456.

Stahl, S. A., & Shanahan, C. H. (2004). Learning to think like a historian: Disciplinary knowledge through critical analysis of multiple documents. In T. L. Jetton & J. A. Dole (Eds.), *Adolescent literacy research and practice* (pp. 94–115). New York: Guilford.

Stanford History Education Group (2012). Charting the future of teaching the past. Downloaded February 27, 2012. Found at http://sheg.stanford.edu/

The Friends of Valley Forge (2011). *Valley Forge legacy, the muster roll project: The encampment.* Downloaded November 21, 2011 at http://valleyforgemusterroll.org/encampment.asp

Tilzer, A. V., & Fleeson, N. (1920). I'll be with you in apple blossom time. [Recorded by The Andrews Sisters]. On *The Andrews Sisters 20 greatest hits* [Record album]. USA: MCA. (1940).

Tomlinson, C. M., Tunnell, M. O., & Richgels, D. J. (1993). The content and writing of history in textbooks and trade books. In M. O. Tunnell & R. Ammon (Eds.), *The story of ourselves: Teaching history through children's literature* (pp. 51–62). Portsmouth, NH: Heinemann.

Tovani, C. (2000). *I read it but I don't get it: Comprehension strategies for adolescent readers.* Portland, ME: Stenhouse.

Tovani, C. (2004). *Do I really have to teach reading? Content comprehension, grades 6–12*. Portland, ME: Stenhouse.

Toynbee, A. J. (1957). *A study of history*, Vol. 2. London: Oxford University Press.

Tunnell, M. O., & Ammon, R. (1996). The story of ourselves: Fostering multiple historical perspectives. *Social Education, 60*(4), 212–215.

van Drie, J., & van Boxtel, C. (2008). Historical reasoning: Towards a framework for analyzing students' reasoning about the past. *Educational Psychology Review, 20*, 87–110.

VanSledright, B. (2002). *In search of America's past: Learning to read history in elementary school*. New York: Teachers College Press.

VanSledright, B. A., & Frankes, L. (1998). Literature's place in learning history and science. In C. R. Hynd (Ed.), *Learning from text across conceptual domains* (pp. 117–138). Mahwah, NJ: Lawrence Erlbaum Associates.

Vygotsky, L. (1986). *Thought and language*. Cambridge, MA: The MIT Press.

Wiggins, G. & McTighe, J. (1998). *Understanding by design*. Alexandria, VA: Association for Supervision and Curriculum Development.

Wineburg, S. S. (1991). On the reading of historical texts: Notes on the breach between school and academy. *American Educational Research Journal, 28*, 495–519.

Wineburg, S. S. (1994). The cognitive representation of historical texts. In G. Leinhardt, I. Beck, & C. Stainton (Eds.), *Teaching and learning in history* (pp. 85–135). Hillsdale, NJ: Erlbaum.

Wineburg, S. S. (1998). Reading Abraham Lincoln: An expert/expert study in the interpretation of historical texts. *Cognitive Science, 22*, 319–346.

Wineburg, S. S. (2001). *Historical thinking and other unnatural acts: Charting the future of teaching the past*. Philadelphia: Temple University Press.

Wineburg, S. S. (2005). What does NCATE have to say to future history teachers? Not much. *Phi Delta Kappan, 86*(9), 658–665.

Wineburg, S. S. (2007). Forrest Gump and the future of teaching the past. *Phi Delta Kappan, 89*, 3, 168–177.

Wineburg, S., Martin, D. & Monte-Sano, C. (2011). *Reading like a historian: Teaching literacy in middle and high school classrooms*. New York: Teacher's College Press.

Wineburg, S., Smith, M., & Breakstone, J. (in press). New directions in assessment: Using Library of Congress sources to assess historical understanding. *Education Week*.

Young, K. M., & Leinhardt, G. (1998). Writing from primary documents. *Written Communication, 15*, 25–68.

INDEX